Structures of Power

Structures of Power
An Introduction to Politics

J.J. Schwarzmantel

Lecturer in Politics
University of Leeds

WHEATSHEAF BOOKS · SUSSEX

ST. MARTIN'S PRESS · NEW YORK

First Published in Great Britain in 1987 by
WHEATSHEAF BOOKS LTD
A MEMBER OF THE HARVESTER PRESS PUBLISHING GROUP
Publisher: John Spiers
16 Ship Street, Brighton, Sussex
and in the USA by
ST. MARTIN'S PRESS, INC.
175 Fifth Avenue, New York, NY 10010

© J.J. Schwarzmantel, 1987

British Library Cataloguing in Publication Data
Schwarzmantel, J.J.
  Structures of Power: an introduction to
  politics.
  1. Political science
  I. Title
  320'.01   JA71

  ISBN 0-7450-0337-0
  ISBN 0-7450-0402-4 Pbk

St. Martin's Press
ISBN 0-312-01208-X
LCN 87-42775

Library of Congress Cataloging-in-Publication Data
C.I.P. Data applied for

Typeset in Times 11/12pt by Witwell Ltd, Liverpool
Printed and bound in Great Britain by
Biddles Ltd, Guildford and King's Lynn

THE HARVESTER PRESS PUBLISHING GROUP
The Harvester Group comprises Harvester Press Ltd (chiefly publishing literature, fiction, philosophy, psychology, and science and trade books); Harvester Press Microform Publications Ltd (publishing in microform previously unpublished archives, scarce printed sources, and indexes to these collections) and Wheatsheaf Books Ltd (chiefly publishing in economics, international politics, sociology, women's studies and related social sciences).

For my parents

Contents

Foreword

This book is based on a course of lectures delivered over a number of years at Leeds University. The book presents the main elements of three different theories of politics—pluralist, elitist and Marxist. It tries to explain the different ways in which each theory deals with questions concerning the state and the distribution of power. It also covers the nature of different state forms—the liberal-democratic state, the communist or Soviet-type state and the fascist state. In the two latter cases the role of the monopolistic parties which sustain such state forms is emphasised. Finally, two short chapters deal with conservative and anarchist perspectives on politics and with the contrasting stance each takes on the nature of the state. The general theme of the book is thus the nature of state power in different political systems, and the various ways in which such state power is conceptualised. It is designed as an introduction, aiming to provide a basic exposition of the various topics with which it deals.

My thanks are due to Anne-Marie Barry, David Beetham, David Cesarani and Janet Wolff, who have each read draft versions of some of the chapters. I am very grateful to them for their helpful comments and suggestions. I also wish to thank my father who has helped me by typing a draft version of the whole manuscript and suggesting several improvements. For any errors, omissions, and other defects I alone am responsible.

J. J. Schwarzmantel
Leeds

Introduction: What is Politics?

What is politics? Everybody has some idea about the meaning of the term, to some people the question may even appear quite superfluous. 'Politics' is what one reads about in the papers or watches on television. It deals with the activities of the politicians, notably the leaders of the political parties. What Mrs Thatcher does today or Mr Kinnock says tomorrow, this surely is what politics is all about. But why, precisely, are these activities 'political' and what defines the nature of politics? If one started with a definition couched in terms of the activities of politicians one might say that politics concerns the rivalries of politicians in their struggle for power. This would certainly be the kind of definition with which most people would agree. There would also probably be agreement that politics refers to the relationship between states on an international scale.

It is not satisfactory to leave the matter there, but such commonsense definitions contain two notions which are essential to the understanding of what politics is about. The activities of politicians are related to their attempt to gain *power* or maintain themselves in a position of *power*. When the question of international politics was touched upon it was noted that this concerned the relationship between *states*. Both terms—*power* and *the state*—are crucial in arriving at an adequate definition of politics. It may be helpful to start by saying that politics deals with relations of power and that it is fundamentally concerned with one central political institution, the state. However, both these terms require further comments.

1

'Politics is about power and how it is distributed.'[1] But power is not an abstract entity floating in the void. It is embodied in human beings. Power is a relationship existing wherever a person (or group of persons) can impose their will on other persons (or groups), making the latter obey whether they want to or not. Hence arises a situation characterised by leadership, a relation of domination and subordination. Max Weber, in his famous lecture of 1918, 'Politics as a Vocation', started by proposing that the concept of politics was 'extremely broad-based and comprises any kind of *independent* leadership in action.'[2] In whatever context such 'leadership in action' exists, there politics is present. In our terms, politics would be the study of power and the sphere of the political would include any situation where power relations existed, i.e. where people were constrained or dominated or subject to authority of one kind or another. It would also include situations where people were constrained by a set of structures or institutions rather than by the subjective will of persons.

Such a broad definition has the advantage of showing that politics is not necessarily a matter of government, nor solely concerned with the activities of politicians. Politics exists in any context where there is a structure of power and struggle for power in an attempt to gain or maintain leadership positions. In this sense one can speak about the politics of trade unions or about 'university politics'. One can discuss 'sexual politics', meaning the domination of men over women or the attempt to alter this relation. At the present time there is much controversy about race politics with reference to the power, or lack of it, of people of different colour or race in various countries. In a narrower sense, however, everything is politics which affects our lives through the agency of those who exercise and control state power, and the purposes for which they use that control. In the lecture quoted above Weber, after initially giving a very broad definition of politics in terms of general leadership, went on to produce a far more limited definition: 'We wish to understand by politics', he wrote, 'only the leadership, or the influencing of leadership, of a *political* association, hence today, of a *state*.'[3] In this perspective the state is the central political association. A political question is one that relates to the state, to the topic of who controls state power, for what purposes that power is used, with what consequences, and so on.

This, then, raises a new issue. What is the state? The question is by no means an easy one to answer, nor is there general agreement as to what the answer should be. It must first be noted that there are various forms of state which differ from one another in important ways. The Greek city state is clearly different from the modern nation-state which has dominated world politics since the French Revolution. The contemporary liberal-democratic state which exists in Britain and Western Europe is different from the fascist-type state of Hitler or Mussolini. It is also different from the state form which exists in the USSR and in Eastern Europe. An important part of the study of politics, and certainly an integral element of this book, is the explanation of what is meant by those terms (liberal-democratic, fascist, etc.). The purpose is to show how each form distinguishes itself from the others and what the significance of such distinction is.

States differ in terms of their political institutions as well as in terms of the social context within which they are situated and which they try to maintain. So, while the liberal-democratic state is characterised by representative institutions such as a Parliament and by an independent judiciary, the fascist state is controlled by a leader (il Duce, der Führer). With respect to the social context, the crucial contrast is between Western and Soviet-type systems in so far as the former are embedded in a society which is organised according to the principles of a capitalist economy, while in the latter case the productive resources of society are owned and controlled by the state. In each case, therefore, the state, itself differently structured, operates in a social framework of a very different kind, and this affects and influences to a large extent the nature of the state and the purposes which it serves.

There are different forms of state but whatever form one has in mind, the state as such is not a monolithic block. To start with, 'the state' is not the same as 'the government'. It rather is a complex of various elements of which the government is only one. In a Western-type liberal-democratic state those who form the government are indeed invested with state power. They speak in the name of the state and take office in order to control the levers of state power. Nevertheless, to change the metaphor, the house of the state has many mansions and of those the government occupies one. In his book *The State in Capitalist Society*, Ralph Miliband registers those different elements which together constitute the state.[4] The first, but by no means the only, element of the state apparatus is government. The second is the administrative element, civil service or bureaucracy. This political executive is, in liberal-democratic systems, supposed to be neutral, carrying out the orders of politicians who are in power. In fact, however, the bureaucracy may well have its own authority and dispose of its own power. Third in Miliband's list come the military and the police, the 'order-maintaining' or repressive arm of the state; fourth the judiciary. In any constitutional system the judiciary is supposed to be independent of the holders of government power; it can act as a check on them. Fifth come the units of sub-central or local government. In some federal systems these units have considerable independence from central government, controlling their own sphere of power where government is constitutionally debarred from interfering. The relationship between central and local government may become an important political issue, as witnessed by the controversy in recent British politics over the abolition of the Greater London Council and the metropolitan counties, the argument about financing local government, 'rate capping', and so on. Sixth and finally, one can add to the list representative assemblies, Parliament in the British system. One may also mention political parties, though they are not normally part of the state apparatus, at least not in a liberal democracy. They play their obvious role in the representative assembly and it is there that, at least partly, the competitive fight between government and opposition is enacted.

This view of the state as a totality composed of various elements opens up perspectives which involve some of the key problems of modern politics. An important fact is that the different elements of the state need not be in harmony. Bureaucracy or the military may well use their sectional powers to slow down or block government initiatives. In extreme cases this may lead to a final clash whereby those sections remove a democratically elected government, as happened in Chile in 1973. Similar conflicts on a minor scale may result in tensions between an elected government and a permanent civil service. The same analysis is also useful in dealing with the different state forms. These can be defined by the specific relationships between the various branches of the state apparatus. Obviously, under a military dictatorship the armed forces and the repressive services will swell out of proportion while the representative institutions will either be abolished or stripped of any effective power. The bureaucracy, while it remains important, becomes the creature of the army. Similarly the transformation of a liberal-democratic into a fascist state involves a massive increase of the repressive sections and, again, the destruction of representative assemblies and of an independent judiciary. This marks the decisive difference from the mutual relationships of the state elements in a democracy. Yet even within a democratic system it is possible for the power of the executive and the administration to be increased at the expense of the representative elements. This development is emphasised by those who suggest evidence of moves towards a 'strong state' in liberal-democratic systems.[5]

All this has not yet given us a full view of what the state is, or how it may be defined, much less of how the power of the state is exercised. There are two basic means by which state power is maintained: coercion and consent. Consent raises the related issue of a process of legitimation through which power is justified and voluntary acceptance of the power holders' authority is achieved.

The point brings us back to Weber and his already quoted lecture, 'Politics as a Vocation'. After arguing that politics is concerned above all with the central political association, the state, Weber continued by maintaining that a definition of the state could not be given in terms of the tasks which it undertook or of the ends it pursued. There was no task which specifically determined the state. Therefore one had to define the state in terms of the specific means which it employed and these means were, ultimately, physical force. The state, Weber wrote, 'is a human community that successfully claims the *monopoly of the legitimate use of physical force* within a given territory.'[6]

There are three distinct elements combined here: a given territory, or geographical area, which the state controls; the use of physical force to maintain its control; thirdly, but most importantly, the monopoly of the *legitimate* use of such force or coercion. This legitimacy must be acknowledged by most, if not all, of those who are subject to the state's power. Weber concluded that for him politics meant 'striving to share power or striving to influence the distribution of power either among states or among groups within a state.'[7]

It was also mentioned that each state exists within a particular social context. The study of politics is vitally concerned with the relationship of state and society. A state-centred perspective on politics does not imply that the study should neglect what happens in the wider sphere of society and how that may, as Weber says, 'influence the distribution of power'.

A further fact cannot be ignored: this is the continued growth and centralisation of state power. If one sees the state in terms of a specialised apparatus of domination, then the history of modern times has been marked by the extension of its scale and grip. The modern state requires an increasingly complex bureaucracy dealing with a mounting variety of tasks. It needs larger and more sophisticated armed forces, more regulative welfare agencies, and engages in a wider range of activities than was the case before. This extension of the state's sphere of action, its growth and development, applies both to liberal-democratic systems in their capitalist socioeconomic context, and to socialist systems with their collectivist economic framework. Weber saw such growth manifested above all in the emergence of a trained, skilled and rationally effective bureaucracy. Someone of quite a different political and theoretical background, Marx, agreed with him on this point. Marx wrote in *The Eighteenth Brumaire of Louis Bonaparte* of the growth of state power in France which he saw as typical of the modern state. He described how

The executive power possesses an immense bureaucratic and military organisation, an ingenious and broadly based state machinery, and an army of half a million officials alongside the actual army, which numbers a further half million. This frightful parasitic body, which surrounds the body of

French society like a caul and stops up all its pores, arose in the time of the absolute monarchy, with the decay of the feudal system, which it helped to accelerate.[8]

Marx, of course, thought that socialism would eventually abolish the state; society would govern itself without a specialised apparatus of repression. Weber, on the contrary, believed that socialism would need even more officials to administer a collectivised economy and society.

Let us return to the question of force, or coercion, as against consent, or legitimation. State power depends on coercion; politics implies, at some point at least, the use of force. If in a particular geographical area no association can successfully monopolise the use of force, then in that area there is no state, or at least it is in danger of collapse and disintegration if such a situation persists for any length of time. Where the state has no power it ceases to exist. The case can be illustrated by the contemporary situation in Lebanon where several competing groups are fighting each other but none can successfully claim a monopoly of power nor a legitimate authority. There is then a situation of 'war of all against all'. Such, according to Hobbes, was the far from attractive yet unavoidable human condition before, by mutual consent, people came to establish a commonwealth, or state system.

The point is that although the state depends on force, it does not rest on force alone. Here the notion of the legitimate use of power comes in. Power in general, and so the power of the state, can be exercised in different ways. Coercion is one form of power and perhaps the easiest to understand, but it is not the only one. Not all power relations are to be understood on the same crude model. If a lecturer through force of argument and breadth of knowledge helps students to form their ideas, such a person exercises a kind of power, though not against the students' will. More to the point, all holders of power try to get those who are subject to their rule to believe in the rightness and justness of the power they wield. This attempt at justification in order to make people consent constitutes the process of legitimation. One can refer to such justified or accepted power as 'authority' to distinguish it from such power as is obeyed only because of a fear of sanctions. In such a situation of legitimate power, or authority, people obey

because they think it is right to do so. They believe, for
whatever reason, that the power-holders are entitled to their
dominant role. They have the legitimate authority, a right to
command. In the words of one recent analysis of power,
'Legitimate authority is a power relation in which the power
holder possesses an acknowledged *right to command* and the
power subject an acknowledged *obligation to obey*.'[9]

According to Weber there are three types of legitimation,
i.e. three methods by which the wielding of power can be
justified. The first type is *traditional* domination. There, power
is justified because the holders of power can appeal to
tradition and habit; authority has always been vested in them
personally or in their families. The second type is *charismatic*
legitimation. People obey the power-holder because of the
exceptional personal qualities displayed by the leader. Finally,
the third type is of the *legal-rational* kind. People obey certain
persons who are authorised by specific rules to command in
strictly defined spheres of action. One might also say that the
first two types are of a personal nature while the legal-rational
type shows a procedural character. As such it corresponds to
the modern conception of political authority. It is, as Weber
says, 'domination as exercised by the modern "servant of the
state" and by all those bearers of power who in this respect
resemble him.'[10]

It is obvious that the power-holders in any system will wish
to have their power accepted as legitimate. Seen from their
point of view such an acceptance will permit a considerable
'economy' in the use of force. People will obey freely and
voluntarily. The means of coercion then will not need to be
constantly displayed; they can rather be concentrated on those
who do not accept the legitimacy of the power structure. In
any political system there will be those who comply with the
rules only because non-compliance will be punished. Clearly,
however, the stability of any political system is enhanced to the
degree that people voluntarily obey the rules or laws because
they accept the legitimacy of the established order. Hence they
recognise the authority of those empowered by the rules to
issue commands. In reality, all political systems are
maintained through a combination of consent and coercion.

These are the reasons why, as C. Wright Mills puts it, 'The

idea of legitimation is one of the central conceptions of political science.'[11] The study of politics is centrally concerned with the methods by which holders of power try to get their power justified, and with the extent to which they succeed. It is crucial in studying any political system to investigate the degree to which people accept the existing power structure as legitimate, and thus how much the structure rests on consent as distinct from coercion. It is also important to ascertain the actual justifications of power which are offered, that is to say, the methods by which a system of power is legitimised. This, as the elitist theorist Mosca points out, is the 'political formula' of any political system. The question of legitimacy, furthermore, is highly important in dealing with the topics of stability and change of political systems. Consent may be granted or withdrawn. It is true that political systems can survive in situations where large sections of the population cease to accord any legitimacy to the system. The case of South Africa at the present time may be cited as an example; similarly that of Poland, where it seems that the Jaruzelski regime has little legitimacy in the eyes of substantial popular elements. The point is that in such a situation a regime has to rely mainly on force. It then finds itself in a more precarious position, vulnerable and open to the impact of fortuitous events. The system may survive for quite a time. However, once it rests on force far more than on consent one condition for a revolutionary change presents itself.

This explains why a revolution is often preceded by a period when the dominating ideas of the system are subjected to sustained criticism. One may call this a process of 'delegitimation' whereby the ideas which justify the existing structure of power come under attack. Long before the fall of the *ancien régime* in France the ideas of Divine Right and of autocracy were ridiculed and refuted by the *philosophes*, the critics of the absolute state. Such a movement of delegitimation contributed to undermine the foundations of the old order. It prepared the way for its revolutionary overthrow.

A case in point in modern times would be the fate of the Weimar Republic when large sections of the German population lost confidence in the democratic regime and, fearing a communist alternative, gave their support to Hitler's National-Socialist party. The result was the fall of the republic without much of a struggle. Similar causes had similar effects all over the Continent. Many Western systems of liberal democracy were overthrown and replaced by fascist or semi-fascist authoritarian systems as happened in Italy, in Spain, in Austria and in Hungary. The conclusion in a general sense must be that any system loses its stability once it ceases to enjoy legitimacy in the eyes of its subjects.

Finally, it must be noted that even in normal times processes of legitimation and delegitimation are permanent features of any political system. The process of legitimation is carried on in more or less subtle ways through many channels available for the legitimation of the existing order. Legitimising ideas are absorbed from the earliest stages of education, diffused through a variety of forms of social interaction, and spread especially through the influence of the press, television and other mass media. Views which are accepted or considered to be within the boundaries of the system are almost forced on readers, listeners and viewers. Action which goes beyond those limits is presented as illegitimate. A range of political alternatives is blocked off by being made to look very unattractive.

There are still more effective methods available to prevent subversive ideas from even arising. They may be intercepted at source, the source being the conscious and even the subconscious mind. An important dimension of power is the capacity to affect and mould people's consciousness so that they will accept the existing state of affairs without ever becoming aware of alternative possibilities. Consent then becomes manipulated consent. To a certain extent we are all affected by the prevailing 'climate of opinion'. From there an ascending scale leads to a position where the moulding of minds, manipulation, is made the deliberate purpose of the state in order to create a monolithic popular mentality. Such was the purpose of Goebbels' propaganda machine, and this is still the purpose of any totalitarian regime.

Manipulation is 'power wielded unknown to the powerless', as C. Wright Mills defines it.[12] Peter Worsley points out that 'the mechanisms by which consciousness is manipulated are of growing importance in modern society.'[13] In Marxist language such manipulated consent would eventually produce a 'false consciousness'. Against that it could be argued that where people are free to choose and to express their choice (between political alternatives, parties, etc.), as in liberal-democratic systems, the manipulation of consciousness is not possible. Manipulation can only occur where free choice does not exist, as in one-party systems. It is also argued that wherever people are free to choose but do not in fact choose an alternative to the existing order—for example, by supporting parties committed to radical changes—it is safe to assume that the existing structure of society is broadly 'what people want'. This would lead to the conclusion that the importance of political choice and the ability to freely express that choice cannot be overrated. However, 'what people want' is to some extent conditioned by various factors. Choice does not take place in a vacuum. In short, the choice itself cannot be considered as completely free from the impact of a process of legitimation.

From the short survey we have so far made of political problems a few points of importance emerge which will recur in the following discussion. They chiefly stem from the fact that state power is structured or broken up, so to speak, into distinct sectors. It has already been mentioned that the specific relationship of the various sectors (or departments) is determined by the political system within which they operate. The internal structure, say, of a liberal-democratic state differs from a fascist regime, or of a communist state. A further question involves the personnel of those sectors. The state, after all, is not a machine, though the phrase 'machinery of the state' may be used. The state is a set of institutions staffed by people whose ideas and basic attitudes are largely influenced by their origin and social environment. The composition of the state elite is an important problem in the study of politics. What is meant by the term 'state elite' can be exemplified with reference to a recent study by J.A.G. Griffith, *The Politics of the Judiciary*. It shows that in Britain 'in broad terms four out of five full-time professional judges are products of public schools, and of Oxford or Cambridge.' In consequence it is not surprising that while discussing 'judicial opinion about political cases' Griffith finds 'a remarkable consistency of approach in these cases concentrated in a fairly narrow part of the spectrum of political opinion.'[14]

It must be noted here that from different theoretical points of view different answers will be given to the question as to how decisive the nature and composition of the state elite are. Elitist theories accord the highest importance to that factor. In their perspective the nature of a political system is best explained by an analysis of its elite, that ruling minority which controls the state apparatus. In this perspective almost everything depends on the talents and abilities of the leaders. A low quality of leadership will have disastrous consequences. For that reason, Max Weber was much concerned with the nature of Germany's political leadership. He was in favour of a strong parliament which, he believed, would provide an adequate training ground to produce leaders willing and capable of responsible action. Alternatively leadership would fall into the hands of the bureaucracy whose training and life style made them unsuitable material for creative leadership.[15]

Marxist theories would view the matter differently. They would accord less importance to the nature of the state elite. The argument would rather be that the purpose and the aims of state activity are determined less by the elite but far more by the social context and the economic framework within which the state system is located. This structure is of greater significance in this view than the character of the personnel that staff the state machine. Generally, 'structural' theories would emphasise the constraints on the government stemming from the social structures within which the government has to operate. Nevertheless, the two types of interpretation ('structural' and 'elitist') need not be mutually exclusive.

This brings us to a final question, which deals with the relation of state and society. The phrase which Marx applied to the Bonapartist state, that its power was not 'suspended in mid-air', can be generalised to apply to all types of state systems. Then several problems present themselves. How does the power structure of society affect and constrain the political leaders? To what extent does the state interfere to maintain and legitimise or, alternatively, mitigate the inequalities of the social system? To what extent indeed is 'civil society' independent of the state? For some theorists the concept of 'totalitarianism' is meant to suggest a situation where society is totally controlled by state power and, therefore, has no independence at all.

The remaining task of this introduction is to set out how it is proposed to deal with such questions. Different theoretical approaches in the study of political power will be presented and evaluated, each being applied to several political systems. The theoretical approaches are:

(a) Pluralism or liberal-democratic theory.
(b) Elite theory and the elitist perspective on politics.
(c) The Marxist approach to the state and to the question of political power.

Under each of these headings fall a number of theories which share a fundamental approach but differ in various aspects. These variations must be noted, but the aim will be to elucidate the basic concepts of each approach and to subject each type of theory to a critical assessment.

Pluralist theories emphasise the dispersal of power among different power centres. They regard Western liberal-democratic systems as conforming to that type of dispersed power. Elitist theories concentrate on the description of an elite as the most important feature of any particular system. Such an elite is seen as inevitably emerging and assuming a leading role under any regime. Elite theories affirm the inevitability of minority rule, but they take different views on the nature of the elite and the source of its power. There are differentiations too within Marxist theories. They all analyse society in terms of class and class conflict. They see the state in a class-divided society functioning to maintain class power, i.e. the power a ruling class derives from its ownership and control of society's economic resources. Yet this common approach is differently developed in various Marxist theories leading to contrasting positions on issues such as the nature of Soviet-type systems or the prospects of transforming liberal-democratic systems.

Each theory, then, has its own basic concepts through which it explains the distribution of power and the nature of political and social conflicts. The contrast between the various political theories will be illustrated by applying them to different state forms.

The liberal-democratic (Western-type) state is characterised by a representative assembly (parliament), a competitive party system, a range of pressure groups and also by some sort of political or constitutional 'separation of powers'. It tries to uphold the twin values of liberalism by controlling the power of the executive and of democracy by inviting the voluntary participation of the people.

Fascist or Nazi states emerge from liberal-democratic state systems in deep social and economic crisis. They are typically characterised by a mass party led by and subordinated to an individual leader (Führer). The masses are always manipulated under fascism. It is not enough that they obey: their active cooperation is demanded. By contrast, other authoritarian and also traditional conservative systems try rather to minimise or prevent any form of popular involvement.

A third, clearly distinct form of state is the Soviet, or East European, type. It shares with fascism the characteristic of a one-party system. Some political writers would in fact place Soviet-type systems under the same heading as fascism, both as specimens of 'totalitarianism'. There are, however, three factors which distinguish the Soviet-type state from either liberal democracy or from authoritarian systems of the Right. First, it exists in the context of a state-owned collectivist economy. Secondly, the Soviet state orginated from a socialist revolution carried out under the banner of Marxism though under conditions different from those which classical Marxist theory envisaged. The third point is that although fascism and the Soviet state both adhere to an ideology which covers all aspects of life, the content of that ideology is completely different in either case. This has important implications for the nature of the state and the purpose for which state power is employed.

There are, of course, other perspectives, some of them taking a critical view of all political theories focused on the state. We shall indeed devote two short chapters to two fundamentally opposed political attitudes. The one is the attitude of political conservatism which sees the state as the defender of the existing social system, the guarantor of its stability and orderly function. The other is the anarchist position. It rejects altogether the state as a coercive institution invading the private sphere of free individuals. In its place the anarchists wish to set the voluntary self-organisation of society. They oppose and criticise each of the three theories we have been considering because such theories are regarded by anarchists as attempts to legitimise a structure of authority and of power. The anarchist critique is then a critique of power in general.

NOTES

1. As was written by one practitioner of politics, the Labour Member of Parliament Bryan Gould; *The Guardian* 2 June 1986.
2. Max Weber, 'Politics as a Vocation', in *From Max Weber: Essays in Sociology*, translated, edited and with an introduction by H.H. Gerth and C. Wright Mills (Routledge & Kegan Paul, London, 1970), p. 77.
3. Ibid., p. 77.
4. Ralph Miliband, *The State in Capitalist Society* (Weidenfeld and Nicolson, London, 1969), pp. 50—4.
5. See, for example, A. Gamble, 'The Free Economy and the Strong State', *The Socialist Register 1979*, edited by Ralph Miliband and John Saville (The Merlin Press, London, 1979), 1—26; Ralph Miliband, *Capitalist Democracy in Britain* (Oxford University Press, Oxford, 1982), Chapter 6, 'The Future of Capitalist Democracy in Britain'; E.P. Thompson, *Writing by Candlelight* (The Merlin Press, London, 1980).
6. Weber, 'Politics as a Vocation', p. 78.
7. Ibid.
8. Marx, 'The Eighteenth Brumaire of Louis Bonaparte', in *Karl Marx, Surveys from Exile, Political Writings*, Vol. 2, edited by David Fernba· (Penguin, Harmondsworth, 1973), p. 237.
9. Dennis H. Wrong, *Power. Its Forms, Bases and Uses* (Blackwell, Oxford, 1979), p. 49.
10. Weber, 'Politics as a Vocation', pp. 78—9.
11. C. Wright Mills, *The Sociological Imagination* (Penguin, Harmondsworth, 1970), p. 63.
12. Ibid., p. 50.
13. P. Worsley, 'The Distribution of Power in Industrial Society', in J. Urry and J. Wakeford (eds.), *Power in Britain, Sociological Readings* (Heinemann, London, 1973), p. 257.
14. J.A.G. Griffith, *The Politics of the Judiciary*, 3rd edition (Fontana Press, 1985), pp. 28, 31.

15. See David Beetham, *Max Weber and the Theory of Modern Politics* (Polity Press, Cambridge, 1985), especially Chapter 4, 'Parliament and Democracy'.

1 The Pluralist View of Politics

1. OUTLINE OF THE PLURALIST VIEW

The aim of the chapter is to expound and assess a particular perspective on politics, which can be given the label 'pluralist'. The basis of this perspective, as the term 'pluralist' indicates, is that there should be in any political system a plurality of different centres of power, political and social. Power should not be concentrated in the hands of any one person or any one group. There should be, on the contrary, a diffusion or dispersion of power. This is held to be the defining characteristic of a pluralist political system. A system where there are competing parties, a network of pressure groups and associations, a 'separation of powers' in some form or other in the constitutional field, is one where, in the pluralist view, the concentration of power would be avoided. These features of political parties, of pressure groups, and of a constitutional division of powers, are the marks of a liberal-democratic or 'Western' political system. The system satisfies the pluralist demands. It prevents the abuse of power, or the unrestricted use of power, which may occur in other systems where power is concentrated in a few hands. Such other systems may be categorised under the heading of totalitarianism or authoritarianism. They lack the range of groups and associations independent of the state and of each other, an independence which constitutes the pluralist system.

The term 'pluralism' is also sometimes used with reference to a tradition of American political science associated with R. A. Dahl and his school. It is applied to his position in the debate concerning the distribution of power in local communities, for example in Dahl's discussion of New Haven, from which more general conclusions were drawn at the 'macro' level of the power structure of American society.[1] Pluralists held that no one group, or 'power elite', was dominant at the local level and that, by implication, the same was true at the broader national level. As against this view the 'elitists' tried to establish the opposite thesis, namely, that a dominant and relatively united group did hold power in the United States at both local and national level. The debate is important and needs to be analysed in order to understand the pluralist view as well as the problems associated with the concept of power. These problems will be considered in section 6, as will the pluralist methodology. The term 'pluralism' can also be used in a much wider context. H.S. Kariel, in his article on 'Pluralism' (*International Encyclopedia of the Social Sciences*) writes:

In the context of public affairs and political thought, pluralism refers to specific institutional arrangements for distributing and sharing governmental power, to the doctrinal defence of those arrangements, and to an approach for gaining understanding of political behaviour. Political pluralism is therefore an historical phenomenon, a normative doctrine, and a mode of analysis. As the exclusively proper way of ordering and explaining public life, it remains the heart of the liberal ideology of the Western world.[2]

If one concentrates on the second of the three aspects distinguished by Kariel, the normative doctrine or doctrinal defence of 'specific institutional arrangements', it can be said that pluralism is linked to a particular political tradition, that of liberalism. The arrangements which the liberal-pluralist tradition seeks to defend are those of the liberal state. It is for this reason that the basic elements of liberal doctrine and of the liberal state need to be discussed. This brings us to the question of the historical and ideological origins of the pluralist doctrine.

2. HISTORICAL ANTECEDENTS OF PLURALISM: THE LIBERAL PERSPECTIVE

The core of the liberal view on politics as it is taken up in the pluralist perspective involves the purpose of checking and controlling all forms of power. This implies the idea of the limited state, of restricting the sphere of the state's action and limiting the range of its activities. A limited state, however, should not be confused with a weak state. In the words of Franz Neumann:

The liberal state has always been as strong as the political and social situation and the interests of society demanded. It has conducted warfare and crushed strikes; with the help of strong armies it has defended and extended its boundaries; with the help of the police it has restored 'peace and order'. It has been a strong state precisely in those spheres in which it had to be strong and in which it wanted to be strong. This state in which laws but not men were to rule (the Anglo-American formula) i.e. the *Rechtsstaat* (the German formula) has relied upon force *and* law, upon sovereignty *and* freedom.[3]

From the point of view of liberalism the highest value is attached to the individual person. The liberal state, therefore, had to preserve and guarantee the basic rights of the individual.[4] They were natural rights. They included, as Locke had argued, life, freedom and property. The state, therefore, had to protect the person against arbitrary interference, whether from other individuals or from the state and its officials. Indeed in the liberal perspective the state officials were more often held to threaten an individual's liberty, precisely because of the political power with which they were invested.[5] By no means the least of the rights to be protected was that of ownership of private property, explicitly mentioned, for example, in that classical declaration of modern liberalism, the French Revolution's Declaration of the Rights of Man and of the Citizen of 1789.[6] The point is that the state was created precisely for the protection of those rights, but it had to be checked and controlled lest it exceeded its limits and infringed civil liberties. Consequently, dividing power between the different centres of the state, splitting up the power holders into mutually controlling groups, was the chief means to secure the desired end.

One of the most influential expressions of this idea in liberal theory has been the demand for the separation of powers and, more generally, for constitutionalism and the rule of law. The arbitrary and unrestricted use of power could be prevented by the very fact, in Locke's words, of 'having a fixed rule to live by.'[7] The doctrine of the separation of powers is defined in a recent study:

It is essential for the establishment and maintenance of political liberty that the government be divided into three branches, or departments, the legislative, the executive and the judiciary. To each of these branches there is a corresponding identifiable function of government, legislative, executive or judicial. Each branch of the government must be confined to the exercise of its own function and not allowed to encroach upon the functions of the other branches. Furthermore, the persons who compose these three agencies of government must be kept separate and distinct, no individual being allowed to be at the same time a member of more than one branch. In this way each of the branches will be a check to the others and no single group of people will be able to control the machinery of the state.[8]

The separation of powers, however, could be interpreted in a wider sense of a system of checks and balances. Those holding power in the state would be checked by the device of competing groups, that is by the introduction of 'opposition parties.'[9] A team of 'outs' would oppose the 'ins' (out or in of government office). If the governing team was unable to govern satisfactorily it could be replaced by the opposing team which, in any case, would already have scrutinised the proposals and the policies of the group in power. A 'loyal opposition' required for its function a representative body, a parliament. This would serve as a forum for debate and would also create suitable procedures of accountability and control.

Historically, it was the case that political parties developed within the framework of such representative assemblies. Initially they were not mass parties disposing of the powerful extra-parliamentary mass organisation characteristic of political parties in modern democratic systems. They were parliamentary groups, cadre parties, in the terminology of Duverger. They were *partis de notables*.[10] In British politics the period preceding the Second Reform Act of 1867 was the golden age of the independent MP, well described by Bagehot in his classic text *The English Constitution*.[11] The parties operated with a weak sense of representation. The Member of Parliament was a representative but not a delegate, not bound by instructions or mandates or policy directives decided by a party conference. The problems which arise here will be discussed in greater detail below. The main point should be clear by now. It is that the concept of the diffusion of power, which is the basis of the pluralist view, is derived from the liberal idea of the state. The institutions of that state were supposed to prevent a concentration of power.

The idea of the liberal state, and of liberalism in general, is by no means identical with the democratic idea. The distinction is in fact attached to the different meanings of the concept of freedom. Freedom may mean freedom from the state or freedom within the state. In the former sense it means that there is a private sphere which the state must never invade. This is the essence of liberalism, based on the idea of civil freedom or liberty. It is also sometimes called the modern idea of freedom because the idea it describes was utterly alien to the ancient Greeks and Romans. This can be contrasted with the democratic idea of freedom. This implies the right of citizens to make their voice heard in determining the actions and the purpose of the state. Freedom then means the right to involve oneself in the democratic procedures of making the law. It involves possessing the rights needed for such citizen participation: the rights of assembly, of coalition and of expressing one's ideas by word or in print. Such active participation is viewed in democratic theory as bound up with the self-realisation or self-development of the individual. As against the liberal view of 'negative freedom' ('freedom from') the democratic idea propagates a positive view ('freedom to'). The distinction is a familiar once since Isaiah Berlin suggested it in *Two Concepts of Liberty*.[12] The point to notice is that in principle the democratic idea sets no limits to the activity of the state as long as such activity is in conformity with or is an expression of the General Will.

This aspect of the liberal-democratic state has been emphasised by C.B. Macpherson. The liberal state, as he observes, was liberal before it became democratic.[13] In so far as the liberal aim of restricting state power is quite different from the democratic purpose of ensuring political participation and popular power, there is an inherent tension within the institutions of the liberal-democratic state. The whole history of the state can be seen and interpreted as a process of democratisation. The struggle for democratic rights, above all for the general franchise, released popular pressures. The demand was for 'the people', the masses, to take their rightful place within the existing institutions of parliament and political parties. This process of democratisation involved a protracted struggle.[14] The other side of the coin was the attempt by those in power to adopt a policy of 'containment' and to resist the pressures for democratisation.[15] So it can be said that the politics of liberal-democracy has been to a large extent concerned with extending the scope of popular participation, or at the very least preventing democratic rights from being eroded. The rights here under discussion would include trade union rights, rights of controlling executive action, guaranteeing freedom of expression, etc. All this is important in order to understand the tensions within the liberal-democratic system and the pluralist interpretation of its politics. In the pluralist view the system and its institutions satisfy both the liberal aim of checking the power-holders and the democratic aim of ensuring popular participation. It is claimed that the existing structures are sufficient to allow the citizens to exert their democratic rights. Elitist critics of pluralism have been doubtful about this claim. We shall return to this point later.

The liberal state developed in a particular social context, that of a capitalist economy based on private ownership. One of the vital rights the liberal state was intended to protect was property. The liberal state was brought into existence by the great 'bourgeois revolutions', such as the English Civil War and the French Revolution of 1789. They overthrew the absolutist state and created the political framework for the development of a capitalist market economy free from state control. The liberal state and the capitalist economy thus developed together. The social system was one of 'free enterprise'. The adjective must be taken literally as denoting the fact that economic enterprise, business, economic decision-making in general, were free from political control. This has implications for the pluralist analysis. It is a question of the type of society within which the liberal state exists and of the significance of the social context of liberal democracy. The nature of pluralist competition will be influenced by the structure of power prevailing in the wider social context. If the social structure is such as to give built-in advantages to some groups over others, then the competition among groups and associations will be on unequal terms. Certain groups will be able to put greater pressure on the political power-holders; they will, socially and economically, have greater power than others and inevitably the state will be more responsive to them. Therefore the nature of the social context of the liberal state and the balance of pluralist competition within its framework will be important elements in assessing the adequacy of the pluralist view of power as applied to liberal-democratic systems.

3. BASIC CRITERIA OF THE PLURALIST PERSPECTIVE

Pluralism, then, is not just a term arising out of recent debates within American political science. It is an aspect of a much older liberal perspective offering diffusion of power as a remedy against its abuse and as a means of controlling power. The pluralist view of the distribution of power can be shown as expressed in a series of arguments which we shall discuss. Defenders of pluralism maintain that they formulate the criteria of the pluralist theory, and also that a liberal-democratic system satisfies these criteria.

A. No single group is able to exercise systematic and pervasive control over more than one range of issues

The argument is that a group may be dominant in one area but its influence will be confined to that area. Liberal-democratic systems are seen as satisfying this demand. There exists in such systems a range of pressure groups which try, often successfully, to influence government or other holders of state power. Such groups include confederations of industry, trade unions, or the representatives of specific branches of the modern economy. Beer, in a comparison of Britain with the USA, refers to them as 'organisations based on the great economic interest groups of modern society, especially the big three of business, labour and agriculture'. They occupy 'the centre of the stage.'[16] Pressure groups can be divided (following S.E. Finer) into groups promoting particular interests, and 'cause' groups who argue for some cause, viewpoint, or policy.[17]

Clearly, not all groups are equal in power. In Britain, the National Union of Mineworkers has more power and influence than the Association of University Teachers. Beer points out that his Big Three 'are bound in turn to influence policy-making more frequently and on the whole more effectively than pressure groups of other types.'[18] The point is that there must be no group dominant over a whole range of different areas. If there were such a group it could constitute in Marxist terms a 'ruling class', or, in elitist parlance, a 'ruling elite' or 'power elite' (Wright Mills). The essence of the pluralist case is to deny the existence of such a cohesive group. If the political process is scrutinised, if the 'key decisions' are examined, whether at the 'micro' level of local community and local government or on a national scale, it will be found that a group may be specially influential on key decisions in one 'issue area' but cannot sustain this dominance in other areas. In this way, it is claimed, different people have power on different issues. Power is diffused. Trade unions might be highly influential on matters relating to wages and working con-ditions; they would have little say in questions of educational or investment policy. Their scope of influence is restricted.

Considering the range of issues arising in a modern democracy, most people would have a say on some issue. The pluralist view points to the existence of a wide variety of groups as well as of political parties. Such proliferation guarantees that there is no concentration of power. The methodology of the pluralist approach consists in looking at the overt decisions which are taken in any community, local or national, and observing the participation of a range of groups in what is called the 'decision-making process'. That methodology needs to be examined more closely and this will be done in section 6 below.

B. There is a rough equilibrium of power between the most important producer groups, those of capital and labour: the assumption of 'countervailing power'

While power is 'tied to issues' a further aspect of pluralist theory can be summed up under the heading of the idea of 'countervailing power'. Pluralists accept that the producer groups in an advanced economy are particularly important. However, it is argued that there is a balance of power between the two main kinds of groups, respectively representing capital and labour. The term 'countervailing power' was coined by J. K. Galbraith to suggest that the exercise of one kind of power will give rise to organisations which counteract that power, for exmple, organisations of buyers will emerge to counteract sellers' organisations.[19] A situation of 'perfect competition' does not exist. However the 'imperfect competition' between capital and labour is not such as to give either side dominance or any built-in advantage. They both hold economic power and so they can influence government and restrain government action. That may happen through strikes, as far as the unions are concerned, or result from the economic power of capital. The assumption is that there exists a rough equilibrium between them.[20]

C. The separation of economic from political power

Against the Marxist view of the interconnection of economic and political power, the pluralist view denies that political power and control of the state are linked to dominant economic interests or are subservient to any particular economic group. With the achievement of universal suffrage, the rise of working-class political parties and the development of trade unions, it is said, the link of the state with the owners of the productive resources of society was broken. All people are citizens; all have the vote. Economic power is no longer the sole or most important source of political power. Politics has become autonomous. Duverger, for example, writes of the 'separation of political power and of economic power' which marks 'a capitalistic or semi-capitalistic economy'. In his view, 'in a liberal capitalistic regime, as it functioned in the nineteenth century, political power had hardly any independent existence; it was little more than a reflection of economic power.' It is only, Duverger argues, 'in the mixed regime of today's capitalistic societies' that the distinction between economic and political power has acquired significance. He does, however, qualify this by noting the 'concentration of economic power in the hands of a few powerful corporations'. Such a concentration of power casts doubt on the notion of 'a multiplicity of independent "centres of decision"', and suggests that those who have economic power have 'powerful means' of influencing those who hold political power.[21]

Furthermore, pluralists argue that governments will be responsive to the wishes of the electorate because they realise that they have to satisfy at least some of those wishes in order to be returned to power. When combined with the activities of parties and interest groups, this puts even more pressure on a government. In that way the responsibility and accountability of the rulers towards the governed is secured. Such is the meaning of the grandly named 'Law of anticipated responses'.[22] It means that a government, in its own interest, will anticipate the wants of the electorate. The implication is that hardly any action on the part of the citizens is needed because the government will take their preferences into account. The result is that the interests of a small group of property owners will no longer prevail. The state will have to act in the general interest.

D. The neutrality of the state

It follows from the foregoing that seen from the pluralist point of view the state appears as the neutral arbiter, impartially controlling the conflicts of classes and other social groups. It supervises and regulates social antagonisms without taking sides. The personnel of the state do not favour any one set of social or economic interests. In this as in other respects, pluralism contradicts Marxist theory. The axiom of the neutrality of the state can be combined with a view of the state as an agent of reform. If the state is not intrinsically linked to the interests of a 'ruling class', state power can be captured and used by 'subordinate' groups (working-class and socialist parties) to bring about significant changes in the socioeconomic structure of society. This view may be called a social-democratic or reformist version of pluralism. The state, it is argued, has put into effect schemes of social welfare and, at least in Europe over the last century, assumed a more active and interventionist role than ever before. Such is the argument presented, for example, by A. Crosland in *The Future of Socialism*. The state, he suggests, is no longer the instrument of the capitalist class. Its power can be harnessed for a variety of social purposes. In short, under a succession of Labour governments a gradual approach, by democratic means, towards a socialist system becomes a distinct possibility.[23]

E. A plurality of ideas: absence of a dominant ideology

Pluralists further argue that liberal-democratic systems are characterised by the absence of a dominant ideology. A plurality or diversity of ideas can all find expression through various channels. It is claimed that, unlike in a totalitarian society, an active and diversified public opinion in democratic countries can raise and sustain a wide range of opinions and perspectives. There is no uniformity of belief. Such a society would satisfy C. Wright Mills' idea of a 'society of publics', as opposed to what he called a 'mass society'. In a 'society of publics' issues would be raised for political discussion and decision by an informed public free to express its various views. Mills contrasted such a society with one where issues were manipulated, handed out in pre-packaged form, and where people were told what to think.[24] In his view, American society no longer approximated, if it ever had, to a 'society of publics'. The domination of the 'mass media of distraction' had eroded any critical and genuine public opinion. American society was now more accurately described in terms of a mass society.[25] Nevertheless, the term 'society of publics' can be applied to summarise the pluralist view that liberal-democratic societies are marked by a spectrum of ideas, the diversity of which constitutes public opinion. Such public opinion is considered a strong social force.

F. Ideas of choice: Competition: Consent and accountability

Finally, the pluralist view sees politics as a process of choice and competition. Diversity rules everywhere. The politics of Western-type systems is marked by choice between, and competition among, a variety of political parties and pressure groups. The multiplicity of such parties and groups ensures the diffusion of power. Governing parties are checked by opposition parties, while elections guarantee the accountability of the power-holders ('Law of anticipated responses'). They provide the means for citizens to choose the government they want. Just as the customer is supposedly sovereign in the market, so are the citizens in the political sphere. The rights of minorities are protected by opposition parties. A pluralist system, then, results in government and the exercise of power by consent. It produces a state of affairs where two purposes are achieved:

(a) the *liberal* aim of the limited state; restrictions on power holders;
(b) the fulfilment of the *democratic* aim, by a network of parties, groups, associations, of all citizens exercising their democratic rights and participating in political action.

4. PLURALISM IN THE POLITICAL SPHERE: POLITICAL PARTIES

One of the two main projects of pluralist theory, as has been said, is the limitation and control of political power. This is achieved through the existence and the working of various political institutions and mechanisms. A competitive party system is one of the most important of these. Political parties (in the words of Gordon Smith) are indeed 'the summation of pluralist traditions'.[26] A liberal-democratic system requires two or more parties competing for electoral support. The party most successful in the electoral competition provides the personnel for governmental office. The party struggle and the existence of opposition parties make power control effective. A diversity of parties, each offering a different set of policies and programmes, each animated by a different ideology, gives citizens a chance to choose. If the party in power does not satisfy the electorate, then through the mechanism of regular elections it can be turned out.

Furthermore, the parties offer their members an opportunity to participate in political work. Modern political parties are mass organisations with an extra-parliamentary structure, annual conferences, policy-making committees, and so on. Their structures cover local constituencies. They contain channels through which party members can make their voice heard. Individual persons can participate in election campaigns, and once involved in the activities of the party they can affect decisions and policy options. Inner-party democracy as well as the regular party conference make the party leader accountable to the rank and file. In this way, participation and democratic control are possible. It is true that parties vary in this respect. Generally speaking, socialist parties, at least in theory, tend to scrutinise the actions of their leaders more closely than is the case with the parties of the Right. The latter are traditionally inclined to grant their leaders a greater degree of autonomy and more freedom from accountability to the party conference and ordinary members. It has been suggested that parties which originated outside the parliamentary system, like the British Labour Party and indeed most socialist and working-class parties, pay more attention to the mood of their rank-and-file followers than those that originally consisted of groupings in parliament.[27] However that may be, political parties function in the way we have tried to indicate. They are essential factors within a democratic system.

The historical evolution of those parties, from factions within the representative assembly to mass organisations, has been traced in summary fashion by Max Weber and, among others, by Duverger.[28] They were initially cadre parties, loosely organised groups functioning solely within the parliamentary context. With universal suffrage, or at least male suffrage, parties changed their nature and indeed their function.[29] Eventually their main function was to mobilise electoral support in order to 'get out the vote'. In between elections they would try to maintain morale and cohesion, to develop forms of political education and instruction. All this required a permanent apparatus, a structured party bureaucracy where the top positions became very important. A new party elite had been created. Especially within the parties of the Left this resulted in tensions between the party staff and the parliamentarians fearful of their autonomy which they felt threatened by the party machine. The party leader had become 'the boss' who controlled the machine. He towered in importance over the person who was a mere parliamentarian or backbencher. Without his authorisation nothing could be done.

Political parties provide the perfect example of the institutional democratisation of the liberal state that was outlined before. The question then arises of the significance of the changes the parties experienced. Was it a genuine process of democratisation? Weber denied it. He held that all that had happened was the emergence of a new and different kind of ruling elite. The party leader had become 'the dictator of the electoral battlefield'.[30]

The divergencies in interpreting the functioning of the party lead now to a crucial problem. This is not merely a problem of academic discourse, but is of vital importance in the field of political practice. It is the problem of representation. What role should be played by those people who represent the many? Are they free representatives, or are they delegates bound by their instructions? Here too we can observe the transition from a liberal to a democratic standpoint. This question is intimately connected with the degree of urgency attached to the demand for universal suffrage.

In the liberal view representation is a trust, and the representative has an open mandate. Representatives cannot be bound or tied by any specific instructions. Whatever the matter that comes up for debate, they speak their mind, they decide to the best of their judgement and as their conscience dictates. Once the decision has been taken they report to those whom they represent, but beyond such reporting back they have no further responsibility provided they have acted in good faith. Any attempt to control their action would be seen as a threat to the representatives' autonomy, implying a doubt as to their ability to take the right decision in the general interest.

The democratic idea of representation is quite different. Basically it is informed by a distrust of all forms of delegation of power, i.e. of entrusting people's interests to anyone other than the people themselves. This distrust takes many forms; it stems from the fear that the representatives may be dominated by their own wishes or interests. The ideal, therefore, remains direct democracy even where for obvious reasons it cannot be achieved. Representation, if not an outright evil, will always remain a second best. In any case the representatives must not substitute themselves or their will for the will of the people.

Their task is to represent in the strict sense, i.e. to express and put into effect the will of the people. They are in fact delegates bound by decisions arrived at in the general meetings of the people or of the party. To go beyond their role of actualising the popular will means the abuse of their power. For that reason there must exist, in the democratic perspective, mechanisms of accountability and control, structures and procedures in the political party as well as in the wider political framework which prevent the democratic delegates from going beyond their terms of reference.

The democratic distrust of representation finds expression in various theoretical as well as practical political perspectives. It underlies Rousseau's insistence on a direct democracy. In his words: 'The deputies of the people, therefore, are not, and cannot be, its representatives; they are merely its stewards.' Suspicion of the character of the people's representatives has often enough been expressed by a range of writers, including Hegel and his observation that 'The Few assume to be the *deputies*, but they are often only the *despoilers* of the Many', as well as Sorel's condemnation of parliamentary politicians 'waiting for the wheel of fortune to turn to their advantage' so that they could become 'republican princes'.[31] An extreme form of distrust is the anarchists' rejection of any kind of representation on the grounds that delegation always involves a loss of liberty. This is one reason for anarchist abstentionism or refusal to get involved in political action. In a different form the problem surfaces in Marx's political views. In his discussion of the Paris Commune of 1871 he invoked the aim of maximising control over the municipal representatives of Paris. They 'were to be chosen by universal suffrage in the various wards of the town, responsible and revocable at short terms'.[32]

In the context of political practice the democratic conception of representation implies that the parliamentary representatives and the full-time officials of the party should be bound by party policy as decided by conference. They thereby receive their mandate. In the British Labour Party a document of 1937 clearly expresses such a democratic as opposed to a liberal idea of representation by emphasising the sovereignty of the party:

In contradistinction to Conservative conferences which simply pass resolutions which may or may not be acted upon, the Labour Party conference lays down the policy of the party, and issues instructions which must be carried out by the Executive, the affiliated organisations, and its representatives in Parliament and on local authorities.[33]

Whether or not the Labour Party in its practice has ever fully implemented the prescription is another matter. The argument, in any case, is that a firm commitment to conference resolutions, and even more to the party manifesto, enables the electorate to make a conscious choice. It ensures that the voters know how they stand with their representative. In this way the mandate creates a democratic legitimacy. Were it otherwise, there would be no control over the leaders and no accountability on their part. There would be 'power without responsibility'.

Of course, there is the counter-argument that the mandate threatens to undermine the sovereignty of Parliament. It might also be argued that the President of the United States is elected to his most powerful position with a minimum of policy commitments. In fact, the British situation recently tends to approximate to the American model in so far as it seems that once installed in office and as long as he or she enjoys the confidence of his or her party, a British Prime Minister disposes of great, one might almost say of dictatorial, power. The question must be left open. What can definitely be asserted is that leadership autonomy is not compatible with the classical theory of democracy. According to Rousseau the sovereignty of the people cannot be transferred. Robespierre adopted the principle. He distinguished between 'le représentant du peuple' and 'le mandataire'.[34]

As far as Britain is concerned, it is not always possible neatly to separate the liberal and the democratic strands for the reason that they are both amalgamated in the texture of British politics. Of course, there was the gradual transformation of a liberal into a democratic system, but the liberal elements have been preserved. The view that power-holders whether elected or non-elected (civil service) should be given more independence from popular pressure and that therefore the democratic aspect of the system should be reduced is still widespread. After all, it seems that even in the Labour Party the democratic pressures are more pronounced in the aftermath of disillusion and electoral defeat, as (for example) after the formation of the 'National Government' of 1931, or after the experience of the Wilson and Callaghan governments ending with the electoral victory of the Conservatives under Mrs Thatcher.

One could argue that the tension between popular pressures and leadership autonomy persists in all liberal-democratic systems. In that case Miliband's view of the British political system as a 'system of containment' might be held to apply generally.[35] There are mechanisms and institutions operating within all democratic systems to 'contain' and reduce popular pressures and the involvement of the rank and file. This is one function fulfilled, as we shall see, by representative assemblies or parliaments.

Party leaders certainly need some freedom of action and manoeuvre. In this respect Sartori has a point when he stresses the importance of the so-called 'vertical' aspect of democracy, by which he means the necessity of leadership.[36] He is no doubt right in warning us of the danger in neglecting this 'vertical dimension'. Similar views have been expressed to point out the bad consequences if leaders are all too responsive to popular demands. Decisions are then taken for short-term reasons to curry electoral favour, the political system is overloaded by attempts to satisfy particular groups, and long-term interests are neglected. Such criticism may be valid to a certain extent, but one must be careful not to fall into line with writers who merely wish to highlight certain questionable features of the democratic system in order to discredit democracy altogether. One might think, for example, of the French right-wing thinker Maurras who emphasised the lack of continuity, especially in foreign policy, due to electoral changes. He also blamed, as inherent in the democratic system, the vacillations of a government always too ready to conform to a volatile public opinion.[37]

The thrust of the democratic argument is that democratic controls must be maintained for two reasons. The one is the 'protective argument'.[38] It says that unless there are structures of control imposed on them the power-holders will try to increase their power. They will overstep limits and ultimately harm the interests of those whom they are supposed to represent.[39] The other argument is developed in classical democratic theory as expressed by Rousseau and J.S. Mill. It suggests that a democratic involvement of the people is necessary not only for protection against abuse of power, but also for reasons of political education. Through participation in politics people became educated, or rather 'self-educated': they develop interests and abilities broader than those relating to a purely private and personal sphere.[40]

Such views may also serve as a standard of criticism of existing democratic (or so-called democratic) systems which do not provide the structures necessary for an effective and genuine participatory democracy. That was the kind of criticism advanced by C. Wright Mills when he wrote that in both the USA and the USSR 'there are no readily available vehicles for reasoned opinions, no instruments for the rational exertion of public will'. He went on to say:

The kind of public that democratic theorists imagined does not prevail in either the USA or the USSR, nor is it the forum within which a politics of real issues is regularly enacted.

The classic conditions of democracy and democratic institutions do not flourish in the power structure of the United States or the Soviet Union.[41]

It is only when we view the political problem placed in its social context that we can properly understand the significance of the liberal, and by implication, of the democratic theory of representation. This will also shed light on the protracted struggle for universal suffrage. The point is that in its liberal interpretation representation means that the liberal rights of the citizen are safeguarded by his or her representatives whether or not he or she has voted for them. Such was Ireton's argument in the army debates which took place at Putney in 1647 during the English Civil War. Ireton maintained that the birthright of an Englishman was that he could freely move through the country always protected by the law. That was what the Civil War had been fought for, Ireton argued: that the law should rule and not one man's (the king's) will. The Levellers had other ideas. They thought the war had been fought to give them a new deal, a deal which would alter the social structure of the realm. If that were to be the case (as in fact it was not), an Englishman's birthright must include his right to cast his vote for men he thought fit to effect such radical changes. The franchise would then be a necessary condition of his freedom though not yet a sufficient one: the representatives had to be controlled. A demand for biennial parliaments was indeed the second point on the agenda of the meeting.[42]

Ireton's argument was taken up by later political figures. It was repeated by the younger William Pitt on 7 May 1783, in a speech he made in opposition to the extension of the franchise: 'For my part', Pitt said, 'my idea of representation is this, that the members once chosen, and returned to Parliament, are in effect, the representatives of the people at large, as well of those who do not vote at all...'[43]

Ultimately all depends on the extent to which the state can affect the life of its citizens. All through the liberal era citizens could safely leave it to their representatives to arrive at their decision. Vote or no vote, whatever happened in Parliament would not drastically affect one's private life or property interests. People might be taxed but the tax would not be crippling. The representatives might decide on war or peace, but even war would not seriously interfere with one's way of life. In this respect it could be written that 'the whole problem of conscription' (in the First World War) 'had nearly split the country, for Britain had never before been in a position where war had to be regarded as an unlimited affair which would seriously upset the everyday life of the ordinary citizen.'[44]

With the coming of democracy and the expectation of an active role for the state, the whole position changed. Universal suffrage became an irresistible demand. It was still delayed because of the fear prevalent since the earliest time that the franchise might prove detrimental to property. This is a point to which we shall revert in the next section.

5. REPRESENTATIVE ASSEMBLIES

In the pluralist view, representative assemblies are seen as no less central to liberal-democratic systems than political parties. They are seen as the forum within which governments are held accountable to the sovereign people, present in the shape of their parliamentary representatives. Certainly some of the most dramatic scenes in the politics of liberal-democratic systems have taken place within the framework of the representative assembly. Apart from such highlights and confrontations, a central part of the everyday business of democratic government, and of the opposition, proceeds. The seal of democratic legitimacy is set on governmental decisions while, at the same time, the task of controlling power-holders supposedly becomes tangible political reality. For that purpose legislatures are equipped with committees and with procedures for inquiry. Opposition parties have rights of question and debate. They can raise issues so that governments have to give account of their actions.

The fundamental principle of democracy is that counting heads is preferable to the breaking of them. Political systems in general contain devices which work to mitigate conflicts.[45] Liberal-democratic systems contain institutions which function as shock-absorbers or 'sponges' to reduce social conflicts, and this is one part of the significance of representative bodies. One can also say that representative assemblies perform a most important task by securing democratic legitimation. The basis of the liberal-democratic system is held to be *consent*: no exercise of power or act of the executive is legitimate unless it has been agreed through a majority vote of the representatives of the sovereign people. No finance can be raised until the budget has been approved. Thus the justification of governmental authority rests with those holding sovereign power, i.e. the people themselves at election times and afterwards their parliamentary representatives.

If the representative assembly is therefore seen as the centre of political life in a democracy, it is also thought to be an educational centre. A people without a parliament lacks that education. It is not only participation but the receiving of daily reports that sharpens the political mind and makes it more alert. To know what is going on makes for a better understanding. In this sense the task of representative institutions is to develop public political awareness and contribute to what has been called the 'continuous election campaign'.[46] The assembly should be the central focus of attention because it is the locus of sovereignty and of the popular will. French republican democratic ideas emphasised this point, as a recent study makes clear.[47] Sovereignty resided with the people, but given the practical impossibility of a direct democracy, the realisation of popular sovereignty lay in the jealously guarded supremacy of the representative assembly.

If parliament thus fulfills an educational function, it may also be regarded as a training ground for politicians where they can develop their ability in debate as well as in political action. Representative assemblies provide a terrain for parliamentarians to develop the skills needed to fill the leadership positions in a democratic system. Weber stressed 'the function of a strong parliament as a recruiting ground for leadership'. While he was by no means an uncritical devotee of parliamentary democracy, he emphasised the need for a strong parliament in Germany. He 'insisted that the low level of political ability in Germany was a consequence of the institutional weakness of the Reichstag'.[48]

The historical development of representative assemblies reflects the transformation of a liberal into a democratic society. Observers have often noted the loss of individual brilliance and of the high standard of debate which were claimed to characterise liberal parliaments. This may well be true, though it must not be forgotten that strong personalities have left their stamp on parliamentary proceedings in modern times, in Britain as elsewhere. Admittedly, modern party organisation imposes a certain uniformity, not to say drabness, on the conduct of its members, as de Tocqueville observed some time ago: 'Members of these associations answer to a word of command like soldiers on active service.'[49] This subordination of once sovereign parliamentary representatives to party rule was largely the result of the coming of universal suffrage. This clearly was of paramount importance and best illustrates the transformation of the political climate. Its introduction met with determined resistance because its opponents were convinced that it would challenge the very foundations of the liberal order. Thus Ireton, in his Putney speech quoted above, sought to prove that the extension of the suffrage was not only unnecessary to secure freedom, but that it also contained a dangerous element since, as he put it, 'All the main thing that I speak for, is because I would have an eye on property.' If those who were 'here today and gone tomorrow', who therefore had no stake in the country claimed the franchise as a natural right, might not by the same right equality in property be claimed ('a freedom to the land, to take the ground')? At that point in the debate Cromwell in the chair concurred: 'the consequence of this rule tends to anarchy, must end in anarchy.'[50]

Freedom, for Ireton, meant the rule of law and security of the person and of his or her property. The fear persisted that if the masses were to take their place within the structure of the liberal state's representative institutions, then the existing social order could not be expected to survive. At a much later date the Duke of Wellington stated that 'a democracy has never been established in any part of the world that has not immediately declared war against property.' His concern was echoed by Disraeli who, in 1859, warned:

If you establish a democracy, you must in due season reap the fruits of a democracy. You will in due season have great impatience of public burdens combined in due season with great increase in the public expenditure.... You will, in due season, with a democracy find that your property is less valuable and your freedom is less complete.[51]

What aroused fear in the defenders of property meant hope to those who tried to reveal the injustice and inequalities which they saw as inherent in the economic system. Marx believed that the coming of democracy would certainly lead to a majority for socialism. 'The carrying of universal suffrage in England', he wrote on the occasion of the Chartists' demand for manhood suffrage, 'would, therefore, be a far more socialistic measure than anything which has been honoured with that name on the Continent.' Engels was even more confident: 'Democracy, nowadays that is communism', he claimed in 1845.[52]

We know today that such fears and hopes were not borne out by the facts, at least not to the extent expected. The democratic, and later the socialist, movements did indeed take their place within the institutions of the liberal state, yet the capitalist system survived these challenges. It is true, however, that with the advance of democratic ideas the state did come to interfere with the economic structure of society, albeit in a fairly limited way. At least it imposed certain demands of taxation on property-owners and did curtail the power of capital to some degree. It seems to follow that at least in certain areas political democracy does exert a levelling pressure and gradually develops, or seeks to develop, from political to social democracy. de Tocqueville remarked that 'Democratic institutions awaken and flatter the passion for equality without ever being able to satisfy it entirely.'[53]

Such considerations may provide at least part of an answer to the question posed by the French historian, Halévy: 'Why no revolution?' – a belated echo of the expectations just discussed.[54] Social and other reforms have indeed taken place within liberal-democratic systems, and have contributed to averting the revolutionary challenge of democracy. But a further element relevant to answering Halévy's question is to be found in a fact already mentioned, the integrative effect of the political institutions of the democratic system.

There are two different aspects of the significance of representative assemblies. They do provide a forum for raising issues, expressing grievances, and promoting different ideological viewpoints. They also constitute essential bulwarks for the defence of democratic rights and act, with varying degrees of efficiency, to control the power of the executive. Nevertheless, participation in the institutions of the liberal-democratic state has a certain demobilising effect. As Przeworski points out—he is speaking of the choices facing a socialist movement—taking one's seat in parliament imposes certain 'costs'.[55] It creates a distance between the representatives and the masses whom they represent. A caste of professional politicians emerges. They have to accept the rules of the parliamentary game. They are caught up in parliamentary structures and procedures which they do not wholly control. A club-like atmosphere in parliament tends to blur class and party differences. The result is a tendency towards deradicalisation of those taking their place in legislative or representative assemblies.

A final word should be said about the limits of that power control which can be exercised by a representative assembly.

First, it must be pointed out that much state action in pluralist systems escapes any form of parliamentary scrutiny. This applies to the military, to sections of the bureaucracy or civil service. Where abuses of power are discovered, *ex post facto* parliamentary inquiries can be started but, obviously, only after the event.

Secondly, where there is strong party control, as in the British system, such scrutiny as the system permits often remains formal. The government can put pressure on its supporters in various ways: by appealing to party loyalty, promising office or promotion to potential dissidents, stressing the need for party unity in the face of opposition, and so on. There are many devices, as we have seen, to subject a government to criticism and hold it to account. It still remains true that in most Western systems, the US Congress being a possible exception, the extent of such oppositional probing can be minimised. Once this is admitted it can be argued that the representative assembly provides governmental action with a sort of democratic façade or a seal of approval. Governments may then claim that their actions have received democratic approval and consent. The claim is not totally meaningless; nevertheless there is little doubt that the reality of democratic control through the agency of representative institutions is considerably less than a formalistic democratic theory might suggest.

In this connection it is worth mentioning what Raymond Williams calls the idea of the 'all-purpose representative'.[56] He suggests that in Western-type systems it is often argued that the parliamentary channel of representation is the only legitimate one. An MP is seen as the 'all-purpose representative' in so far as he or she represents the members of the constituency on a whole range of possible issues. In consequence the representation of interests outside the parliamentary sphere would be severely limited or even seen as utterly unacceptable. Such a view rather contradicts the general thrust of pluralist theory, which attributes the representation of interests to a variety of sources. These, as we shall see in the next section, include pressure groups or interest groups outside parliament. Interest representation should, therefore, not be restricted to the activity of the parliamentary representative.

Finally, it should be said that to point to the functions of representative assemblies as institutions for absorbing or containing conflict, and for providing democratic legitimacy, is not in any way meant to suggest that these exhaust the significance of representative assemblies. An effective parliament is a crucial institution for a system which aims to control the power-holders. That is best suggested by the fact that whenever authoritarian regimes come to power, they either dismantle parliamentary institutions altogether or they convert them into passive tools for the achievement of their own purposes. Hitler had an Enabling Act passed which 'enabled' him to rule without any reference to the Reichstag. A parliament then becomes the platform where the bombastic declarations of a leader are received and duly applauded.

6. PLURALIST PRESSURE GROUPS – PLURALIST METHODOLOGY

This section aims to clarify two points: first, the purpose is to show the importance which the pluralist point of view attaches to pressure groups and interest groups as means of interest representation and of the diffusion of power. The second aim is to show something of the methods by which the pluralist case is established, in other words, the methodology of pluralist theory.

The pluralist theory is by no means confined to the formal political institutions we have considered so far, namely political parties and representative assemblies. It is a theory concerned with the distribution of power in 'civil society'. It is claimed that power is dispersed among various groups which are independent of the state and independent of each other. This, in the pluralist view, avoids two constellations which may be labelled *statism* on the one hand, and *corporatism* on the other. Where groups or associations lose their power to the state, so that it is concentrated in the state, there statism rules. This is an authoritarian type of political order. Civil society – the whole range of social interests – has no longer any separate existence or freedom from state control. Such a situation reaches its culmination in the totalitarian state. 'Society ceases to be distinguished from the state; it is totally permeated by political power.' This permeation, in the words of Franz Neumann, is achieved by the 'transition from pluralist to totalitarian social controls'. It includes the leadership principle, the 'synchronisation' of all social organisations, the atomisation and isolation of the individual. Such a situation is at the opposite pole from a pluralist system.[57]

Pluralism, then, is the antithesis to totalitarianism. The relation of pluralism to corporatism is less clearly defined.[58] Within a corporatist system the presentation and defence of particular interests is the task, or privilege, of professional groups such as business organisations, trade unions and various professional associations. The extent to which the various groups, which here represent social interests, are mutually independent, as well as the extent of their independence from the state, may vary. There are degrees of corporatism. In an extreme case corporatism and statism amount to much the same thing. Such would be the case of a corporate state in the fascist sense of the term where the tight control of the state over the producer groups of the economy approximates to a totalitarian society. In general, a society with a very high degree of integration between pressure groups and the state would fall short of the pluralist ideal.

On the other hand, there is no necessary conflict between a pluralist perspective and the admission of some elements of corporatism in Western-type democratic systems. Traditionally, the kind of corporatism envisaged in such systems has been a tripartite corporatism of state–business–labour. It imparts what a recent author (K. Middlemass) has called a 'corporate bias' to political decisions.[59] Basically, the argument in favour of corporatism has always been that direct collaboration of employers and employees, in and between the professional associations, might mitigate if not eliminate class conflicts. One could here refer to recent political developments in the German Federal Republic, and also in Austria, where both sides jointly attempt to establish wage norms as well as lines of planned economic advance, in the process known as *Mitbestimmungsrecht*.

Corporatism can here signify a situation where certain groups are in an interlocking relationship with the state, business and labour organisations meeting with the state on equal or almost equal terms. This position of interlocking negotiation may involve the exclusion of other groups from the corporate heights. Some groups reach the 'plateau' of corporate representation while others are excluded, with the result that they are weaker in power and influence. Those who have some kind of 'privileged' relationship with government (which can be called a 'corporate' relationship) are more powerful. This corporate relationship may be mediated through committees or institutions where civil servants and interest representatives develop an intimate relationship of mutual concessions and compromises to the exclusion of outsiders. Such would be the case where a powerful interest group had 'colonised' the civil service or part of it, meaning by this a situation where one particular group was seen as the sole legitimate representative of a social interest. It would then be viewed as an important source of information, and its demands readily responded to by holders of state power. Such 'outsiders' as had not gained access to the corporate plateau might then have to resort to more extreme measures to get some response to their grievances.[60]

The pluralist view of liberal-democracy as a system of countervailing tendencies and their resolution by compromise might be seen as typical of a 'balancing society'. Here, 'the state subject to the control of a free electorate, was to be the responsible trustee, the impartial umpire, the expert broker of conflicting interests and contending powers.'[61] But does the idea still faithfully reflect actual political reality? C. Wright Mills called it 'romantic pluralism'. By that he did not mean that the pluralist analysis was wrong, but that it was valid only within certain chronological and social limits. The picture it yielded of American society was correct up to the time, approximately, of the First World War. Later it still remained valid, but only with reference to the 'middle levels of power'. In Mills' view, the vital decisions, those that matter, no longer emerge from an equilibrium of social checks and balances. They are now taken by a small power elite. The elite is composed of prominent politicians, heads of the big corporations and military chiefs (the war lords). They do not act in the interest of any class. There is no class rule. They have common beliefs, a community of outlook, values and basic assumptions, stemming from education, professional principles, and social intercourse. They take their decisions, according to their judgement, in the interest of the state. It is not necessarily the interest of the American people.

In turning now to the second topic of this section we intend to clarify the way in which the pluralist case is established. In other words, we shall discuss the methodology of pluralism. In fact, much of the critique of pluralism has focused on its methodological assumptions.

One important strand of pluralist theory is represented by the American political scientist, Robert Dahl. It draws empirical support and verification from studies of power at local community level. Two important concepts are used.

1. The first is the concept of 'scope of influence' – the area or sphere within which a person or group is influential.
2. The second is the concept of 'key decisions'.

Examination of both concepts, and of the pluralist use of them, goes some way in explaining the pluralist view of power.

As regards the scope of influence, we have already drawn attention to the pluralist demand that the dominating influence of any person or group should be restricted to one area only. This simple idea is a basic element in the pluralist perspective. Examination of the power structure at local level, as in Dahl's study of New Haven, was intended to verify this empirically. It was shown that, while a person or group had power in one 'issue area', i.e. on one set of issues, other persons formed the group influential on other issues. The conclusion is that if there is no one group dominant over a whole range of issues, a pluralist power structure prevails. In Dahl's words: 'a leader in one issue-area is not likely to be influential in another ... Leaders in different issue-areas do not seem to be drawn from a single homogeneous stratum of the community.'[62]

The implications are clear. In every political community a wide range of issues is to be settled. Political power will be unequally distributed; there will be a distinction between leaders and led. However, no one leader is dominant over a wide range of issues. Pluralist systems are systems of 'dispersed inequalities', as opposed to 'cumulative inequalities'. There are indeed inequalities of power, a distinction between leaders and led, in the society as a whole and in its various sub-groups. However, such leaders are limited in their sphere of power. In Dahl's study of New Haven, those who were influential in nominating party members for elective office were not important in the issue-area of urban development. In turn, the scope of influence of either group did not extend to education policy.

The fact of 'dispersed inequalities' is also explained with respect to the varied bases of power. Everyone has some 'resource' which can be turned into a political resource. Dahl charted the development of the leadership structure of the New Haven community from the domination of the 'patricians' through that of the 'entrepreneurs' to those he called the 'ex-plebs'.[63] Each leadership group had a different source of power, illustrating the variety of power resources in the community. The powerbase of the patricians was their social standing. The entrepreneurs possessed the political resources of wealth and of economic power. As for the 'ex-plebs', they had the ability to get out the vote, to mobilise support through their control of the political organisation and of the party machinery. In Dahl's words: 'A political system dominated by one cohesive set of leaders had given way to a system dominated by many different sets of leaders, each having access to a different combination of resources. It was, in short, a pluralist system.'[64]

The implication for political analysis generally is that there is a variety of powerbases which can be turned into political power. Political knowledge, wealth or other economic resources, skill and ability to control political organisations, specialised knowledge, military power, social standing – the list could be extended – can all provide a basis for political power. Any person or group has access to some such political resource, individually or collectively, and so power is not concentrated. That does not mean that everybody has an equal share of the power available. It guarantees that it is not concentrated in a few hands.

It has been argued that just as important as the notion of scope of influence is the concept of 'key decisions' in the pluralist view. Power is defined as the ability to get one's way in those key decisions. A conclusion pointing to the existence of a dominant group, or class, is only tenable if a series of overt decisions is examined and if this shows that one group regularly succeeds in having its preferences win the day.[65] The pluralist method involves looking at cases of open conflict where definite outcomes can be observed. The classical expression of the method is provided by Dahl in *Who Governs?*: 'A rough text of a person's overt or covert influence is the frequency with which he successfully initiates an important procedure over the opposition of others, or vetoes policies initiated by others, or initiates a policy where no opposition appears.'[66]

So, if one took a pluralist view of the conflict between organised business and labour, one would have to look at cases where the interests of the two groups were in collision. If neither side regularly prevailed, there would be evidence that the conflict took place within a pluralist system. There would be no ruling class and hence no concentration of power. Accordingly, the bulk of *Who Governs?* is devoted to examining decisions in three 'key areas', seeing which group or individuals participated in those decisions, whether the same group was dominant in all areas, or if there was what Dahl calls 'specialisation of influence'. In such terms the pluralist methodology is couched and the notion of power discussed.

7. CRITICAL EXAMINATION OF PLURALIST THEORY

Having surveyed the pluralist view of the distribution and exercise of power in Western-type systems, we must add a few critical remarks. The critique of pluralism can be summarised under three headings:

(i)   The question of the methodological procedure of pluralism.

(ii) The pluralist view of the state and the social context of pluralist systems.

(iii) The internal structure of social groups (the vertical aspect) and their mutual relations (the horizontal aspect).

(i) This criticism is directed against the concentration of the pluralist method on overt conflict and key decisions. The point is not that the competition of interests does not take place on equal terms, though that may well be true. The question is of what has been called the 'mobilisation of bias', a structure of power which works to filter out certain issues and stop them coming to the stage of overt conflict. Here the metaphor of 'two faces of power' can be used, the term coined by Bachrach and Baratz.[67] They suggest that the pluralist approach is inadequate because power may also be exercised to prevent certain issues from ever reaching the stage of open discussion. A group may be powerful enough to determine 'the agenda' of politics and to make sure that certain items are never put on that agenda. Bachrach and Baratz give the example of a lecturer who has a grievance, but who does not raise the issue through the appropriate channels of his or her institution. A pluralist observer might then assume that in the absence of any complaint everyone was perfectly satisfied. However, there might have been a number of reasons why the lecturer did not complain. The lecturer might have hesitated to offend the political views and attitudes of his or her colleagues. In any case he or she might have known that the complaint would not have any effect, given the power structure of the university and the attitudes of most of its members. Or the lecturer might have been afraid that a complaint would be considered an act of disloyalty to the institution. Alternatively there might be the fear of sanctions applied against a 'trouble-maker'. The latter case would have been one of 'reputed power', the college authorities being reputed to possess a power which they might use. In sum, although no overt action was taken, the 'non-decision' of the lecturer reveals a hidden power.

The question is of more general applicability. It raises the problem of the importance of values and beliefs as affecting people's decisions. This in turn refers to the whole area of power which in Marxist terms is called ideology, in other terms legitimation. For instance, the alternative to the existing Western system of power is sometimes presented in extremely unpleasant terms as if any radical change would necessarily imply repression and the destruction of individual liberty. The point is that if such arguments are widely spread and accepted, the beliefs they reflect become dominant or 'hegemonic' within the system. Those in power could then dispense with, or largely reduce, coercion because the prevailing climate of opinion would prevent 'subversive' attitudes from emerging. Here too the fact that no overt action could be observed would not prove that no power relations were operating. Power, in other words, can be inherent in ideological and belief systems. A 'one-dimensional' view of power ignores the power which is derived from beliefs and value attitudes.[68]

This 'second face' of concealed power, which pluralist studies do not take sufficiently into account, applies to structures as well as to ideas and beliefs. The structure of a system within which decisions are made may be such as to secure a built-in advantage for one or the other group. The whole process of overt conflict is then skewed respectively to the advantage or detriment of one party. We shall revert to the point when considering the social context which conditions the working of a pluralist system.

Pluralist theory, then, operates with too limited a view of power. C. Wright Mills was quite aware of the various forms power can assume. 'Coercion is the final form of power', he wrote,

but we are by no means constantly at the last resort. Authority (power that is justified by the beliefs of the voluntarily obedient) and manipulation (power that is wielded unbeknown to the powerless) must also be considered, along with coercion. In fact the three types must be sorted out whenever we think of power.[69]

It is true that some proponents of pluralist theory, and this includes Dahl, are quite aware of the problem of the context within which the overt conflict takes place. In its more subtle versions the pluralist perspective does have a view of what is called 'indirect influence'. In the case of urban redevelopment in New Haven the debate, as Dahl points out, was held within the limits of the existing socioeconomic system.[70] The implication is that the conflicts which form the material for the pluralist interpretation take place within a particular context. Not only will this, generally speaking, curtail the range of debate, but if the existing socioeconomic system is such as to involve a particular distribution of power, it will skew the terms of the contest between the competing groups.

(ii) The critical examination of the view pluralism takes of the state centres on two points. The first is that pluralist theories underrate the independent power or the 'might' of the state. The second criticism calls into question the apparent neutrality of the state, its impartiality in balancing conflicting interests.

Classical pluralist theory arose in the struggle against a sovereign state which had become the undisputed holder of all political authority. The pluralist tradition assumes a limited state which has no purposes of its own. It functions merely to control and balance competing social forces, achieving an equilibrium of pressure groups. As against this, the increasing and ever more centralised power of the modern state was noted in the introductory chapter above. It was mentioned that thinkers as different as Marx and Weber were in agreement in acknowledging the phenomenon. The pluralist theory then appears rather outdated in failing to grasp the growth of state power.

From the Marxist point of view, as we shall see in Chapter Three, this increased state power serves the interests of an economically dominant class. The recognition of greater state power goes hand-in-hand with a view of the state's lack of neutrality in being an agent of capitalist interests. From the basic starting point that capitalist interests dominate society and can harness the state to their service, the conclusion is that the increased power of the state will only strengthen the dominance of those class interests. It may even happen that in the event of a serious challenge the state will override the democratic consensus by authoritarian methods in an attempt to preserve capitalist power.

Not all versions of socialist thought accept the Marxist view connecting the greater role of the state with its function as defender of capitalist power. Social-democratic theorists would agree that the contemporary state plays a more active part than that assigned to it in pluralist theory. Yet they reject the Marxist argument that this role is necessarily one of serving capitalist interests. State power can be captured by a party representing the majority of the population, and used in a democratic context against the power of the capitalist class.

This is the point of Crosland's book, *The Future of Socialism*, which has been mentioned above. Crosland recognised 'the greater influence of the government', but denied that this was always used 'to buttress the power, and underwrite the actions of private business'.[71] In his view the state is seen as neutral; it is the instrument available to whichever party gains the democratic majority vote. The same point was made in a more popular form by Harold Wilson when he said that the state was like a motor car which could be driven anywhere depending on who was in the driving seat.

The pluralist view of power diffusion and of the limited role of the state is also criticised by elite theory, for example in the 'power elite' version offered by C. Wright Mills. Mills argued that there existed a power elite which took the vital decisions affecting society, American society in his case. This 'power elite' was different from the Marxist view of an economically dominant ruling class. Its powerbase was not, as in Marxist theory, the ownership of the means of production, but stemmed from control over large organisations—military, business and political. Yet the critique of pluralism is much the same. Power at the top level is in the hands of a small cohesive group which dominates civil society. The pluralist vision fades and becomes completely extinguished. There is no dispersion of power in such a society.

How do pluralist theorists respond to such criticism? In answer to the question concerning the increasingly centralised power of the state, pluralists could point to the fact that the state itself is not a monolithic bloc. There are different centres of power within the state, various sections of the state apparatus which mutually check each other. Secondly, even while making allowances for the state's greater power, it is argued that in liberal-democratic systems the state system remains subject to group pressure from a variety of sources. The state does not challenge nor seek to undermine the independence of diverse groups and centres of power outside the state system. State power may indeed be greater than that of the pressure groups of civil society, but the state remains open to influence from business associations, unions, 'cause groups' of various kinds. As long as such groups preserve their autonomy, the increased power of the state is compatible with a considerable degree of diffusion of power, and the pluralist thesis is not refuted. Similar arguments are used in the pluralist view to answer the charge that the state is not a neutral arbiter. It is held that the diverse range of interests both within and outside the state system in a pluralist polity make it impossible for the state to be systematically and permanently linked to any one set of social interests. The state cannot be seen as the instrument of an economically dominant ruling class (Marxist critique) nor of a power elite (Mills' view). There are too many interests capable of making themselves heard for the state to be anything other than neutral.

In turn, critics of the pluralist view seek to show the inadequacy of this pluralist response. Three factors are referred to, to establish that the state is indeed not a netural agency. Each factor can be interpreted in a Marxist or elitist fashion. The three factors are: (a) the nature and structure of state institutions themselves; (b) the nature of the personnel of the state machine; and (c) the social context within which the state system is placed.

Marxist theory, of course, rejects the idea of state neutrality out of hand. It considers political power as subservient to the economic power of a single class, the capitalist class.[72] In more general terms, it could be said that the state is intended to, and does, maintain the existing social order. Its institutions, therefore, reveal a certain bias or 'structural selectivity' in favour of those interest groups which are also the main beneficiaries of the social system.[73] Such 'selectivity' has been defined as follows: 'The structural selectivity of the state means that it is not a neutral instrument equally accessible to all social forces and equally adaptable to all ends; instead, it has an in-built form-determined bias that makes it more open to capitalist influences and more readily mobilised for capitalist policies'.[74]

Furthermore, the fact that the state is composed of different branches can be used in criticism of the pluralist approach, rather than in its defence. It is true that the state comprises a number of elements, of which the government is only one, along with the civil service, the army, and the police, among others. All of these are 'permanent' and as such in a different position from the relatively transient members of government.

Yet such 'permanence' could be used to maintain the role of the state in defending particular established social interests. Crosland's ideas of using a parliamentary majority for the enactment of radical reforms do not take sufficient account of that factor. The events in Chile under the Allende government, and the *coup* which destroyed that reforming government in 1973, may serve as a warning. The government was overthrown by a section of the state apparatus, namely the military, as a means of preventing any structural social reforms. It has indeed been pointed out that holding governmental office is not necessarily the same as holding power.[75]

Apart from such extreme and dramatic events as in Chile in 1973, the continuous influence of the personnel that serves the machinery of state must not be underrated, in particular the attitude of the civil service. Hegel called its members 'the universal class', meaning that they were not biased towards any particular sectional interest of civil society, towards any class or party. This claimed impartiality of the bureaucracy has been questioned from various theoretical standpoints, and with regard to different case-studies of bureaucratic power. Max Weber stressed the enduring influence of the outlook of the social class from which civil servants were mainly recruited, and his brother Alfred expressed the same view.[76] Many studies of the French political system, to take a further example, point out the importance of the key group of top civil servants (*les grands fonctionnaires*) in the political process in France. This elite group supplies much of the personnel of the French state elite, including ministers and prime ministers, as well as the staff for the administration. It comes from a relatively restricted background; some social groups are much over-represented in the *grand corps*. Studies of the French administrative elite also suggest that *pantouflage*, the moving out of the civil service into private business concerns, builds up a network of connections.[77] This means that the state administration is more receptive to certain pressures. Business pressure in the way of discrete intervention can be made more effectively by those who are themselves ex-administrators. For futher empirical illustrations of such 'structural selectivity' one could refer to the observations made in a recent comparative study of corporatist trends in France and Italy.[78] Any realistic view of power must take into account the nature of the state elite, meaning here the social origin, composition, and beliefs of the people who staff the various branches of the state. The criticism of pluralist theory is based on the charge that the theory does not sufficiently consider this factor, and its implications for the neutrality of the state.

The question of the bias in state structure and the links between state power and particular social groups leads to the topic of the social context of the state. While the pluralist view does not entail that all people or even all groups are equal in power, it does assume an equilibrium between capital and labour. The pluralist system is one of 'countervailing power'.

There are really two points in question. The first, already considered above, is that certain groups may have privileged access to the power-holders and that the state may favour them. The second problem is that pluralism neglects the terms on which groups compete, especially capital and labour.

Socialist arguments generally would see the advantage of capitalist interests as inherent in the social framework which constitutes the context of political power. R.H. Tawney referred to that context in his book *Equality* where he regretted the lack of a suitable word to describe 'a type of society which combines the forms of political democracy with sharp economic and social divisions'.[79] One may suggest that Tawney really meant what is known in Marxist terminology as 'bourgeois democracy', or what a contemporary author, Miliband, calls 'capitalist democracy'. This he defines as a system, like the British one, where

Democratic institutions and practices provide means of expression and representation to the working class, organised labour, political parties and groups, and other such forms of pressure and challenge from below; but the context provided by capitalism requires that the effect they may have should as far as possible be weakened.[80]

In pluralist systems 'sharp economic and social divisions' prevail, and such divisions cannot but affect the nature of politics within the systems.

Pluralist systems are marked by competition between parties and groups representing diverse and mostly conflicting interests. The democratic rights which make such interest representation possible must not be undervalued. Nevertheless, the groups do not compete on equal terms. Business groups have, on the whole, more resources, staff and money than groups representing labour interests. There is also, at the apex of large firms or corporations, an 'inner circle' of persons holding interlocking directorships, who are well informed about industrial interests and the impact of government decisions on business. This 'inner circle' has recently been studied by M. Useem.[81] Perhaps even more important is the fact that the individuals constituting that circle are in a position to make 'key decisions' on investment, employment and economic resources. They are hardly subject to any form of accountability or democratic control. There are, therefore, within the structure of pluralist societies groups (classes) which are economically dominant, and groups economically subordinate. The former hold the initiative in far-reaching decisions. Thus, for example, when it comes to the relationship between trade union and employer groups, the former are usually in a defensive role, reacting to decisions on investment and employment taken elsewhere. It is this factor which pluralist theories tend to neglect.

The advantage of the intiative has another consequence. The privileged position in the socioeconomic context of a pluralist society, occupied by the groups controlling the economic resources and hence taking key decisions, means that they have a greater influence on the holders of state power. This is due to the fact that their interests weigh more heavily in the framework of a privately owned and controlled economy. Here again it appears that some pluralists, or erstwhile pluralists—like C.E. Lindblom in *Politics and Markets*—are aware of the structural power of capital and of the 'veto' power stemming from the privileged position of capital in a free enterprise economy.[82]

Finally, the socioeconomic context has other effects as well. It creates as a climate of opinion a dominant ideology. This in itself runs counter to the pluralist view of a diversity of perspectives. The dominant role of corporate business is the material basis for a pervasive process of legitimation which works through a variety of channels. One could point here to the private ownership of mass media, especially newspapers, and in general to the advantages possessed by the defenders of the existing economic order. In this respect the words of H. Laski writing in 1925, in his *Grammar of Politics*, remain true today. They are worth quoting at some length.

There is all the difference in the world between a power informed and conscious of its strength and a power so latent and suppressed that its holders are hardly aware that they may exercise it.... The disparity of influence between those who defend and those who attack an existing system is, therefore, immense. The one can appeal to a solid and tangible reality; the others ask for a leap into a dark hinterland which requires effort and imagination to be understood. The members of a democracy cannot be said to possess their power until they have been deliberately trained to use it. We are still far from such a time.[83]

(iii) The first set of objections against pluralism dealt with its methodology, and the second set with its view of the state. A third set is concerned with the structure of groups. Here we distinguish between a vertical dimension revealing the internal structure of groups and a horizontal dimension, in other words the structure of their interrelations.

In its broadest sense pluralism asserts that within a pluralist system groups and parties offer an opportunity for voluntary paticipation and citizen involvement. Unlike totalitarian systems where participation is enforced, and unlike an authoritarian system which permits no popular participation, a pluralist system is seen as containing institutions which make it possible for the citizen to be politically active. The extra-parliamentary organisations of the big parties provide suitable channels for that purpose. Parties are the training ground where political leaders are selected. Pressure groups provide a further chance for citizens to organise and promote their ideas. There is ample scope, it is claimed, for a participatory democracy.

Against that claim the elitist arguments suggest that the supposed democratisation of parties and pressure groups has not, in fact, led to any genuine democracy. The classical formulation of that argument is Michels' 'iron law of oligarchy'. It states that as parties expand their organisation they become ever more bureaucratic. The result is the supremacy of a new bureaucracy. Democracy requires organisation, observes Michels, but 'who says organisation says oligarchy'. The point is that Michels' dictum would apply to any sort of organisation, including pressure groups. Their existence in a pluralist system would no longer provide structures for democratic participation. They would each be dominated by an oligarchic elite which would take the key decisions. Power might still be diffused among the elites, but not among the masses.

It must be observed that the argument, if correct, would be more detrimental to the idea of democracy than to pluralism as such. The reason for this is that one could imagine a pluralist system where each of the groups within the system was led and controlled by an oligarchic elite, but this would not be a genuine democracy without the active cooperation of the masses.

There is a further argument proposed by supporters of a 'radical democracy' in which participation is seen as both desirable and attainable, but not in fact yet attained. In this argument, the participation possible in Western democracies is criticised as being restricted to voting in periodic elections. Any more active participation is constrained by the oligarchic structure of parties. Furthermore, from the point of view of this perspective, certain crucial areas where key decisions are taken, the economy and the workplace, are not opened up for popular action nor to democratic accountability. Decisions relating to working conditions, for instance, are taken without consultation and no mechanisms exist for participation in these areas of social life.[84]

We have already referred to C. Wright Mills' view of the interlocking power structure, as he saw it, of American society.[85] Mills' critique facilitates the transition to the second aspect of the structure of a pluralist society, the interrelationship of the groups and parties supposedly competing with each other. To see how this involves a questioning of the pluralist position, it is necessary to look first at the occupational interchangeability of the persons who constitute the power elite. Mills argued that while they come from three different groups, military, political and industrial (the corporations), members of one elite group can and do move into another elite group with ease. The military chiefs like the top business executives enter politics, politicians and 'warlords' take office in industry, and so on. This means that the most important pressure groups, which were at one time independent of each other, no longer compete. They devise policies and start military or industrial projects in concert with each other.

In a wider and more general sense, the argument is that there is indeed a variety of groups in liberal-democratic systems, but the degree of their competition is not as high as at least some versions of pluralist theory would have us believe. It is argued that although political parties do offer different policies and represent different interests, they operate within a consensus limiting the range of opinions and actions; that is to say, they operate within a framework of shared assumptions about the political system and the socioeconomic structure of society.[86] It might also be adduced that while trade unions in liberal-democratic systems act as pressure groups to promote the interests of their members against management and employers' organisations, yet they work within certain limits. They define their task as improving 'wages and conditions' within a context taken as given, respecting (on the whole) management prerogatives and controls over employment and investment. This is not to say that there have never been challenges to the industrial power structure, but they do not arise in the 'normal' context of industrial and trade union relations. The fact also remains that parties of the Left tend to narrow the range of debate and to marginalise members who think that more could be achieved. This has to do with the pressure of electoral competition, the need to gain a majority of votes. It pushes the parties towards accommodation with such elements as occupy the centre ground of the political scene.[87] Whatever the reasons, the range of attitudes in pluralist systems is limited and the fact must be taken into account.

As against this, it must not be forgotten that some degree of consensus is necessary for any democratic system to survive. There must be a common platform on which the conflicts of beliefs and interests are fought out. In the absence of such a platform (in the widest sense of the word) democracy ceases to work. It can no longer work wherever majority and opposition meet in uncompromising hostility because the gulf dividing the classes has become unbridgeable. The fact is illustrated by the modern history of European countries where democratic systems broke down to give way to fascism.

Altogether, if such types of argument (as discussed under (iii)) seem to cast a shadow on the idea of democracy, we may find encouragement in de Tocqueville's final conclusion. 'The vices and weaknesses of democratic government', he writes, 'are easy to see; they can be proved by obvious facts, whereas its salutary influence is exercised in an imperceptible and almost secret way. Its defects strike one at first glance, but its good qualities are revealed only in the long run.'[88]

NOTES

1. R.A. Dahl, *Who Governs? Democracy and Power in an American City* (Yale University Press, New Haven and London, 1961); Nelson W. Polsby, *Community Power and Political Theory* (Yale University Press, New Haven and London, 1973).
2. H.S. Kariel, 'Pluralism', *International Encyclopedia of the Social Sciences*, edited by David L. Shils, Vol. 12 (New York, 1968), p. 164.
3. Franz Neumann, *The Democratic and The Authoritarian State. Essays in Political and Legal Theory* (The Free Press, New York and London, 1957), p. 22.
4. Anthony Arblaster, *The Rise and Decline of Western Liberalism* (Basil Blackwell, Oxford, 1984), p. 15.
5. For example, Bentham wrote in his *Leading Principles of a Constitutional Code, for any State* of 'those evil-doers, whose means of evil-doing are derived from the share they respectively possess, in the aggregate of the powers of government. Among these, those of the highest grade, and in so far as supported by those of the highest, those of every inferior grade, are everywhere irresistible'. B. Parekh (ed.), *Bentham's Political Thought* (Croom Helm, London, 1973), p. 199.
6. Article 2 of this Declaration stated that 'The aim of all political association is to preserve the natural and imprescriptible rights of man. These rights are liberty, property, security and resistance to oppression.' J. Godechot (ed.), *La Pensée révolutionnaire en France et en Europe 1780–1799* (Armand Colin, Paris, 1964), p. 115.
7. See John Locke, *Second Treatise on Civil Government*.
8. M.J.C. Vile, *Constitutionalism and the Separation of Powers* (Oxford University Press, Oxford, 1967), p. 13.
9. On the idea of opposition, see R.A. Dahl (ed.), *Political Oppositions in*

Western Democracies (Yale University Press, New Haven, 1966); and G. Ionescu and I. de Madariaga, *Opposition. Past and Present of a Political Institution* (C. A. Watts, London, 1968).

10. M. Duverger, *Political Parties* (Methuen, London, 1954); Klaus von Beyme, *Political Parties in Western Democracies* (Gower, Aldershot, 1985).

11. Walter Bagehot, *The English Constitution*, with an Introduction by R.H.S. Crossman (Collins-Fontana, London, 1963). In his Introduction, Crossman writes: 'Of the modern party, Bagehot had not even a premonition—partly because he had never visited America where it was already dominant when he wrote. Throughout *The English Constitution* he describes party organisation as weak at Westminster and almost non-existent outside', (p. 39).

12. I. Berlin, 'Two Concepts of Liberty', in Isaiah Berlin, *Four Essays on Liberty* (Oxford University Press, Oxford, 1969), pp. 118–72; and, more generally, Z. Pelczynski and J. Gray (eds.), *Conceptions of Liberty in Political Philosophy* (Athlone Press, London, 1984).

13. C.B. Macpherson, *The Real World of Democracy* (Clarendon Press, Oxford, 1966), p. 6; and see also C.B. Macpherson, *The Life and Times of Liberal Democracy* (Oxford University Press, Oxford, 1977).

14. Göran Therborn, 'The Rule of Capital and the Rise of Democracy', *New Left Review*, 103 (1977), 3–41.

15. See Ralph Miliband, *Capitalist Democracy in Britain* (Oxford University Press, Oxford, 1982), for an analysis of the British political system in terms of 'containment' of popular pressure.

16. Samuel H. Beer, 'Group Representation in Britain and the United States', in A. Pizzorno (ed.), *Political Sociology, Selected Readings* (Penguin, Harmondsworth, 1971), p. 194.

17. S.E. Finer, *Anonymous Empire, A Study of the Lobby in Great Britain* (Pall Mall Press, London, 1966), p. 3.

18. Beer, 'Group Representation', in Pizzorno (ed.), p. 194.

19. J.K. Galbraith, *American Capitalism* (Penguin, Harmondsworth, 1963), pp. 122–49.

20. This is not true of some more recent 'neo-pluralist theories', such as C.E. Lindblom, *Politics and Markets. The World's Political Economic System* (Basic Books, New York, 1977), which talks of the privileged position of business. For a discussion of 'neo-pluralism', see John F. Manley, 'Neo-Pluralism: A Class Analysis of Pluralism I and Pluralism II', *American Political Science Review* 77 (1983), 368–83.

21. M. Duverger, *The Study of Politics* (Thomas Y. Crowell, New York, 1972), p. 90.

22. G. Sartori, 'Anti-Elitism Revisited', *Government and Opposition* 13 (1978), 58–80, p. 72, where he quotes the 'law' on the basis of C.J. Friedrich, *Constitutional Government and Democracy* (Boston, 1941), ch. XXV.

23. A. Crosland, *The Future of Socialism* (Jonathan Cape, London, 1964).

24. C. Wright Mills, *Power, Politics and People* (Oxford University Press, New York, 1963), pp. 35–8. For a discussion of Mills's view of 'the

transformation of a community of publics into a society of masses', see J.E.T. Eldridge, *C. Wright Mills* (Ellis Horwood, Chichester, 1983), p. 82.

25. Mills, *Power, Politics and People*, p. 37.
26. G. Smith, *Politics in Western Europe* (Heinemann, London, 1972), p. 48.
27. Duverger, *Political Parties*, pp. 182–202.
28. For Weber, see 'Politics as a Vocation', in H.H. Gerth and C. Wright Mills, *From Max Weber: Essays in Sociology* (Routledge and Kegan Paul, London, 1948), pp. 99–111.
29. Ramsay Muir, *How Britain is Governed. A Critical Analysis of Modern Developments in the British System of Government* (Constable, London, 1930), p. 123.
30. Weber, 'Politics as a Vocation', p. 106; Max Weber, *Gesammelte Politische Schriften* (J.C.B. Mohr (Paul Siebeck), Tübingen, 1971), p. 535.
31. Rousseau, *The Social Contract*, Book III, Chapter XV (Everyman edition, translated by G.D.H. Cole, Dent, London, 1968), p. 78; Hegel, *The Philosophy of History*, translated by J. Sibree (Dover Publications, New York, 1956), p. 448. Hegel's dictum is a pun, as can be seen from the original German 'Sie vertreten die Vielen, aber sie zertreten sie auch'; Sorel, *Reflections on Violence*, translated by T.E. Hulme and J. Roth (Collier-Macmillan, London, 1961), p. 226.
32. Marx, 'The Civil War in France', in K. Marx, *The First International and After, Political Writings*, Vol. 3 (Penguin, Harmondsworth, 1974), p. 209.
33. Cited in L. Minkin, *The Labour Party Conference* (Manchester Univerity Press, Manchester, 1980), p. 20.
34. Robert Michels, *Political Parties*, translated by Eden and Cedar Paul (Dover Publication, Inc., New York, 1959), p. 37.
35. Miliband, *Capitalist Democracy in Britain*.
36. Sartori, 'Anti-Elitism Revisited', p. 60.
37. For Maurras' views, see, for example, Charles Maurras, *Kiel et Tanger 1895–1905. La République française devant l'Europe*, 2nd edition (Librairie Nationale Française, Paris, 1913).
38. C.B. Macpherson, *The Life and Times of Liberal Democracy*, Chapter II: 'Model 1: Protective Democracy'.
39. This argument was classically expressed by James Mill in his *Essay on Government* (1820). See J. Lively and J. Rees (eds.), *Utilitarian Logic and Politics* (Oxford Univeristy Press, Oxford, 1978), which contains the text of James Mill's *Essay on Government*.
40. See G. Duncan and S. Lukes, 'The New Democracy', *Political Studies* 11 (1963), 156–77; reprinted in S. Lukes, *Essays in Social and Political Theory* (Macmillan, London, 1977), Chapter 2.
41. Mills, *Power, Politics, and People*, p. 228.
42. See *Puritanism and Liberty, the Army Debates from the Clarke Manuscripts*, selected and edited by A.S.P. Woodhouse (J. M. Dent, London, 1974), p. 72.
43. R.J. White (ed.), *The Conservative Tradition* (A. and C. Black, London,

1964), p. 136.

44. Thomas Jones, *Lloyd George* (Geoffrey Cumberledge, Oxford University Press, London, 1951), p. 60.

45. See Duverger, *The Study of Politics*, p. 19.

46. This was the term used by B. Crick, *The Reform of Parliament* (Weidenfeld, London, 1970), p. 26. But of course the idea of the representative assembly as developing public awareness of political issues is an old one in the liberal tradition. See J.S. Mill, 'Considerations on Representative Government', in J.S. Mill, *Three Essays* (Oxford University Press, Oxford, 1975), p. 226: '... the Parliament has an office ... to be at once the nation's Committee of Grievances, and its Congress of Opinions'; or W. Bagehot, *The English Constitution*, p. 152: 'The third function of Parliament is ... the teaching function.... It ought to teach the nation what it does not know.'

47. For a discussion of the role of the representative assembly in the Third French Republic, in the context of a discussion of republican ideas, see Claude Nicolet, *L'idée républicaine en France (1789–1924), Essai d'histoire critique* (Gallimard, Paris, 1982), p. 431.

48. David Beetham, *Max Weber and the Theory of Modern Politics* (Polity Press, Cambridge, 1985), p. 99.

49. A. de Tocqueville, *Democracy in America*, edited by J.P. Mayer and Max Lerner (Collins, Fontana Library, London, 1966), Vol. I, p. 240.

50. *Puritanism and Liberty*, pp. 57–59.

51. White, *The Conservative Tradition*, p. 155 (Wellington) and p. 168 (Disraeli).

52. Karl Marx, 'The Chartists' (*New York Daily Tribune*, 25 August 1852), in K. Marx, *Surveys from Exile, Political Writings*, Vol. 2 (Penguin, Harmondsworth, 1973), p. 264; Engels, quoted in R.N. Hunt, *The Political Ideas of Marx and Engels*, Vol. 1 (Macmillan, London, 1975), p. 135.

53. de Tocqueville, *Democracy in America*, I, p. 243.

54. E. Halévy, *A History of the English People in the 19th Century*, 6 vols (Cass, London, 1949–52). See also W. G. Runciman, *Social Science and Political Theory* (Cambridge University Press, Cambridge, 1965); P. Worsley, 'The Distribution of Power in Industrial Society', in J. Urry and J. Wakeford (eds.), *Power in Britain* (Heinemann, London, 1973), pp. 247–66, p. 253.

55. Adam Przeworski, 'Social Democracy as a Historical Phenomenon', *New Left Review* 122 (1980), pp. 27–59, p. 29; reprinted as Chapter 1 of Przeworski, *Capitalism and Social Democracy* (Cambridge University Press, Cambridge, 1985).

56. Raymond Williams, *Towards 2000* (Penguin, Harmondsworth, 1985), p. 125.

57. Neumann, *Democratic and Authoritarian State*, p. 244.

58. For a discussion of the vast literature on corporatism, see P.J. Williamson, *Varieties of Corporatism. A conceptual discussion* (Cambridge University Press, Cambridge, 1985).

59. Keith Middlemas 'Corporate Bias', in D. Held *et al.* (eds.), *States and*

Societies (Martin Robertson, Oxford, 1983), pp. 330-8 (extract from K. Middlemass, *Politics in Industrial Society* (André Deutsch, London, 1979)).

60. Henry W. Ehrmann, 'Interest Groups and the Bureaucracy in Western Democracies', in *European Politics, A Reader*, edited by Mattei Dogan and Richard Rose (Macmillan, London, 1971), pp. 333-53, p. 340.

61. C. Wright Mills, *The Power Elite* (Oxford University Press, New York, 1956), p. 119; p. 244 for 'romantic pluralism'.

62. Dahl, *Who Governs?*, p. 183.

63. Ibid., pp. 85-6.

64. Ibid., p. 48.

65. R.A. Dahl, 'A critique of the ruling elite model', *American Political Science Review* 52 (1958), pp. 463-9; also in A. Pizzorno (ed.), *Political Sociology*, pp. 126-35.

66. Dahl, *Who Governs?*, p. 66.

67. P. Bachrach and M.S. Baratz, *Power and Poverty. Theory and Practice* (Oxford University Press, New York, 1970), Chapter 1; this appeared first as P. Bachrach and M.S. Baratz, 'Two Faces of Power', *American Political Science Review* 56 (1962), pp. 947-52.

68. S. Lukes, *Power: A Radical View* (Macmillan, London, 1974).

69. Mills, *Power, Politics and People*, p. 23.

70. Dahl, *Who Governs?*, p. 138.

71. Crosland, *The Future of Socialism*, p. 7.

72. See N. Poulantzas, 'The Problem of the Capitalist State', and R. Miliband, 'Reply to Poulantzas', both in R. Blackburn (ed.), *Ideology in Social Science, Readings in Critical Social Theory* (Fontana, London, 1972), pp. 238-65.

73. Claus Offe, 'Structural Problems of the Capitalist State', in K. von Beyme (ed.), *German Political Studies*, Vol. I (Sage, London, 1974), 31-59.

74. Bob Jessop, 'The Capitalist State and the Rule of Capital: Problems in the Analysis of Business Associations', *West European Politics* 6 (2), 1983, pp. 139-63, p. 141.

75. Ralph Miliband, 'The *Coup* in Chile', in Miliband, *Class Power and State Power* (Verso, London, 1983), pp. 79-107.

76. Beetham, *Max Weber and the Theory of Modern Politics*, p. 66, quotes Alfred Weber as saying: 'It is a fundamental error to imagine that bureaucracy has the characteristic of being independent of any social basis. It finds its social basis in those power groups which control the organisation of society.'

77. See, for example, P. Birnbaum, *Les Sommets de l'état. Essai sur l'élite du pouvoir en France* (Seuil, Paris, 1977), p. 139.

78. M. Salvati, 'May 1968 and the Hot Autumn of 1969: the response of two ruling classes', in S. Berger (ed.), *Organising Interests in Western Europe. Pluralism, Corporatism, and the Transformation of Politics* (Cambridge University Press, Cambridge, 1981), p. 345 (on France): 'The plan was supposed to provide an area in which the unions could make their voice heard, but the executive was quite impermeable to

their demands and based incomes policy on simple power relations, actively intervening to limit the advance of wages'; p. 352 (on Italy): 'The power system the Christian Democrats created in the postwar period was based on a relative under-representation of working-class demands and institutions (the parties of the Left and the unions) with a relatively greater access to state resources for other groups and classes through clientelistic relations.'

79. R.H. Tawney, *Equality* (Allen and Unwin, London, 1964), p. 78.
80. Miliband, *Capitalist Democracy in Britain*, p. 1.
81. Michael Useem, *The Inner Circle. Large Corporations and the Rise of Business Political Activity in the U.S. and U.K.* (Oxford University Press, New York and Oxford, 1984).
82. Lindblom, *Politics and Markets*, p. 346. See the discussion of Lindblom's work in David Marsh, 'Interest Group Activity and Structural Power: Lindblom's *Politics and Markets*', *West European Politics* 6 (2), 1983, pp. 3–14, and J. F. Manley, *APSR* 77 (1983), pp. 368–83 (footnote 20 above).
83. H. Laski, *A Grammar of Politics* (Allen and Unwin, London, 1970), p. 101. But for another perspective see N.Abercrombie and B.S. Turner, 'The dominant ideology thesis', in A. Giddens and D. Held (eds.), *Classes, Power, and Conflict. Classical and Contemporary Debates* (Macmillan, London and Basingstoke, 1982), pp. 396–415.
84. P. Bachrach, *The Theory of Democratic Elitism* (Athlone Press, London, 1969), p. 102.
85. Mills, *Power, Politics and People*, p. 38; and *The Power Elite*, p. 244.
86. R. Miliband, *The State in Capitalist Society* (Weidenfeld, London, 1968), p. 71 ff.
87. Przeworski, 'Social Democracy as a Historical Phenomenon'.
88. de Tocqueville, *Democracy in America*, Vol. I, Part II, p. 285.

2　The Elitist View of Politics

1. GENERAL STATEMENT OF THE ELITIST PERSPECTIVE

The pluralist view, we have seen, emphasises the diffusion of power in society and the division of political influence among competing centres of power. It also leads to a democratic conception of politics implying popular participation. The elitist perspective is quite different. We have here a view which stresses the concentration of power, not its diffusion. In its most basic form the elitist argument asserts that in any society political power is concentrated in the hands of a comparatively small group, an elite. Elitists differ on the factors which secure this leading group its power, but they agree on the inevitability of minority rule.

The ancestor of all elitism is Plato. In his *Republic* he describes the selection, training and way of life of a ruling elite, the Guardians. The point is that his republic is a utopia. He tells us what ought to be the case in an ideal commonwealth. Modern elitists are no utopians. They want to state the facts as they are. They claim to discover sociological laws. The classical exponents of modern elitism are the Italians Vilfredo Pareto and Gaetano Mosca. To them must be added the Swiss sociologist Robert Michels, mainly on the strength of his important book *Political Parties*. Max Weber's theory of society also contains many elitist elements. Among recent representatives of elitist thought we single out Schumpeter and Sartori.

It was Michels who claimed to have discovered 'the iron law

of oligarchy'. His statement implies that democracy in its core meaning of the exercise of popular power and of popular participation in the running of a society's affairs can never in actual fact be realised. In all political systems power is and remains the privilege of a dominating minority. Often enough, however, so the proponents of elite theory assert, this fact is disguised. The minority tries to veil its effective power, to hide it under some formula which masks its domination. Alternatively it attempts to justify its rule by some argument that will elicit the consent of the masses to their submission. The task of the political scientist using the tools of analysis is then to penetrate the myths, the political 'formulas', to show them up for what they are: devices masking the harsh reality of elite rule. Democracy is nothing but such a device. A democratic system, in the elitist view, is not one where people govern themselves or have effective control of the government. Such a state of affairs is not possible. A democratic society is one where the perpetual fact of minority rule is concealed by a myth asserting popular sovereignty or proclaiming the rule of the masses, also implying that the system does indeed express the will of the people. Such assertions have no scientific value; they 'cannot override a sociological law.'[1] Nevertheless, they may fulfill an important practical task by ensuring the stability of the so-called democratic system.

In liberal-democratic systems, therefore, as in all political systems, there is an 'establishment', a 'political class', a ruling group or controlling minority—the term may vary, the main idea remains the same. One of the reasons why that group is so powerful is precisely that it is small in size and cohesive. The division is between a creative, self-conscious leadership group, sure of its power and willing to use it, and, on the other hand, a mass submissive to that elite. Elite and mass—these are the elementary terms of elite theory just as parties, groups and their competition formed the core concepts of pluralism. The often-quoted words of Mosca can serve as an authoritative statement of the basic tenets of elite theory:

Among the constant facts and tendencies that are to be found in all political organisms, one is so obvious that it is apparent to the most casual eye. In all societies – from societies that are very meagrely developed and have barely attained the dawnings of civilisation, down to the most advanced and powerful societies – two classes of people appear – a class that rules and a class that is ruled. The first class, always the less numerous, performs all political functions, monopolises power and enjoys the advantages that power brings, whereas the second, the more numerous class, is directed and controlled by the first, in a manner that is now more or less legal, now more or less arbitrary and violent, and supplies the first, in appearance at least, with material means of subsistence and with the instrumentalities that are essential to the vitality of the political organism.[2]

How this ruling class varies in terms of its character and composition is something which we shall have to consider. Elites in their relationship to the masses, as Mosca indicates, use force and manipulation to different degrees, varying blends of consent and coercion. They differ in the means they use to secure their position as well as in the 'political formula', or justifying principle, which is intended to legitimise their rule. They differ in the extent to which they open or close their ranks or recruit new members. The present point is that in contradistinction to that variety elitist writers tend to see the mass as an unstructured and unorganised multitude, inherently inferior in intelligence and character to the elite. This is a particularly striking feature in Michels' study. The field of his investigation is rather restricted. While Pareto's monumental four volume *Trattato* ranges over all history from ancient Greece and Rome to the ministry of Waldeck-Rousseau in late nineteenth-century France, Michels concentrates on the social-democratic parties in contemporary Europe. The elite for him is the leaders of those parties, the mass their members. Here he finds any amount of empirical data, facts and statistics, but whatever he finds, the mass is always characterised in the same way. Michels speaks of 'the political immaturity of the mass'; 'the organic weakness of the mass'; 'the need which the mass feels for guidance'; 'the apathy of the masses and their need for guidance'. This leads Michels to the conclusion that 'The incompetence of the masses is almost universal throughout the domains of political life, and this constitutes the most solid foundation of the power of the leaders.' From 'the recognition of the political immaturity of the mass' can be inferred 'the impossibility of a complete practical application of the principle of mass sovereignty.'[3]

The problems raised by the basic elite–mass dichotomy with its corollary, accepted by all elite theorists, of the passivity and incompetence of the masses, will be discussed at a later stage. It is, however, worth noting now the contrast with the pluralist view, according to which the mass does not at all remain static. People organise in a multiplicity of groups and parties. They are members of such groups, indeed of more than one – what are called 'cross-cutting cleavages'. They organise themselves and take action.

Equally, the elitist view is incompatible with the Marxist interpretation of social class and of class conflict. Here it is admitted that, initially, the workers form an unorganised mass, but in the course of their struggle for economic and social as well as political rights, that mass turns into an organised and cohesive class movement.

Returning to elite theory, it follows that although the most violent changes and revolutions may occur in history, they will not change the basic structure of society. An elite may decay to be replaced by another elite. Such in fact is the normal course of historical evolution, as Pareto points out. The Roman Senate, the Catholic Church, the French aristocracy all lost their power. The English nobility escaped this fate only by accepting into their ranks a rising bourgeoisie and amalgamating with it. By admitting talented individual members from the mass, an elite may change its composition. Whether such assimilation happens in a peaceful way, or whether the elite is overthrown by force, it amounts to exchanging one elite for another. As the psychologist Le Bon wrote of the French Revolution: 'The Revolution of 1789 had as its real object the substitution of the power of the nobility by that of the bourgeoisie; that is, an old elite which had become incapable was to be replaced by a new elite which did possess capacity'.[4] In the same way, if a socialist revolution overthrew the present ruling elite of the bourgeoisie, it would produce a new elite, a socialist one. The masses would remain just as much in submission. They would have exchanged their masters. The forms change, the essential structure remains. The sociological law cannot be defied.

2. ORIGINS AND SOCIAL CONTEXT OF CLASSICAL ELITISM

Liberalism and democracy have their roots in the tradition of the Enlightenment. The Enlightenment considered humanity as a rational being. It believed that humanity guided by reason would progress for ever. When after all the turmoil of history and the struggle between revolution and reaction the Third Republic was eventually established in France in 1870, it was confidently believed that democracy was now victorious and progress assured. Yet at the very hour of their triumph those ideas were called into question. As measured by the highest hopes ever aroused by a historic enterprise, the final results of the Revolution could not but be felt disappointing. The sorry spectacle of party politics, the arrogance, incompetence and often corruption of democratic politicians, suggested a belief that the Revolution had after all been a failure. Similar conditions promoting similar attitudes prevailed in Italy. At the same time the political participation of the masses, such a significant feature in revolutionary times, became somehow suspect, something which had to be resisted.

This movement must be seen in the wider context of a European development which could be, and has been, given the title of 'the revolt against reason.'[5] Only its more general features can be suggested here. Its origins can be traced back to the protest of the Romantic movement which exalted sentiment over reason. In German philosophy Schopenhauer accorded priority to Will as against Reason. Where he left off Nietzsche continued. Metaphysical Will was transformed into a Will to Power. Nietzsche influenced the French philosopher Bergson, and both inspired Sorel, a key figure in this movement of ideas.

The age of the 'revolt against reason' was still an age of science, though it is significant that the recently developed science of psychology came to attract more interest than the science of logic. This was not surprising. As long as people were considered essentially as rational beings the important question was what people thought and whether their thought was rational and correct. On the other hand, once it was assumed that the primary impulse was will and that people were driven by their emotions and passions, the crucial question was what motivated their will. Eventually the problem would be one of knowing how to manipulate people, stimulating their emotions to make them not only carry out, but even wish and desire what they were expected to do.

The alliance between an anti-rationalistic and an anti-revolutionary attitude is well illustrated in the work of Gustave Le Bon. Le Bon had made a psychological discovery in his analysis of the crowd. The crowd was a collection of individuals held together neither by an idea nor by a common interest, but solely by a centre of attraction on which its attention was focused: a chance event, a sudden catastrophe or the appearance of a dominating personality under whose spell it came. The crowd was no longer rationally motivated, but swayed by its emotions. The individual members lost their very personality; as Le Bon put it, their 'conscious individuality vanishes in the unconscious personality of the crowd.'[6] But Le Bon thought that his crowd psychology had given him the clue to interpreting history, in particular the history of the French Revolution. He made the most of the 'mystic spirit of the leaders of the Revolution' and of a mystic Jacobin mentality which, he claimed, had so far escaped the attention of the historians. The Assembly itself was a crowd. In all revolutionary movements 'the unconscious collective mind of the crowd seems bound up with the mind of the leader. The latter gives it a single will and imposes absolute obedience.'[7] The activity of the masses was thus divested of any meaning. In turn the French writer Sorel, though from a different perspective and with utterly different objectives, argued in his *Reflections on Violence* that no theory but only a myth could stimulate and guide the action of the masses. Whether the partial statements contained in the myth were true or not was irrelevant. It was the myth in its entirety that mattered. It carried the political movement. The movement was for Sorel the socialist movement and it found its symbolic expression in the dramatic picture of the General Strike.[8] Such was the intellectual background of classical elitism.

The elitists, of course, were rationalists. They were men of science. Pareto indeed tried 'to construct a system of sociology on the model of celestial mechanics, physics and chemistry'.

Starting his career as an engineer his quest was for scientific empirical laws which he knew could be 'nothing more than experimental uniformities'. In pursuing his research he followed what he called the 'logico-experimental method'.[9] Yet logically minded as he was and intent on keeping his analysis on strictly rational lines, uncontaminated by emotions, prejudice and unwarranted *a priori* assumptions, experience taught him that the object of his enquiry did not reveal the same logical structure. People as social beings were by no means guided by reason alone and, what seemed to him still more significant, even when they sincerely believed that they were acting rationally in proclaiming the truth of their ideas as the very source of their action, they misunderstood themselves. Quite unconsciously they used their reasoning powers as tools to justify their behaviour. Accordingly all social ideas were merely derivative: they served to rationalise sentiments which as such had their roots outside the logical sphere.

The bulk of Pareto's great treatise is therefore devoted to the study of non-logical conduct. But such conduct is, in his view, not exemplified by the emotional outbursts of a crowd. It rather imitates the process whereby starting from experienced facts we arrive by logical inference at practical conclusions. In the social field the unconscious starting points are certain manifestations of sentiments which have never changed throughout history. Pareto calls them 'the residues'. They are at the basis of a pseudo-logical process which gives rise to what Pareto called 'derivations'. Arguments, supposed proofs, misleading analogies, are freely used to achieve at least the semblance of rationality. The results are the 'derivations', social theories or political systems, which finally find the support of the masses and guide their action. They are now sincerely believed in, and it needs a deeper analysis to reveal that such beliefs are merely the masks non-logical conduct is made to wear and which it is the task of sociology to tear off in order to lay bare the things they hide from view.[10] The things, of course, are the sentiments unchangeably inherent in human nature. The masks are a variety of ideological systems proclaimed and offered as the ultimate wisdom, the highest summit of morality, of their time. As such in his own time Pareto identifies the ideas of humanitarianism, of democracy, and of socialism.

Generally, in their revelation of what they regarded as the myths of democracy, classical elite theorists laid emphasis on the irrational aspects of human behaviour and the manipulation of the masses. The mass is not merely apathetic and disorganised, it is basically irrational. Gone is the democratic idea of the calculating citizen, rationally defending his or her interest, a feature of some democratic theories, notably of what C. B. Macpherson calls 'protective democracy' as in James Mill's *Essay on Government*.[11] The stress on the irrationality of human behaviour is an important strand in elite theory, though it is stronger in some versions than in others, stronger in Pareto and Michels than in Mosca. It is important because it provides a further reason for the necessity of leadership. The leaders, as Michels puts it, thus become all the more indispensable to the movement. They 'continue to think and to act tranquilly on behalf of the rank and file', even though – as in the case of socialist parties and trade unions – they might be 'in opposition to the rank and file at once theoretically and practically.'[12] In recent elite theory the same argument is used to justify a view of democracy which seeks to minimise popular involvement and pressure. Since the mass is irrational and manipulable, too great a degree of popular involvement may lead to support for demagogic leaders of a fascist type who destroy the consensus and the limits of liberal democracy. Hence the dangers of excessive participation and the threat of mass mobilisation are emphasised. This is used to back up arguments 'in praise of apathy'.[13]

If democracy and the myth of popular sovereignty formed one target of the elitist attack, socialism formed the other. The two were most explicitly related by Mosca. Elite theory would offer a realistic corrective to the myth of democracy by showing the impossibility of popular power. At the same time it would prove the impossibility of socialism with its idea of a classless and egalitarian society. Indeed, some versions of elite theory even maintained that a socialist society could only strengthen the power of the elite. The argument went on two lines, first, that the idea of an egalitarian society contradicted the indisputable fact of an inherent inequality of human abilities. Second, and more related to socialism, collectivism would concentrate economic and social power in the hands of the political elite and, therefore, reinforce the elite's domination. Both these themes were worked out in Weber's writings on socialism as well as in those of Mosca.[14] The connection between democracy and socialism was demonstrated by Mosca. Unrestricted democracy would eventually produce a socialist system and this would further strengthen the power of a socialist elite. Democracy as well as socialism would endanger the liberal values which Mosca cherished, those of individual liberty and of private property. His concept of 'juridical defence' was the medium through which he expressed those ideas. By 'juridical defence' Mosca understood a system of values implying the defence of the individual's rights and of a rule of law. Ultimately 'juridical defence' meant 'government by law'. It depended, more than on anything else, on what he called 'the political organisation proper, the organisation that establishes the character of the relations between the governing class and the governed and between the various levels and various sections of the ruling class'.[15]

A dangerous situation, utterly inimical to the liberal concept of juridical defence, would arise with the existence of a governing class which 'can permit itself anything in the sense of a sovereign who can do anything'.[16] Such despotism would be the result of an unlimited democracy where the masses would want the state to do everything for them irrespective of any legal guarantees or power limitation. The next step would be a tyrannical socialism. It would create an ever more centralised and dominating oligarchy. Socialism, Mosca suggested, was based on sentiments of class hatred and envy. Its consequences would be disastrous because collectivism meant the fusion of economic and political power. 'If, then, all the instruments of production pass into the hands of government, the officials who control and apportion production become the arbiters of the fortunes and welfare of all.' These officials would constitute 'a more powerful oligarchy, a more all-embracing "racket" than has ever been seen in a society of advanced civilisation.'[17]

What Mosca did here was to advance a traditional liberal

argument of a conservative type. It is significant that he opposed the introduction of universal franchise. His ideal was a cultured elite which would strictly observe the limits of the state's activity. At the same time, he repeated the fears which had always been associated with the progress of democratic ideas, that they might prove detrimental to property rights. 'Social democracy' he called 'the intellectual malady of our age'. Mosca warned that:

Absolute equality has never existed in human societies. Political power never has been, and never will be, founded upon the explicit consent of majorities. It always has been, and it always will be, exercised by organised minorities, which have had, and will have, the means, varying as the times vary, to impose their supremacy on the multitudes.[18]

In Mosca's view, as in the view of other elitist thinkers, the forward march of socialism, that logical extension of democracy, could only be halted by a grasp of the laws of political science, such as elite theory revealed. It was indeed the task of the social scientist to announce those great constant laws of society, and thereby to demonstrate the futility of socialist aspirations. His message would prove even more effective if it was addressed to the intellectuals and to the educated classes who might otherwise be attracted by the illusions of a democratic socialism:

In the world in which we are living, socialism will be arrested only if a realistic political science succeeds in demolishing the metaphysical and optimistic methods that prevail at present in social studies – in other words, only if discovery and demonstration of the great constant laws that manifest themselves in all human societies succeed in making visible to the eye the impossibility of realising the democratic ideal. On this condition, and on this condition alone, will the intellectual classes escape the influence of social democracy and form an invincible barrier to its triumph.[19]

Social science and the discoveries of elite theory were thus a prophylactic to be used against the temptation of socialist ideas. If despite this warning socialism was to be put into practice, it would not fulfill its promises. It would create a new elite, more powerful than the elite of liberally inclined societies which were imbued with the spirit of juridical defence.

The attack on both democracy and socialism is the common feature of all classical elite theories. At the same time the elitists were aware that the ruling class of their time, which was the bourgeoisie, was decaying in a process of disintegration. Pareto denounced their rule as feeble and ineffectual; they were digging their own grave. He surmised at first that the succession might fall to the socialists and he did not like the prospect. Mosca for his part would have preferred the bourgeoisie to regain its vigour and to recover, so to speak, its liberal conscience. However, if it was doomed as a ruling class, if both radical democracy and socialism were thought unrealisable as well as undesirable, what was the alternative? The question was not answered by any of the thinkers concerned. It was answered by history when Mussolini marched on Rome and the fascists took power in Italy. Mosca never accepted fascism. It went too much against his liberal principles; besides he thought the fascists were an uncultured lot. Pareto, on the other hand, then nearly at the end of his life (he died in 1923) believed the event was 'a splendid confirmation' of his theory.[20]

Michels was altogether a different case. For him politics was not mainly a matter of academic research. He had started his career as a revolutionary socialist, indeed as a syndicalist. In 1907 he attended the Stuttgart Congress of the Second International as a delegate from the syndicalist faction of the Italian section.[21] Soon afterwards he left the socialist movement. As a syndicalist he would never have been satisfied with the parliamentary tactics of the social-democratic parties. After he got a teaching appointment at Turin University he came under the influence of Mosca and Pareto. In 1911 he published *Political Parties* analysing the disappointment of his socialist activities. He ended as a wholehearted supporter of Mussolini. In 1928 he accepted a professorship in the fascist faculty of political science at Perugia, which he held until his death in 1936.[22]

3. THE NATURE OF ELITES

A political elite is a minority group. It holds effective power even in societies which call themselves democratic. The fact, however, is disguised; it needs to be 'unmasked' by a realistic political science. The ruling group is differently named by the various protagonists of elite theory. It is called 'political class' by Mosca, 'governing elite' by Pareto, 'oligarchy' by Michels. This difference in terms reflects the various ways in which the power base of the elite is defined. Nevertheless, one feature is common to all versions of elite theory: they all reject the Marxist assumption of the economic basis of political power. One of the core concepts of Marxism is that of a ruling class whose power is based on its ownership and control of the means of production. Elite theory does not completely neglect the economic factor, but it does interpret political power as chiefly determined by other, that is, political or psychological factors. Such factors are superiority of intelligence or character, political skill, ability to manipulate the masses, heroism and fighting skill; their manifestations are organisation and cohesion. They are non-economic factors, though it is acknowledged that power may facilitate the acquisition of wealth which in turn reinforces political power. If thus the difference of Marxist and elite theory is marked, they both oppose a pluralist theory in so far as they find power concentrated in a few hands while pluralism sees it diffused.

Mosca, we said, calls the elite a 'political class'. As such it has the advantage of organisation and cohesion while the passive majority cannot be coordinated: '... the dominion of an organised minority, obeying a single impulse, over the unorganised majority is inevitable.' The crucial factor, however, which guarantees that minority its power is that its individual members 'are distinguished from the mass of the governed by qualities that give them a certain material, intellectual, or even moral superiority.' Those qualities which form the criteria for elite superiority vary; they are relative to the standard of the society in question. As Mosca puts it: 'members of a ruling minority regularly have some attribute, real or apparent, which is highly esteemed and very influential in the society in which they live.' It might be military skill where this is vital, or ownership of land, or in a religiously-oriented society membership of a 'priestly aristocracy'. When for whatever reasons a need is felt for different qualities or characters, 'the old capacities, therefore, lose some of their importance or changes in their distribution occur.' The old ruling class will lose its position to be replaced by a minority group better endowed with those qualities which are now valued. The shift in the nature of the ruling group will be precipitated by a tendency of the ruling group to seal itself off from the non-elite, a sign of decay. When such things happen, 'when their talents and the services they render lose in importance in the social environment in which they live' then a new elite emerges:

The whole history of civilised mankind comes down to a conflict between the tendency of dominant elements to monopolise political power and transmit possession of it by inheritance, and the tendency towards the dislocation of old forces and an insurgence of new forces; and this conflict produces an unending ferment of endosmosis and exosmosis between the upper classes and certain portions of the lower.[23]

Thus the elite is not entirely impervious to pressures from below, from the non-elite. One reason is that to some degree it is open to the 'insurgence of new forces', and so may be receptive to new blood. What is more likely is that the elite's tendency to monopolise political power will induce it to seal itself off. In that case change will lead to its wholesale replacement by a new counter-elite. These ideas correspond to Pareto's concept of 'the circulation of elites'. However, as long as the elite keeps its organisation intact, and as long – and this is really the decisive point – as its character qualities are those required by its society, it remains in power. It remains the 'ruling class' though not in the sense in which the term is used by the Marxists. It forms 'the Establishment'.

As such, the elite justifies its functions by some 'political formula' which provides the 'legal and moral basis, or principle, on which the power of the political class rests'. The formula might invoke the divine right of kings or it might make the democratic claim of fulfilling the will of the people. Different societies employ different formulas – derivations, in Pareto's terminology. They do not correspond to the real power structure of society, therefore they have no scientific value. They serve to cover up the reality of elite rule. Yet, for Mosca at least, the formula answers a real need of human nature, the need 'of governing and knowing that one is governed not on the basis of mere material or intellectual force, but on the basis of a moral principle'.[24] Similarly, in Pareto's system, the elite rules not by force alone but, partly at least, by consent, in so far as it appeals to the psychological constants (the residues) inherent in human nature.

Pareto's theory of the circulation of elites has greater coherence, if not in logical then in psychological terms, than Mosca's. To begin with, Pareto points out that an elite exists in every sphere of human activity. It is composed of those who excel in a particular activity and that sets them apart from the rest. Just as there is a political elite so there is an elite of artists, of footballers, even of thieves. Within the elite category we find the distinction between the governing elite and the non-governing elite. The former consists of the men and women who excel in those activities which are relevant to political power. Their skills must include the ability to manipulate the sentiments and feelings of the masses. Obviously this is the elite we are mainly interested in.

Here we may use Pareto's famous picture of the social pyramid. The pyramid symbolises society. Its narrow top is occupied by the elite, its middle area and its base by the masses. This is the static aspect of society which needs to be supplemented by a dynamic interpretation. The members of the elite are persons of superior intelligence and ability, strength of purpose and character. In the natural course of life they might lose their efficiency; in any case they will grow old and die. On the other hand, throughout the social pyramid men and women are born at every moment gifted enough to be potential leaders and they will gradually rise to the top. There is then a continuous circulation and in due course the elite will have entirely changed its composition. The nearer this ideal schedule is approximated and the smoother the flow of circulation, the better society will function and the healthier it will be. But it does not happen that way, as the elite theorists emphasise.

For in actual fact every elite once in power closes its ranks. It constitutes itself as a corporate body, as a 'ruling class', and bars the way to newcomers. While it maintains in its top ranks those of its members who without such support would be unable to survive in the elite because of their failing ability, it also replaces them at their death by their relatives and descendants. It adopts a system of nepotism. That is how an elite perpetuates its rule. Owing to its artificial isolation it no longer represents talent and merit; gradually it declines but still clings to power.

The closed shop of the elite is of course never so closed in an absolute sense. There will always be means for some individuals to cross the line. The promotion of the clergy, access to nobility by distinction in war or in the civil service, offer such opportunities. However, even in the best case the flow will be obstructed and the circulation unduly retarded. An effective barrier runs across the social pyramid and against it a double pressure is now exerted: a pressure from below due to an increasing number of talents who find their way blocked, and a pressure from above in hostile reaction to their demands. As the tension increases social unrest and disturbances follow. How does an elite keep itself in power? First, by killing its most dangerous enemies, an efficient means up to a point though socially undesirable because of the waste of talent it entails; by persecution, imprisonment, financial ruin, exile and ostracism—unavailing procedures which spur the opposition to even greater efforts and bestow on them the halo of martyrdom; finally, by admitting to its ranks some selected leaders of the counter-elite, on the understanding that henceforth they will serve the interests of the ruling elite. In the end, however, as history so often has demonstrated, all those remedies fail. The tension in society becomes unbearable, and unless the elite in power voluntarily opens the sluices, as happened in England, the flood breaks the dam: the revolution triumphs.

Here we must remember the derivations out of which systems of social ideas and ideals are produced. The revolutionary and the ruling elite, each living under different conditions, will be using different ideologies. The former, now facing its revolutionary task, must look for support which they can only find among the broad masses. Therefore, they will proclaim their particular derivations as the new principles of truth and social justice, principles of a 'new order' which once established will deliver mankind from all evils. The people, who have their grievances at all times, will readily accept the message and lend their support to the new leaders, believing that in overthrowing the old regime they can secure their own happiness while in fact they merely exchange their masters. All the same the change is beneficial to society as a whole, not because the new form of government, say democracy, is intrinsically better, nor because the new ideas are superior to the old ones, but for the simple reason that the new leaders, eager to consolidate their position, will display far greater vigour, energy and efficiency, than the members of a decaying elite. A reservoir of unused talent becomes available as a sluggish circulation quickens its pace; so after every such transformation the prosperity index of society rises sharply, hence the illusion of progress. This happened when the Plebeians of ancient Rome overthrew the rule of the Patricians; it occurred when the ideas of the Reformation triumphed, and again as a result of the English and of the French Revolutions. In due course, however, once the new elite is firmly established it will behave just in the same way as did its predecessors, things will go back to normal and the old levels will be approached again. Once more history has repeated itself:

By the circulation of elites, the governing elite is in a state of continuous and slow transformation. It flows like a river, and what it is today is different from what it was yesterday. Every so often there are sudden and violent disturbances. The river floods and breaks its banks. Then, afterwards, the new governing elite resumes again the slow process of self-transformation. The river returns to its bed and once more flows freely on.[25]

If, then, ideas are not the real determinants of social action but rather serve to justify that action, the question arises: what does determine human behaviour? The answer, in terms of Pareto's system, can only be that it is the residues. These residues are comparatively small in number. They remain unchanged, permanent 'features of human nature, but are unevenly distributed in different societies, even among the various strata of a given society. An exhaustive classification of the residues cannot be given here, but two of them with their corresponding syndromes of behavioural traits are of paramount importance. They are the residues of 'combination' and those of 'persistence of aggregates'. Associated with the former are, in the words of Talcott Parsons' presentation of Pareto, 'innovation, inventiveness, projecting and scheming';

with the latter, 'steadfastness and directness, willingness to accept open conflict, a tendency to override obstacles and hence to use force, traditionalism rather than innovation, an absence of cleverness and resourcefulness.'[26] The human types as they are characterised by those syndromes Pareto calls 'the Lions' (persistence residues) and 'the Foxes' (combination residues). He seems to suggest that for a ruling class to remain stable and successful an essential condition is that it contains a judicious mixture of both types among its members. The preponderance of either the one or the other type signals danger, the elite's chances of surviving and holding on to power being somehow reduced. He was sure that the parliamentary system, especially in the Italy of his own time, produced too great a proportion of Foxes. The skills required for the exercise of power in the democratic system were rather those of compromise and of 'wheeler-dealing'. As he says: 'There seems to be a very close correlation between "democratic" evolution and increasing use of that method of governing which resorts to artifice and clique-politics as opposed to the method which has recourse to force.'[27] The predominance of Foxes resulted in a bourgeois elite unwilling to use force in its defence while adhering to what Pareto thought were decadent humanitarian ideals. He feared that such an elite would be overthrown by a vigorous socialist elite unrestrained by humanitarian scruples and quite willing to resort to force. This could only be prevented by an influx of Lions, i.e. the emergence of an equally determined bourgeois elite. Pareto's view of the humanitarian decadence of the bourgeoisie is illustrated in an exchange of letters with Prezzolini, dealing with the question 'Can the bourgeoisie survive?' His own letter seems to suggest as an answer a definite No!

I have been reproached for my belief that the bourgeoisie of today is in decline and on its way to being replaced by another elite springing from the working classes; it seems to me on the contrary that every day new facts appear which confirm my argument.... Does it not seem to you that there is a big gap between the energy and activity of the socialists and that of the bourgeoisie?[28]

The appeal to force and praise of violence links Pareto with the fascist movement. It makes him an intellectual contributor to fascism. Mussolini's success relieved him of his fear of socialism. He regarded fascism, as we have seen, as the final confirmation of his theories.

It remains to add that Pareto by no means ignores or utterly neglects the problems of social utility. Even social ideas, whatever their political function, are not devoid of all truth. Indirectly and through the residues which motivate them, they are connected with the actual living conditions of a society. If that was not the case, and social reasoning was mere fantasy, ideas would never be accepted or else a society that did accept them would be doomed to perish before long. As it is, Pareto suggests, those ideas have a limited value and might yield some results if their truth was not shrouded in sentiment, and the reasoning that supports them did not follow a line of emotional and often fanciful arguments. What is worse, their limitations are disregarded and the need to modify them according to common sense and experience is neglected. So, in the end, social theories are pushed to extremes; they establish their absolute claim and are offered as holy and eternal truth to the masses. Hence the tendency of derivations to evolve into idealisations and myths. This ideological transformation is on the whole the work of the intellectuals. They take so much delight in handling abstract concepts that they become enslaved by their own arguments, to the detriment of a society which allows itself to be guided by them. If we regard the derivations as what they are, not dogmas but expressions of human sentiments and, at their best, crude approximations to the truth, we might even gain some benefit from them. 'But in politics and political economy the day is still far distant when theory will be in a position to lay down useful prescriptions. . .'[29]

Social utility Pareto terms 'ophelimity' and he postulates a state of equilibrium where each individual member of a society receives a maximum of ophelimity. In this respect he makes a distinction between the utility *for* a society and the utility *of* a society, the one indicating the total amount of utilities of which society disposes, the other referring to their distribution among the individual members. However, these are not problems of our immediate concern.

Michels started from an empirical basis. His socialist activities had made him familiar with the working of the German Social-Democratic Party, with the attitudes of its leaders as well as of their followers. It is here that his analysis of political parties starts. He then proceeds to wider generalisations, though whether these are always correct and justified remains questionable. What is remarkable is the confidence Michels shows in the laws he thinks he has discovered. For Pareto laws were 'experimental uniformities' and he was well aware that any time a law might be counteracted, apparently suspended, by another law. For Michels a law is inviolable. At one place he speaks of an 'established historical law' that dooms races and social classes alike once they have lost faith in their own future. Elsewhere he points out that the syndicalists are not immune 'against the action of sociological laws of universal validity.' His basic 'sociological law' of oligarchy is 'iron', so that even the anarchists cannot break it. It is this law that makes democracy an 'indiscoverable treasure', in the sense of being an aspiration which can never be realised. The leaders will always dominate the masses. The evidence is chiefly to be found in the actual circumstances, seen as a test case, of the German socialist party. The facts are summarised by Michels under three headings: technical, psychological and intellectual.[30]

He starts from the proposition that direct democracy is impossible for technical, that is to say practical, reasons. People simply have not got the time, nor could practical arrangements be made, for popular participation on a large scale. Democracy then, has to be practised by representation: 'But permanent representation will always be tantamount to the exercise of dominion by the representatives over the represented.'[31] The problem of delegation versus representation, which we have discussed before, resurfaces here. In Michels' view a gap opens between the representatives and those they represent, and the former constitute themselves as an elite. Such tendencies are structural, inherent in any large-scale organisation. They do not depend on anybody's excessive lust for power, nor altogether on the conscious will of either leaders or led.

Secondly comes the psychological condition of the mass.

The mass is incapable and always passive. It not only accepts, it wants leadership, is happy to be led. It worships its leaders and in fact is grateful to them for taking on the arduous task and the responsibility of political power. In other words, the multitude never wants to play an active part in politics. Far from being challenged, the leaders are confirmed in office by re-election, hence the continuity of leadership in socialist parties and the ease with which socialist leaders keep their posts. But this precisely assists their transformation from 'servants of the people' (or of the party) into an almost permanent elite, separating them even more from the ordinary party members.

Finally, the third factor is the intellectual gulf as it develops between leaders and followers. It is not necessarily due to the leaders' innate superior intelligence, but rather to structural factors, to the logic of organisation. It is the result of the professional nature and the specialisation of leadership roles. They 'learn on the job' and so acquire the irreplaceable 'know-how'. They have to deal with a wide range of matters; the length of their tenure gives them an overview and practical ability to grasp issues, qualities unattainable by those who turn up at party meetings worn out by a hard day's work. Sometimes there are party schools where those expected to occupy leading positions are trained, but however the intellectual superiority is acquired, it sharply opposes the leadership to the rest.

So far the argument has gone against a possible achievement of true democracy. We might note that as a syndicalist Michels would already have been initially averse to the idea of representation and rather in favour of a direct democracy. But his main concern was always socialism. So his scepticism reaches further and poisons at source his most cherished ideal. If democracy fails, can socialism survive? It transpires through the pages of his book *Political Parties* that Michels was deeply disappointed by the attitudes of the German socialist party, leadership and rank and file alike: 'The workman's ideal is to become a petty bourgeois.' True, he summons Jaurès as witness that things are no better in France.[32] Nevertheless, what is a psychological trait and a vague aspiration in the manual worker becomes a potent if unconscious motive, and eventually a fact, once the worker has been promoted to leadership. 'The proletarian leader has ceased to be a manual worker not only in the material sense, but psychologically and economically as well.'[33] Such is the effect of bureaucratic oligarchy. It equally affects the leader of middle-class origin. They all could not be unaware of their controlling power. They had become specialised professionals, having attained their positions through working their way up in the organisation. The minutiae of day-to-day administration and routine tended to absorb their time and energy. Such tasks blotted out the ends for which the organisation was supposed to be fighting. The means took over from the ends and the maintenance of the organisation was given priority. What was worse, the leaders would feel that they had 'made it'. They now occupied power positions within the party organisation, hence within the wider society. Thus they would be reluctant to put the organisation (party or union) at risk. They developed conservative inclinations, accommodating themselves to the existing order, and almost reconciled with that order: 'What interest has now for them the dogma of the social revolution? Their own social revolution has been effected.'[34]

Democracy and socialism were both refuted by 'the iron law of oligarchy'. The question then must be asked: How iron is that law? In introducing Michels' theories we emphasised his almost inordinate confidence in universal sociological laws. As Beetham notes, 'the typical structure of his [Michels'] theorising was derived from a model of social science pursuing universal laws.'[35] Beetham's suggestion is very important; it concerns the status of historical and sociological laws. The point is that there are no such laws as apply everywhere and at all times. The laws themselves are subject to change and accordingly social relations change. What Michels utterly fails to take into consideration are the particular historical circumstances under which his sociological laws are supposed to work.

In the argument as it is presented in *Political Parties* the elite will always win over any challenge. Michels tries to demonstrate how the party elite will respond to such challenges. They might pretend to accept criticism or even take the lead in making the issue their critics were advancing their own, or they might threaten to resign in order to prove their indispensability. Alternatively they might have to absorb, by co-optation, some of the most vociferous critics into the leadership. This is Michels' equivalent to Pareto's circulation of elites.

As against that it might be queried whether the analysis is valid under all circumstances. Should it not be possible to create a structure of accountability which effectively checks the party elite? In fact, things have already changed. Some British Members of Parliament belonging to the Labour Party may read with melancholy regret Michels' passages on 'continuity of leadership' when they have just been told that they will not be re-selected as candidates for the next general election. Undoubtedly in the present inner-party situation in the Labour Party a tendency prevails towards greater accountability as far as the leadership is concerned, a demand that the representative should pay attention to the wishes of his or her constituency. Even within the trade union movement, as ballots become more frequent, the leaders are not all that sovereign. While such developments are connected with the general assessment of the activity of the masses, the point of course applies to all versions of elite theory. As Beetham says in another place, one does not have to go to the extreme of seeing 'the people' as the repository of all virtue and political initiative, but the fact is that there have been and are political and social movements which 'the masses' have organised.[36] As an actual instance in our time one could cite a movement like the Campaign for Nuclear Disarmament. Irrespective of its merits or demerits, this is a spontaneously organised enterprise which developed 'from the bottom up', involving ordinary people but not an elite. It may well be that later on a rising need for organisation will bring with it the danger of professionalism and oligarchic leadership. Nevertheless, the fact that mass movements exist seems to prove the possiblitity of people organising themselves and taking the initiative on their own accord. Another example would be feminist movements which have insisted most strongly on 'fragmented' modes of organisation, on a principle of non-hierarchical and non-bureaucratic organisation.[37] So in any case it is possible to envisage and, at least to a certain degree, to realise a social movement that minimises, if it cannot altogether avoid, oligarchic tendencies.

If finally one wishes to go beyond such bare statements of fact, one might envisage a society in which norms of participatory democracy were deeply ingrained. In consequence sentiments of deference, of gratitude to leaders for shouldering the burdens of office, would be completely absent or only survive to a very small degree. Within such a system there would be a tradition of citizenship urging people to be eager for office; there would be a general acceptance of democratic processes of accountability and public control. It may well be that under present conditions such a picture seems utopian. Certainly the difficulties of bringing it to life should not be underestimated. However, such a 'culture of participation' is presumably what Rousseau had in mind when he warned of the danger inherent in the attempt to substitute representation for direct democracy. He pointed out that once citizens were willing to pay for substitutes to attend the Assembly in their place, society was in a bad way since the civic virtues were in decline. This was the danger he wished to avert.[38] Other writers, like J.S. Mill, hoped that if political participation were extended, people would get a taste for political activity; they would want more participation, although Mill hoped such participation would be guided by a restraining and wise educated elite, as we shall see.[39] Given such extended participation the elite–mass dichotomy would be broken and replaced by a system of radical, or participatory, democracy. This suggests that the opposition of a creative elite against a passive mass may not be an ineradicable feature of political life. Rather in today's mass democracy the apathy of the citizen body, if such exists, reflects a perception that there is a lack of structures permitting genuine democratic involvement. Therefore, one might just as well withdraw into a 'private sphere' and cultivate one's garden. Thus the criticism of elite theory is that the elite–mass dichotomy is 'culture relative', as are the psychological and political dispositions attributed to the masses. 'Oligarchy' then might be the realistic description of a particular society which lacks the opportunities for genuine democratic participation. Such a society will foster an ethos of 'knowing one's place' and letting one's leaders or 'betters' get on with the job. But other systems can be imagined. Elite theory has failed to establish that such more democratic and participatory structures of power are impossible. These would require and instill into people a stronger desire for involvement. They would imply more criticism and a far greater control of leaders.

On the other hand, Michels' reflections on socialism rest on a very narrow empirical basis, the behavioural aspects of European socialist parties, mainly the German SPD, at the turn of the century. This is leaving aside the question whether there is altogether much point in making the future of the socialist idea depend on psychological considerations. The more interesting question then seems directed at the reasons which made Michels desert the socialist camp. Were they all rooted in his theoretical conclusions? If so, he would be the rare specimen of a type that abandons a cherished ideal for the sake of an abstract scientific truth, a strange psychological phenomenon. Why then his fascist conversion? His dislike of the bourgeoisie, the rejection of the system their rule implied, were genuine and must be significant. Would not his despair at seeing German socialism never reach the revolutionary stage let him try to place in its stead the fascist movement? There he would find what can be called the substitute revolution which indeed apes the outward manifestations of a true revolution—its enthusiasm as well as its cruelties—while it remains forever sterile in its intentions.

4. ELITE THEORY AND DEMOCRACY

In concluding this survey the main problem still to be considered is the relation of elite theory to the theory and practice of democracy. In the elitist view power always lies with a small ruling group, and what is true of society as a whole is true of the associations (such as parties) within society. There will be a central political elite but also one or, more likely, several sub-elites among the parties and groups which constitute the political system. These sub-elites mediate between the central political class and the masses; they provide channels for the training of members who will rise to join, eventually, the top class. One of the functions of political parties is to provide such a training ground. But whether at the macro level of the political system or at the micro level of sub-systems, the elite minority takes the initiative. The flow of power is from top to bottom. A representative system cannot avoid this inescapable fate. Mosca went as far as to say:

What happens in other forms of government, that an organised minority imposes its will on the disorganized majority, happens also, and to perfection, whatever the appearance to the contrary, under the representative system.

He was also of the opinion that even in electing their representatives voters had only a limited choice. The only candidates offered to them were those 'whose candidacies were championed by groups, by committees, by organised minorities'. So, in the end it could be said: 'The truth is that the representative has himself elected and, if that phrase should seem too inflexible to fit some cases, we might qualify it by saying that his friends have him elected.'

Nevertheless, Mosca recognised that the 'organised minorities' which play such an important role 'represent the organisation of a considerable number of social values and forces'. The representative system, therefore, while it in no way secured majority rule, resulted 'in the participation of a certain number of social values in the guidance of the state'. It meant that 'certain sentiments and passions of the "common herd" come to have their influence on the mental attitudes of the representatives themselves'. In so far as the voter had an albeit limited choice, the ruling group could not be totally impervious to the wishes and feelings of the non-elite.[40]

Mosca, as was mentioned, did not welcome fascist rule, and when it came, towards the end of his life, his attitude to representative democracy mellowed. He now thought that representative government had certain advantages. It was likely to be more stable because different social forces and values could exercise at least some influence. In 1925 he wrote:

Although the representative system is not, as the official dogma has it, the rule of the popular majority, yet of all types of government it is the one in which the rulers on the whole will be affected by the sentiments of the majority, the one which furnished the best means of judging and debating governmental acts. In other words, it is a rule of freedom, to the extent to which that term can still have real meaning in our time of super-states with their immensely complicated structures.[41]

Mosca's attitude, then, was that of a conservative liberal, fearful of any extension of democracy which might lead to socialism, yet wishing to hold the ranks of the elite open so that the varied forces of a modern society could find expression. Like Pareto he believed that the ruling elite had to admit 'new blood'. In his 1933 study of Political Doctrines, Mosca praised what he called 'mixed regimes' which combined the aristocratic and liberal principles. The aristocratic tendency would be 'tempered by a gradual but continuous renewal of the ruling class, enabling it thus to absorb the better elements into its ranks.'[42]

In the attempt to relate elitism to a democratic pluralism the following questions arise: (1) To what extent is the elitist conception of a creative elite standing over and against a passive mass justified? (2) Is society dominated by one elite only or are there a number of different elites to be found in every society? This question is related to (3), Is elitism incompatible with democracy as classical elite theory asserted or is it possible to conceive of a pluralist democratic elitism? and (4) What constitutes the identity and the composition of the elite group?

(1) As regards the elitist assumption of a passive and always disorganised mass, we have already queried the proposition, and mentioned one or two cases which seem to contradict it. What concerns us now is a matter of principle. The point is that the elitist attitude largely conforms to Le Bon's description of the crowd. If, as Le Bon saw it, the crowd is an amorphous mass of isolated individuals held together by nothing but their submission to a common centre of attention, the only possible social relation within the crowd is the leader—follower relation. What Le Bon did not appreciate was the fact that the crowd is not the only form to unify a multitude of individuals. The second, and more important, paradigm of a social synthesis is the group. The group may concentrate its attention on a focal point: it may attend a

lecture or stage a demonstration, but when the event is over, unlike the crowd, the group does not disintegrate. It persists because it has a purpose. Also its members, individually, fulfil functions, aspire to office, and so on; in any case there is interrelation, intercommunication, between all members. The atmosphere within the group is not emotional but basically rational.

The question never asked by elitist theory is whether our society, destined as it is to be a mass society, should be such a one on the crowd model or on a group pattern. One might suggest that the former is the model of a fascist or national-socialist community with its leadership worship, its predominantly emotional appeal, its dissolution of individuality in the mass movement, even its feeling within the mass of heightened power. Democracy, on the other hand, must be built up on a pattern of groups. These groups, we may add, need not be political groups. Or, as Karl Mannheim writes:

What people mostly tend to overlook is that democratisation may take place in any field, not merely in the political one. A gang of workmen, a study group or an artistic group can all be organised on democratic lines. When it occurs in such small groups, democracy usually produces spontaneity and self-determination. But in a big state, a mass society, its healthy influence is largely checked. This is because democracy is only efficient if the individual feels that much depends on his peculiar and special decision and if others realise the importance of his contribution. But in a mass democracy the feeling that one is only a small and insignificant unit often discourages initiative.[43]

(2) and (3) Pareto tells us that there is an elite in every field of human activity. In his famous picture of the social pyramid the ruling elite appears in its struggle with an opposing elite emerging from the base; in the same way Mosca speaks of elite and counter-elite. It all depends on how the competition between two, or perhaps more, elites is decided. If the decision is taken through the ballot box, nothing prevents us from accepting the democratic-pluralist model with an elitist proviso. Each group then is led by an elite but it is the privilege of the masses to decide by their vote which will be the ruling elite. We shall presently see how so different writers as Max

Weber and Schumpeter are in agreement on such a model of what may be called 'elitist democracy'.

The French philosopher and sociologist Raymond Aron joins in the 'affirmation of the "oligarchic fact" in society as a whole as well as in its sub-systems', by which are meant the parties and groups composing the pluralist system. So far Aron accepts the 'elitist hypothesis' but not the postulate of a single elite. There are elites, he asserts, but no one elite rules unchallenged. The power structure of liberal-democratic societies is seen by him as being one of a 'differentiation of ruling hierarchies'.[44] In other words, there is a set of different organisations, each with its own elite. They compete with each other. They are 'dissociated'. The picture is one of a range of peaks, or tops of different pyramids of power, which do not fuse into one pyramid and therefore do not constitute one cohesive elite. This view reconciles elitism with pluralism. There are still leaders and a relatively passive mass but the necessity of gaining power through electoral victory makes the ruling elite receptive to pressure from below (the masses) and also ensures that no one elite will always command the machinery of the state. There is thus a transformation in the ruling elite which is not due to a revolutionary upheaval but to the normal process of electoral politics. The elitist-pluralist view combines the realistic recognition of elite power with an insistence on elite multiplicity.

Such a perspective of elite pluralism seems very similar to the pluralist ideas presented in the previous chapter. There is a difference to be drawn, however, between what could be called a *liberal elite pluralism* and a *democratic pluralism*. The former is represented by someone like Aron, developing some ideas found in Mosca. In this perspective, the diversity of elites and their competition, electoral and otherwise, achieves the liberal aim of checking and controlling power. There is no unified elite, and so power concentration is avoided. However, the masses still remain passive; democratic participation of any real kind is viewed as impossible. To the extent that it is possible, it is undesirable and needs to be resisted. By contrast, the pluralist views, explained in the previous chapter, take a more positive attitude to democratic involvement, which is held to be desirable and is secured through the network of groups and associations characteristic of a pluralist society. In such a society the pluralistically competing groups provide structures within which citizens can participate, and an effective democracy is realised, avoiding the dangers of a mass society. The elite pluralist view under consideration here regards any degree of democratic participation with scepticism, if not hostility. Multiplicity of elites prevents dictatorship, but does not secure the democracy valued by more democratically inclined pluralists.

The view of the multiplicity of elites has been criticised for reasons advocated by, among others, C. Wright Mills. Mills, as has been mentioned, argued that in American society the leaders of the three most important institutional orders—military business, political—were closely linked in values and convictions, and often worked interchangeably in the three spheres. 'The top of American society is increasingly unified,' he wrote, and while he recognised that there were different and distinct hierarchies of power, he did not believe they were in competition.[45]

Similarly, writers on French politics have pointed to the links between the peak positions in what initially might appear to be different and countervailing structures of power. The Fifth French Republic has earned the title of *La République des fonctionnaires* (the civil servants' republic) because of the way in which a stratum of top civil servants has, in the first place, monopolised the top posts of all sections of the civil service and, secondly, formed the pool from which ministers, even Presidents of the Republic, are taken. The fact of *pantouflage* is also mentioned in this connection. Thus even in the days of the Fourth Republic, it is argued, what gave cohesion to a political system racked by ministerial instability was a bureaucratic elite imbued with a strong sense of *dirigiste* purpose and well connected too with the world of large business.[46]

Our point here is that the mere existence of different hierarchies may suggest, but does not conclusively prove, the case of elitist pluralism. There is considerable evidence in Western-type systems of interlocking elites with shared attitudes resulting in common action to maintain a dominant consensus.

(4) Finally, what is the origin and basis of the power which

the elites wield? The question has far-reaching implications. In a pluralist system there are several bases of power and on each basis power is derived from the social importance or relevance of the activities carried out there. By contrast, the Marxist analysis finds power concentrated in the economic sphere and therefore the privilege of those who command the economic heights. In one respect alone classical elitism conforms to the Marxist model in so far as here too there is one group that is in control and is powerful. This is the elite and on this point only the elite corresponds to what is called 'the ruling class' in Marxist theory. On the other hand, compared with both Marxism and pluralism, within elite theory power remains materially undefined. While Marxism as well as pluralism give an objective definition of the source from which power emanates, that is to say of the powerbase, in at least some versions of elite theory it is subjective and psychological characteristics which enable the elite to occupy otherwise vacant power positions, to maintain and defend them. The psychological foundation of Pareto's 'circulation of elites' is significant because it implies a cyclical interpretation of history. Democratic pluralism is progressive in that it envisages an ever higher level of rationality, and increasing participation. Socialism is even more optimistic. Beyond the class struggle the picture of a free society at leisure and in peace is revealed. In contrast the elitist perspective offers only an eternal cycle of elite decay and renewal. Such indeed was the pessimistic conclusion of the defiant 'revolt against reason'. History has no meaning. 'Once one has read Herodotus, one has read enough history,' advised Schopenhauer. This was echoed by Pareto: 'If, for instance, one would clearly understand what happened in ancient Athens, one must consider what happened in France beginning with the ministry of Waldeck-Rousseau.' The story was always the same.[47]

However, it is true that not all versions of elite theory see the powerbase of the elite in such terms of the personal abilities and characteristics of leaders. Mills' perspective of a 'power elite', for example, does not see the elite's power stemming chiefly from its political skills and ability to manipulate the masses. This power elite theory offers a more 'structural' view of power; power does not stem from the outstanding qualities of particular individuals. It is derived from organisational factors. Those in power are those at the top of the dominant organisations of society (military, business, and political).[48] Mills' view of a power elite is thus different from elite pluralism on the one hand, because it emphasises the cohesive interlocking nature of the ruling group. It is critical of the Marxist view on the other hand; both see the basis of power in terms of a structure, and not of individual qualities of leadership, but for Mills the structural basis of power was not ownership and control of economic resources. Power was derived from the command of large bureaucratically structured organisations. This is a theme which we have noted as an essential element in the theories of Mosca and Michels, though combined in the latter with more psychological explanations. There are thus contrasting explanations within elite theory for the power of the controlling minority group.

5. PLEBISCITARY DEMOCRACY

The idea of combining elitism and pluralism remains problematical. Nevertheless, ideas of 'elite pluralism' are used as the basis of a theory which in turn attempts to combine elitism and democracy. What is involved is a view of democracy which is called realistic in so far as it takes account of the 'vertical dimension' of democracy, the need for effective leadership. This perspective has been given various names, such as 'the theory of democratic elitism' or 'the competitive theory of democracy'. It is put forward by authors such as Schumpeter, Mannheim, and more recently Sartori. Some of the elements of the theory can be traced back to Max Weber.

'Democratic elitism' makes two important points:

(a) Michels' 'iron law of oligarchy' is accepted as valid in the sense that direct democracy is not a possible system except in the simplest and smallest organisations. However, the existence of several competing elites eliminates the anti-democratic consequences which the classical elitists thought unavoidable. This is most true of political parties which compete for electoral support. In elections, the passive and

disorganised mass becomes, as Sartori puts it, the arbiter of
the political conflict. The facts of elections and of the plurality
of elites restrict elite power and enable the masses to remove
from power an elite which is unresponsive to their wishes.[49]

(b) The second point is the allegation that Michels, in his
refutation of democracy, uses an unrealistic criterion of
democracy. Classical elitism thought it had proved that
democracy was an illusion because it could show that direct
popular democracy was impossible. However, that was to
apply a wrong standard. The fact that the masses have a choice
between different elites satisfies all the requirements of a
democratic system. Organisation implies oligarchy, as Michels
asserted; democracy needs leadership. In this sense the
elite–mass distinction is preserved and the analysis remains in
the elitist tradition. On the other hand, it is a necessary and
sufficient condition for a democratic system that at stated
intervals the masses decide which elite is to rule.

The most influential proponent of such a theory was Joseph
Schumpeter. In some respects the theory is foreshadowed by
Max Weber's concept of a 'plebiscitary democracy'. There,
important questions are raised concerning the role of
leadership in democratic systems, or what Sartori calls the
'vertical' aspect of democracy. However, before probing this
question of leadership, Schumpeter's version of the theory
must be discussed more fully.[50]

Schumpeter might be blamed for presenting the classical
theory of democracy in somewhat exaggerated terms. He calls
democracy a political system with the purpose of effecting 'the
people's will'. A system would be called democratic to the
extent to which political leaders carried out the clearly
expressed will of the people. This will is seen as being unitary,
undivided and unequivocal in its implications. One of the main
points of Schumpeter's attack is that there is no such thing as
'the will of the people'. His elitist assumptions and his
acceptance of the framework of the elitist analysis are quite
clear. The mass, he thinks, may be capable of discussing an
issue of local politics or one closely bound up with their
everyday life, on which they can form a view. This does not
apply to general political issues nor to the great options of
state policy. On Schumpeter's analysis the 'will of the people'

would be what Pareto calls a fiction, Mosca a 'political formula'. Not only are the people as a whole ill-informed; public opinion on political issues is shaped by the statements and actions of political leaders, the very agenda of politics is determined by those leaders. The elite, or elites, will decide what the issues are. A political issue does not become one until it is called into life by the leaders who make it an issue and put it on the agenda. There are any amount of problems which need to be solved or at least paid attention to, but only those which the leaders nominate as worthy of public discussion become political issues.

Schumpeter gives Gladstone's campaign in 1879 on the subject of Turkish atrocities as an example. He presents Gladstone as fulfilling the role of a true leader in a democratic society. The issue was not one on which public opinion had expressed itself. Most people knew nothing of the events. Yet Gladstone breathed life into the matter, elevated it to the rank of a political issue, then 'stomping the country' to keep the matter in the public eye he finally came to power on the basis of support for the issue. The 'will of the people' was moulded both in form (people's feelings) and in content (the actual matter) by a political leader.

It will be seen that in Schumpeter's view the initiative goes from top to bottom while in classical democratic theory the reverse is true. In the latter case the leaders are supposed to carry out the public will. They are the delegates of the people. The people are sovereign, the government a mere agent of their will. In Schumpeter's view the leaders have considerable autonomy. They decide what the issues will be and invite public opinion to express itself. Once the people have elected them they must be left free to carry out their own policies. The electorate must exercise what Schumpeter calls 'democratic self-control', one of the necessary conditions for a stable, well-functioning political order. This democratic self-control has various aspects. It implies that:

the voters outside of parliament must respect the division of labour between themselves and the politicians they elect. They must not withdraw confidence too easily between elections and they must understand that once they have elected an individual, political action is his business and not theirs.

The result (as Schumpter himself states) is quite at odds with the democratic notion of the delegate who is bound by instructions. The democratic element is preserved in the crucial sense that at the end of their period in office the leaders must submit to the judgement of the electorate. However, as long as they are in office there must be a considerable distance separating leaders and led. This is seen as a necessary condition for a healthy democratic order. The 'vertical dimension' of democracy must be respected, otherwise a leadership might become too responsive to popular pressure. In that case the leadership elite might take decisions out of short-term considerations. They might follow what Sartori calls 'the politics of envy'—envy on the part of the masses who want to maximise their immediate gains at the expense of long-term benefits.[51]

This is reminiscent of the concerns of traditional liberals like J.S. Mill and de Tocqueville, who realised that the entry of the masses into politics could hardly be averted, yet feared the consequences of democratic advance. They were apprehensive that majority rule, i.e. a democratic system, would produce what Mill in *Representative Government* called 'class politics'.[52] This meant actions taken for the benefit of the majority but virtually incompatible with the 'wise' measures necessary for the good of the country. The latter would only be appreciated as necessary by an educated minority. Hence Mill's proposals were in favour of more votes for university graduates so that (supposedly) wise counsels would prevail and democratic pressures be mitigated. The same flavour is noticeable in contemporary writings issuing from the camp of 'democratic elitists'. From Schumpeter's concept of democratic self-control it would follow that the political leaders have freedom of manoeuvre while in power; they should not be confined by tight controls of accountability. This touches on one of the most important issues of democratic theory. There is the danger, on the one hand, that leaders might be freed from any accountability, on the other hand that they would be so closely bound that they had no flexibility to respond to changing events or situations. There is built in to democratic elitism a tendency towards strong leadership. This must not be understood in any sense of an authoritarian leadership totally free from democratic controls. In Schumpeter's as well as in Sartori's view the indispensable element in a democratic system is open and competitive elections. The political leaders must submit to the masses for confirmation in office or replacement by another party or another team of leaders. In the interval between elections democratic self-control must be observed.

In this perspective elections fulfill the functions of a plebiscite. Except in a very broad and general sense, they are not expressions of the will of the people; they do not determine particular policies. They are plebiscites in so far as they accept or reject a particular team of leaders. It is this view of a plebiscitary democracy which has its origin in Max Weber's political thought and in his ideas of a 'leadership democracy'. The same ideas reappear in Schumpeter's work though in an unacknowledged and somehow concealed form. In Weber's view the political leader took the initiative and appealed for support to the masses. That was the meaning of plebiscitary elections. As Weber wrote: 'It is not a question of the politically passive "mass" throwing up a leader of itself, but rather of the political leader recruiting a following and winning the mass by demagogic appeal.'[53] The leadership, in Weber's view, had to gain electoral legitimation. This was the change which democratic politics had brought about, though the coming of mass democracy had not changed the necessity of leadership. The leader would control the party machinery which provided the necessary means to 'get out the vote'. Thus a new political elite was created in the place of the party of notables characteristic of the pre-democratic age. This new party elite might take the form of the 'party boss' in the USA (the 'Tammany Hall' phenomenon). The leader needed a general staff so that he could mobilise the masses and get their plebiscitary approval. In true elitist fashion, Weber insisted that the relationship of domination and subordination, of the few dominating the many, would not change. He believed that the idea of democracy as expressing the 'will of the people' was utterly meaningless. As he wrote in a letter to Michels: 'How much resignation will you still have to put up with? Such concepts as "will of the people", genuine will of the people, have long since ceased to exist for me; they are fictions. All ideas aiming at abolishing the dominance of men over men are utopian.'[54] It appears that Weber, in a conversation with Ludendorff, really spoke his mind: 'In a democracy people choose a leader in whom they trust. Then the chosen leader says, "Now shut up and obey me". People and party are then no longer free to interfere with his business.... Later the people can sit in judgement. If the leader has made mistakes—to the gallows with him!'[55] In a milder form this presumably is what Sartori meant by the 'vertical aspect' of democracy.

In all such theories democracy becomes a method, a means to an end. The end is the election of competent leaders who are subject to the minimal democratic control of periodic elections. The popular will is dissolved; it does not exist in any meaningful sense. In Schumpeter's words, 'the role of the people is to produce a government'. This purpose is achieved through 'an institutional arrangement for arriving at political decisions in which individuals acquire the power to decide by means of a competitive struggle for the people's vote.'[56] It has often been argued that this is to take a rather instrumental view of democracy. The chief value of democracy, sustained and active popular participation, becomes rather downgraded, in fact it disappears.

Schumpeter lists five factors as necessary if the democratic method is to be a success.[57] First, the 'human material' must be of high quality, there must be a group of adequate leadership ability. The only effective guarantee for this would be 'the existence of a social stratum, itself a product of a severely selective process, that takes to politics as a matter of course.' In the language of classical elitism, there must be an elite, trained and skilled in the art of politics, and also an adequate 'sub-elite', forming a pool of talent from which the elite can renew itself. Secondly, Schumpeter says, 'the effective range of political decision should not be extended too far'. Certain matters should be left to experts and specialists and not dealt with by politicians. Thirdly, in the list is the requirement of a well-trained bureaucracy which, Schumpeter insists, 'must be a power in its own right'. Fourthly, comes the concept of 'democratic self control' which was discussed above; and fifthly, the requirement of 'tolerance for difference of opinion'.

What is involved here, though Schumpeter does not use the word, seems to be an idea of consensus. He refers to 'allegiance to the structural principles of the existing society', an allegiance that must be extended over 'all the interests that matter'. Democracy, he argues, 'may cease to work at all as soon as interests and ideals are involved on which people refuse to compromise'. This raises important issues. It could mean that the breakdown of democracy (the collapse of liberal-democratic systems and their replacement by authoritarian or fascist-type systems) occurs when certain key groups refuse to accept democratic procedures.[58] Schumpeter wrote: 'Democracy cannot be expected to function satisfactorily unless the vast majority of people in all classes are resolved to abide by the rules of the democratic game.' This would imply agreement on the fundamentals of the institutional structure. The decision of key elites to abandon the democratic system, for example in Europe between the two World Wars, was in fact to a large extent prompted by the fear that the institutional structure of the system was politically and socially advantageous to working-class interests. The dominant elements in the system were then prepared to call for a strong state, or even an authoritarian anti-democratic regime, because this seemed the only way to oppose the challenge to their economic and social dominance.

When all this is said, it still remains true that the basic conditions for a democratic system, as defined by the theories here under discussion, are the institutions of two or more competing parties and of free and open elections. Democratic self-control, if taken strictly, seems to exclude the activities of pressure groups in the interval between elections because such activities would interfere with the power-holders' job of governing the country. Other versions of the theory, however, relax this rather rigorous restriction and allow for pressure groups to bring particular interests and grievances to the notice of the government. This appears to be a more realistic interpretation because otherwise the political activity of the electorate, i.e. of the masses, could be seen as restricted to casting a vote every five years. Nevertheless, even if a larger amount of political activity is allowed, the masses remain in their passive condition. Sartori, for example, invokes the 'law of anticipated responses' to demonstrate that in a system of 'polyarchy', i.e. of competing parties, every elite wishing to be re-elected must pay some attention at least to the demands of the masses. Yet in his view a participatory democracy is unattainable, and therefore an unrealistic idea; so the gap between elite and masses remains. Even where 'the unorganised majority of the politically inactive becomes the arbiter in the contest among the organised minorities of the politically active', the characteristic feature of the masses is still their relative political passivity.[59] The question then is whether the acceptance of the elite-mass dichotomy is compatible with anything that genuinely could be called democracy.

6. CRITICAL EXAMINATION OF DEMOCRATIC ELITISM AND GENERAL CONCLUSION

If we now want to sketch out an assessment of the attempted reconciliation of elitism with the democratic idea we must first list the arguments allegedly in favour of the attempt, points which strengthen the hypothesis. These can be listed under three headings:

(i)   that this democratic elitism is a realistic description of how Western-type political systems do in fact work;

(ii)   that an alternative system of democratic participation could, for practical and psychological reasons, not work;

(iii)   that an alternative, even if possible, would not be desirable in view of the irrational character of the masses.

As regards the first point, the claim is made that the perspective under review is realistic in its assessment of the role of political leaders, in particular of their ability to influence and manipulate public opinion. Surely their opportunities in this respect are today greater than ever. On the other hand, as regards the masses, is it not true that on the whole they are politically inactive, 'sovereign' only on election day? The 'average citizen' is basically not very interested in politics which should be left to professional politicians and an activist leadership elite. In short, democratic elitism gives a correct description of the political reality in European and North American countries with liberal-democratic systems.

Secondly, it is argued that a system of radical democracy involving large-scale participation is not workable. It must fail because of the impracticability of direct democracy, but would also not be in accordance with human nature. People just do not want to participate to any great extent; they prefer to follow their private pursuits. The fund of civic virtue is strictly limited with most people. The point is that public activity involves a 'cost', at least in time, which only a very small and dedicated minority will bear.[60]

Finally, the argument goes that sustained and active participation of the masses would by no means help to maintain a healthy democratic order. The masses are not necessarily defenders of democracy. They are easily led astray by demagogues and manipulated in the interest of movements which threaten democratic institutions. In any case too much pressure on democratic leaders would result in instability and in measures taken in favour of short-term interests. That is what Sartori means by the 'politics of envy'. He argues that:

Too much compliance (of leaders or governments with popular pressures) has already landed—an increasingly frequent reality with local governments—on the shores of bankruptcy. Thus the problem and the crying need becomes 'responsibility', the other constituent element of representation. And the more we have indulged in responsiveness, the greater the need for independent responsibility—which is what leadership is really about.[61]

All such arguments have a certain force. They cannot be lightly dismissed. There is, in contemporary Western systems, a gap between ruling elites and the masses. Participation is limited, the system is rather one of 'containment'. Moreover, movements of popular origin, such as we have mentioned before, occur in the 'interstices' of normal political practice. Equally the 'cost' of participation, whether in time or, often, money terms, cannot be altogether denied. Oscar Wilde's quip that 'the trouble with socialism is that it takes up too many evenings' is still relevant. Michael Walzer has taken up the point, seeing here a problem for the Marxist vision of 'the withering away of the state'. Would this not create the need for a host of citizens' committees to administer the affairs of a complex industrial society?[62]

When all this is admitted the question remains whether democratic elitism can still justifiably be called democratic. The point is that the theory is elitist but no longer democratic. Of course, this is largely a matter of definition. But if the term 'democratic' refers, as is our opinion, to a system where there is a substantial amount of popular power and of citizen involvement, then the situation as described by democratic elitism is not one of democracy. A system of competing elites, subject to periodic elections, would satisfy the liberal idea of checking and controlling the executive. It might also ensure some degree of responsiveness of leaders to led. The 'law of anticipated responses' is true enough as far as it goes. Democracy however means more than this and a democratic system must conform to criteria other than the fundamentally liberal ones of sufficiently controlling the power-holders.

The classical theory of democracy, in any case, is not compatible with an elitist interpretation. To let the politicians 'get on with the job' is, in terms of Rousseau's political philosophy, nothing else but a surrender of sovereignty. Rousseau scoffed that the English people were well deceived if they thought themselves free. They were free only at the time of election.[63] The point is that democratic theory is not merely descriptive. It requires a substantial amount of citizen participation in the absence of which no system is democratic. But the theory is also normative, setting up a standard by which any existing system of power must be judged. In other words, it not only describes what is, but, setting up the norm or goal of political activity, it also states what ought to be. Rousseau and after him Mill maintained that through self-education and by extending the sphere of mass participation the conditions for a real democracy would be created. Democracy had to be seen in a 'dynamic' rather than a merely 'static' framework. It had to be seen as emerging from a process of political and social transformation. To change political institutions meant improving human capacities; it even meant changing human nature. People would no longer form a herd-like passive mass; they would approach the democratic ideal of a rational, active and participatory citizenship.

The principal criticism of a theory of democratic elitism is then that it cuts out from democratic theory its very heart—the idea of participation. It takes a purely static view accepting the features of present-day mass society fixed for ever instead of envisaging a process that would transcend the elite–mass dichotomy. The stability of the existing order is thus made the chief value, and democratic involvement then appears to threaten that value. This criticism is levelled by Duncan and Lukes against those accounts of voting behaviour which offer empirical proof of citizens' lack of political knowledge yet estimate that lack a virtue rather than a vice of the system.[64] Democratic elitism misconceives what democracy is and what a democratic society ought to be like. In insisting that democracy is merely a method for choosing leaders it accepts as legitimate the passivity of the mass. Yet the chief value of classical democratic theory was self-determination or autonomy. In the view of Rousseau and of Mill such autonomy could only be realised by extending political participation. Initially, perhaps in a limited way and at local level, people would gradually develop their abilities, later embracing wider fields of policy at higher levels. They would expand their horizon and increase their competence. The gap between an elite of professional politicians and an ignorant mass would be narrowed; perhaps in due course altogether eliminated. This at least was the ideal goal of democracy.

It is strange in a way that the elitist theory acknowledges arguments of education and self-development in certain respects. So Michels in *Political Parties* argues that the gap between leaders and ordinary party members is not so much due to the former's higher inborn intelligence but rather to the fact that they 'learn on the job'. They acquire knowledge and political skill in the course of their political activity, an opportunity denied to the masses. But could it not just as well be said of those masses that they would develop their abilities if they were given the chance? Then those who now are 'unused to public speaking' might soon show their organisational and administrative, even their leadership, talents. Such a system of spreading political culture is the criterion of a truly democratic system. It makes democracy a process extending over long historical periods.

In a further criticism of democratic elitism, more from a practical point of view, it is argued the definition which the theory employs of 'the political' is too narrow.[65] It is quite correct that political (i.e. party) elites have to submit themselves for re-election but the fact is neglected that many other groups which carry the elite distinction do not. There are bureaucratic or civil service elites who have crucial influence in the exercise of power but are not fully responsible or accountable to the general public. There are also economic elites who take vital decisions concerning employment and investment. Those decisions in turn have political implications of great importance. All such 'key groups' escape from electoral sanctions. As against this, elite pluralists would argue that the elites in their diversity and competition check and control each other. Business elites are challenged by trade unions, civil service elites are supposedly under the control of ministers who are politically responsible to the people, and so on. However, we have already considered arguments to the effect that a fairly homogeneous Establishment modifies and to a certain extent even eliminates elite competition. This flow of arguments and counter-arguments leads us towards a final estimate of elite theory in general.

The strength of elitist theory is derived from the fact that throughout the course of history effective political power appears always to rest in the hands of a select minority. One can, of course, point to instances of popular power. The Paris Commune of 1871; the Soviets in 1905 and, for a short period, in 1917; the Spanish Civil War; these provide such episodes. Yet they were episodes which stand out as the exceptions within a pattern of 'normal' elite power. To admit this, however, is not to concede the elitist case that elite rule is unavoidable and that it will never be possible to create an enduring non-elitist situation. The elitist view exaggerates the extent to which elitism cannot be mitigated or perhaps be prevented altogether. The reason is that it pays too little, if any, attention to factors of political socialisation, that is, factors relating to the 'political culture' of a definite period. A 'deferential' elitist political culture will accept as natural a division of labour between those who rule and those who are ruled. It will tend to detect in the latter a sense of their own inadequacy or incompetence. Yet such incompetence, if and where it exists, might well be the result of certain historical patterns, institutional structures or patterns of behaviour, all of which could change. In this sense elitism is too deterministic, one might even say ideological, in so far as the assumption of the incompetence of the masses would make people accept the futility of any attempt to change the basic situation. In other words, elitism elevates the facts to the rank of a norm, the validity of which can never be challenged.

This brings us at the end to a point already touched upon above. We then tried to explain that the elitist theory in some versions neglects to investigate the objective factors, or conditions, from which a leading group, an elite, derives its power. In this respect elitism is weak compared with a Marxist and indeed also compared with a democratic-pluralist interpretation of society. It concentrates on a variety of 'non-economic' factors. The consequence is that leadership, and the whole phenomenon of elitism, can only be explained in subjective psychological terms, as some sort of charismatic leadership. But while we found before that the psychological interpretation results in an utterly pessimistic and cyclical conception of history, matters are not improved if for the psychological analysis a more 'structural' sociological analysis is substituted. The point is that there are no sociological laws, such as Michels claims to have discovered, so 'iron' as to remain valid at all times and all places. The reason is that just as human attitudes, in a sense the very elements of human nature, change in the course of history, so—and even more so—the social consciousness of people changes. In a wider sense, this implies that the historic law is a changing law and that for this very reason history is a process: a progressive movement. But for the elitist with a static conception of society the motto can only be: *lasciate ogni speranza* (Abandon all hope).

NOTES

1. Robert Michels, *Political Parties. A Sociological Study of the Oligarchical Tendencies of Modern Democracy*, translated by Eden and Cedar Paul (Dover Publications, Inc., New York, 1959), p. 35. (Hereafter referred to as Michels, *PP*.)
2. Gaetano Mosca, *The Ruling Class (Elementi di Scienza Politica)*, edited and revised, with an introduction, by Arthur Livingston, translated by Hannah Kahn (McGraw-Hill Book Company, New York, Toronto, London, 1939), p. 50. (Hereafter referred to as Mosca, *RC*.)
3. Michels, *PP*, pp. 87, 56, 57, 205, 86, 87.
4. Gustave Le Bon, *The Psychology of Revolution*, translated by Bernard Miall (T. Fisher Unwin, London, 1913), p. 64. Le Bon, of course, was a psychologist, but his seminal book *The Crowd, A Study of the Popular Mind*, was very influential, as was the one quoted here. Le Bon will be referred to later in the course of this chapter.
5. See, for example, Georg Lukács, *The Destruction of Reason* (Merlin Press, London, 1980).
6. Le Bon, *Psychology of Revolution*, p. 102.
7. Ibid., p. 109.
8. Georges Sorel, *Reflections on Violence*, translated by T.E. Hulme and J. Roth, with an introduction by E.A. Shils (Collier-Macmillan, New York, 1961). On the myth, see especially p. 122, and pp. 124–5.
9. Vilfredo Pareto, *Sociological Writings*, selected and introduced by S.E. Finer, translated by Derick Mirfin (Pall Mall Press, London, 1966); paragraph numbers refer to paragraphs of Pareto's *Trattato di Sociologia Generale* (English translation: *The Mind and Society, A Treatise on General Sociology*, Dover Publications, New York, 1963). Para. 20, p. 181; para. 99, p. 182; para. 17, p. 181.
10. Pareto, *Sociological Writings*, para. 249, p. 194.
11. C.B. Macpherson, *The Life and Times of Liberal Democracy* (Oxford University Press, Oxford, 1977), Chapter II.
12. Michels, *PP*, p. 86.
13. W.H. Morris-Jones, 'In Defence of Apathy', *Political Studies 2 (1954)*, 25–37.
14. For Weber, see his essay on socialism in *Max Weber, Selections in translation*, edited by W.G. Runciman (Cambridge University Press, Cambridge, 1978), pp. 251–63; for Mosca, see Mosca, *RC*, Chapter XI.
15. Mosca, RC, p. 130.
16. Ibid., p. 134.
17. Ibid., p. 143.
18. Ibid., p. 326.
19. Ibid., p. 327. For interpretations of Mosca, see E.A. Albertoni, *Gaetano Mosca. Storia di una dottrina politica. Formazione e interpretazione* (Giuffré, Milan, 1978); E.A. Albertoni (ed.), *Studies on the Political Thought of Gaetano Mosca. The Theory of the Ruling Class and its Development Abroad (Giuffré, Milan and Montreal, 1982); J.H. Meisel,*

The Myth of the Ruling Class. Gaetano Mosca and the Elite (University of Michigan Press, Ann Arbor, 1962).

20. The victory of fascism Pareto called 'a splendid confirmation of the predictions of my Sociology'; quoted in David Beetham, 'From Socialism to Fascism: The Relation Between Theory and Practice in the Work of Robert Michels. II: The Fascist Ideologue', *Political Studies* XXV (2), June 1977, pp. 161–81, p. 165.

21. Michael Löwy, *Georg Lukács* – From Romanticism to Bolshevism (New Left Books, London, 1979), pp. 47–48.

22. David Beetham, 'From Socialism to Fascism: The Relation Between Theory and Practice in the Work of Robert Michels. I: From Marxist Revolutionary to Political Sociologist', *Political Studies* XXV (1), 3–24 and Part II, cited in note 20 above.

23   Mosca, *RC*, pp. 53, 53, 53, 65, 66, 65.

24. Ibid., pp. 70–1.

25. Pareto, *Sociological Writings*, p. 250 (Trattato, para. 2056).

26. Talcott Parsons, *The Structure of Social Action* (The Free Press, Glencoe, 1949), p. 279. In Parsons' words, 'With this general contrast goes a somewhat more special one in matters of great social importance. Men strong in "combinations" tend to value the present above the future, the immediate above the distant future, "material" over "ideal" goods and satisfactions and the interests of the individual over those of any collectivity such as the family, the local community or the state. Men strong in "persistence aggregates", on the other hand, value the future above the present, the ideal above the material, and subordinate their personal interests far more to those of the collectivities to which they belong. Hence for Pareto's theory some of the most important properties of any given society depend upon the relative proportions in its members of these two classes of residues.'

27. Pareto, *Sociological Writings*, p. 269 (Trattato, para. 2259).

28. A. Lyttelton (ed.), *Italian Fascisms, from Pareto to Gentile* (Jonathan Cape, London, 1973), pp. 128–33.

29. Pareto *Trattato* (*The Mind and Society*), para. 1786; and for 'ophelimity' and 'utility' see *Sociological Writings*, p. 85.

30. Michels, *PP*, p. 243; p. 347; p. 360; p. 405 ('Democracy is a treasure which no one will ever discover by deliberate search'). On p. 406 Michels writes: 'Historical evolution mocks all the prophylactic measures that have been adopted for the prevention of oligarchy.'

31. Ibid., p. 40.

32. Ibid., p. 289; p. 305 (Jaurès).

33. Ibid., p. 299.

34. Ibid., p. 305.

35. Beetham, 'Robert Michels – From Socialism to Fascism. II', *Political Studies* XXV (2), p. 178.

36. David Beetham, 'Michels and his critics', *European Journal of Sociology*, XXII (1981), pp. 81–99, p. 98.

37. For example, S. Rowbotham, H. Wainwright and L. Segal, *Beyond the Fragments* (Merlin, London, 1979).

38. Rousseau, *The Social Contract*, Book III, Chapter XV (Everyman edition, translated by G.D.H. Cole): 'As soon as public service ceases to be the chief business of the citizens, and they would rather serve with their money than with their persons, the State is not far from its fall', p. 77.

39. J.S. Mill, *Considerations on Representative Government*, Chapter VIII: 'Amongst the foremost benefits of free government is that education of the intelligence and of the sentiments, which is carried down to the very lowest ranks of the people when they are called to take part in acts which directly affect the great interests of their country.' J.S. Mill, *Three Essays* (Oxford University Press, Oxford, 1975), p. 274.

40. Mosca, RC, p. 154.

41. Quoted in Meisel, *The Myth of the Ruling Class*, p. 324. An interpretation of Mosca as a conservative liberal is given by E.A. Albertoni, *Gaetano Mosca. Storia di una dottrina politica*.

42. Quoted in Meisel, *The Myth of the Ruling Class*, p. 390.

43. Karl Mannheim, *Essays on Sociology and Social Psychology* (Routledge and Kegan Paul, London, 1953), p. 283.

44. Raymond Aron, *Progress and Disillusion. The Dialectics of Modern Society* (Penguin, Harmondsworth, 1972), p. 56.

45. C. Wright Mills, 'The Structure of Power in American Society', in C. Wright Mills, *Power, Politics, and People* (Oxford University Press, New York, 1963), pp. 23–38, p. 38.

46. P. Birnbaum, *Les Sommets de l'état. Essai sur l'élite du pouvoir en France* (Seuil, Paris, 1977). English translation: *The Heights of Power: an essay on the power elite in France* (University of Chicago Press, Chicago and London, 1982); E. Suleiman, *Politics, Power and Bureaucracy in France. The Administrative Elite* (Princeton University Press, Princeton, 1974); and also Henry W. Ehrmann, 'Interest Groups and the Bureaucracy in Western Democracies', in M. Dogan and R. Rose (eds.), *European Politics, A Reader* (Macmillan, London, 1971), 333–53.

47. Pareto, *Trattato* (*The Mind and Society*), para. 2450. In the preceding paragraph, Pareto writes that 'in the quest for social uniformities, past and present throw a reciprocal light upon each other ... when the past parallels the present in one relationship or another, it forms the groundwork for our introduction that those relations constitute a uniformity – are a law.'

48. C. Wright Mills, *The Power Elite* (Oxford University Press, New York, 1956). For example, p. 296: '... the political directorate, the corporate rich, and the ascendant military have come together as the power elite, and the expanded and centralized hierarchies which they head have encroached upon the old balances and have now relegated them to the middle levels of power.'

49. G. Sartori, 'Anti-Elitism Revisited', *Government and Opposition* 13 (1978), 58–80, p. 71.

50. J.A. Schumpeter, *Capitalism, Socialism, and Democracy* (Allen and Unwin, London, 1943), Chapters XXI and XXII.

51. Schumpeter, p. 295; Sartori, p. 65.

52. Mill, *Representative Government*, p. 281.
53. Quoted in David Beetham, *Max Weber and the Theory of Modern Politics* (Polity Press, Cambridge, 1985), p. 106 (Weber, *Gesammelte Politische Schriften*, p. 389).
54. Quoted in Wolfgang J. Mommsen, *The Age of Bureaucracy. Perspectives on the Political Sociology of Max Weber* (Basil Blackwell, Oxford, 1974), p. 87; and in general, Chapter IV on 'Plebiscitarian Democracy'.
55. Quoted in H.H. Gerth and C. Wright Mills, *From Max Weber: Essays in Sociology* (Routledge and Kegan Paul, London, 1948), p. 42.
56. Schumpeter, p. 269. For a critical discussion of Schumpeter's theory of 'competitive democracy', see P. Bachrach, *The Theory of Democratic Elitism* (University of London Press, London, 1969), pp. 17–25.
57. Schumpeter, pp. 289–96.
58. See J.J. Linz and A. Stepan, *The Breakdown of Democratic Regimes* (Johns Hopkins University Press, Baltimore and London, 1978).
59. Sartori, p. 71.
60. For a critical discussion of some of these issues, see David Beetham, 'Beyond Liberal Democracy', *The Socialist Register 1981*, edited by R. Miliband and J. Saville (Merlin Press, London, 1981), 190–206.
61. Sartori, p. 66. See also Bachrach, *Theory of Democratic Elitism*, pp. 26–48, for a discussion of the argument concerning the anti-democratic tendencies of the masses.
62. M. Walzer, 'A Day in the Life of a Socialist Citizen', in M. Walzer, *Obligations. Essays on Disobedience, War, and Citizenship* (Harvard University Press, Cambridge, Mass., 1971), 229–41.
63. Rousseau, *Social Contract*, Book III, Chapter XV translated by G.D.H. Cole (Everyman edition), p. 78: 'The people of England regards itself as free; but it is grossly mistaken; it is free only during the election of members of Parliament. As soon as they are elected, slavery overtakes it, and it is nothing. The use it makes of the short moments of liberty it enjoys shows indeed that it deserves to lose them.'
64. G. Duncan and S. Lukes, 'The New Democracy', *Political Studies* 11 (1963), 156–77; reprinted in S. Lukes, *Essays in Social Theory* (Macmillan, London, 1977), Chapter 2.
65. See Bachrach, *Theory of Democratic Elitism*, p. 97.

3 The Marxist View of the State

1. INTRODUCTION

The present chapter deals with a third view of politics, different from both the pluralist and the elitist view. It is the Marxist view which is here taken as referring to the theories of the founders of Marxism, Karl Marx and Friedrich Engels. The many variants of Marxist theory, including contemporary attempts known under the heading of 'Western Marxism', will therefore be disregarded.[1] Moreover, we have to abstract from the manifold aspects and purposes of the original writings. Our intention is to concentrate on the sphere of politics within the overall work of Marx, and to give an exposition of his ideas about the state and the nature and purpose of political power.

These ideas are essentially different from those put forward by the pluralists or by the elitists. The former, as was shown, consider the state as a neutral agency responding to pressures from various groups of society, but not linked to any particular set of social interests. The Marxist view rejects this perspective of the state as a neutral arbiter. As far as elitist theories go, Marx might agree that in all societies up to now (with the exception of primitive communism) a minority group has held effective power. However, while in elitist theories the ruling elite owes its prominent position to personal characteristics and to political skill, in the Marxist view those who hold power are 'the minority group qualified and called to rule by the given degree of economic development'.[2] The powerbase then is the ownership and control of society's productive resources. Thereby the ruling elite is transformed

111

into a ruling class. Furthermore, elitist theory, as we have seen, implies a cyclical conception of history; it asserts the inevitability of minority rule. By contrast it is essential in Marxist theory to understand history as a process tending towards a final goal, which is a classless society.

Engels posed the question: Why are there classes at all? His answer was that owing to the hitherto insufficient development of production 'historical progress as a whole was assigned to the activity of a small privileged minority while the great mass remained condemned to produce by their labour their own meagre means of subsistence and also the increasingly rich means of the privileged.'[3]

Class division gives rise to class struggle. 'The history of all hitherto existing society is the history of class struggles.'[4] Class division and the ensuing class struggles are by no means absent from liberal-democratic systems such as we have described in the foregoing chapters. From the Marxist point of view they are seen as specimens of 'bourgeois democracy'. The term fits well enough Tawney's previously cited description of a system that 'combines the fact of political democracy with sharp economic and social divisions'.[5] The divisions themselves are manifestations of a class-divided society. If Marx himself did not use the term 'bourgeois democracy' frequently it was for reasons worth considering briefly.

Marx believed that the unconditional grant of democratic rights, and in the first instance the general franchise, would inevitably lead to the revolutionary transformation of society. The ruling class would lose its power. Alternatively, the bourgeoisie, aware of that danger, might rather abandon the democratic rules of the game. In either case 'bourgeois democracy' referred to a highly unstable political situation rather than to a stable form of state. Marx thought he had found the historic case confirming that theory in the events of the French Second Republic of 1848–51. In *The Eighteenth Brumaire of Louis Bonaparte* he described, as we shall see in greater detail, how the property-owning classes switched their support from the parties operating within the context of a democratic republic by transferring their allegiance to Louis Bonaparte who abolished the parliamentary system by his *coup d'état*.

In fact, of course, bourgeois democracy has proved a far more stable political system than Marx envisaged. General franchise and democratic rights have not had the revolutionary consequences which he hoped for and expected and which, on the other hand, were feared by the defenders of the established order. The reason why the democratic development did not lead to a socialist outcome raises the topic of reform and its relation to revolution, a topic central to the Marxist view of politics. The term 'bourgeois democracy' has proved its usefulness in so far as it pinpoints such questions, but even more so because it focuses attention on what in Marxist theory appears as the key to an understanding of the power structure of Western democratic systems. This key is the social and economic context in which the democratic systems are embedded. It is seen as one of bourgeois class power.

It remains to add that Marx would by no means deny the value of democratic forms and institutions, nor did he think that they would always remain associated with bourgeois rule. On the contrary, his argument was that democracy was the means to end class division and would in fact attain its full development in a classless, i.e. socialist society. Ultimately, democracy as a form of state would disappear in a fully communist, and hence stateless, society.

2. SYSTEMS OF CLASS POWER

Bourgeois democracy means then a political system as seen from the Marxist perspective, which under the more familiar name of liberal-democracy we have discussed before. This political system or form of state is characterised by a plurality of parties, a representative assembly, and a range of pressure groups. The point however in the Marxist view is that all these institutions exist within a system of capitalist class power. Class division as such is not a unique feature of capitalism. Class-divided societies have existed throughout history. We have seen how Engels traced their origin and explained the necessity of classes as long as humanity could not master nature. There were slaves and free Greek or Roman citizens in

Antiquity, serfs and feudal lords in the Middle Ages. There are capitalists and proletarians in the modern world. Capitalism, according to Marx, marked a crucial new stage in the progress of humanity. It made the conquest by mankind of nature a distinct possibility. It spread civilisation all over the world. Accordingly the bourgeoisie 'has been the first to show what man's activity can bring about.... It has accomplished wonders far surpassing Egyptian pyramids, Roman aqueducts and Gothic cathedrals; it has conducted expeditions that put in the shade all former exoduses of nations and crusades.'[6]

With all that, capitalism could not eradicate the evils which have always beset the human race: oppression, exploitation, wars.[7] Ultimately they are all due to the basic fact of class rule, of the domination of some people over others. But here the unique feature of the capitalist class division reveals itself. Throughout history ruling classes decayed and were replaced by new ones. Such change was due to changes in the productive forces; its outward manifestations were revolutionary upheavals. The English and the French, nowadays we may add the Russian, Revolutions are historic instances. Capitalism, by basing its class distinctions not on natural and personal characteristics like being a slave or a lord, but on abstract economic relations, has simplified the class structure. Instead of the many subclasses like patricians and plebeians, guildmasters and journeymen, the vast majority of propertyless citizens confront their capitalist rulers. Marx argued that the resulting socialist revolution would not produce a new ruling class, but would abolish classes. It would create a classless society.

It must be noted that following the ideas of Marx, especially as he expressed them in his early writings, capitalism, while determined by the forces of production, cannot be interpreted and judged in purely economic terms. Its basic feature is the exploitation of the working class, but beyond that its influence affects the minds and the lives of all, even of the dominant class. Capitalism produces a 'disenchanted world', a world of reification and alienation. It is a world where quality is necessarily quantified because this world is supremely dominated by money.[8]

With regard to exploitation expressed in general terms, the

point is that the subjected class who form the majority of the population lack ownership and control of the productive resources of society, of the means of production. They are the primary producers, but can only produce in dependence on the owners (the capitalists) and 'at a cost'. Marx defines this cost as surplus labour.[9] In the case of the slave or the serf, it is obvious that they labour for their master under the pressure of brute force. In the case of the wage worker no such force can be exercised, the pressure here applied is of an economic nature. Under the threat of starvation the workers are compelled to sell their labour power as a commodity. The price of a commodity is its production costs. The workers, therefore, receive a subsistence wage barely enough to cover their maintenance and that of their offspring. The fact, however, is that the productivity of their labour power by far exceeds that cost of life. The difference (surplus value) is appropriated by the capitalist and appears in the capitalist's balance-sheet as 'profit'.

A point which is often overlooked must here be made. The costs of living—what Marx also calls 'necessary wants'—represent a relative value not only in money terms but also in respect of the comforts that are required.[10] Or, as Marx wrote:

On the other hand, the number and extent of his (i.e. the owner of labour power, the worker) so-called necessary wants, as also the modes of satisfying them, are themselves the product of historical development, and depend therefore to a great extent on the degree of civilisation of a country, more particularly on the conditions under which, and consequently on the habits and degrees of comfort in which, the class of free labourers has been formed. In contradistinction therefore to the case of other commodities, there enters into the determination of the value of labour power a historical and moral element.[11]

The observation that in Western countries workers may own their house, a car and other commodities contains therefore no valid argument against Marx's theory of exploitation. The question is not one of mere physical survival. The question is what in contemporary society (at least in Western countries) are considered 'necessary wants'.

3. THE STATE AND SOCIETY

The characteristic feature of Marxist theory is that politics in general, and the state in particular, are seen as the chief means by which a system of class domination is maintained. Political power finds its organised expression in the state, which as such is an indispensable institution in any class-divided society. There are different forms of state as there are different forms of class society. The liberal-democratic state, like any other state, exists for the purpose of defending and maintaining the economic and social power of the dominant class.

In the *Communist Manifesto* Marx and Engels wrote: 'Political power, properly so called, is merely the organised power of one class for oppressing another.'[12] However, the relationship between state and ruling class is of a more subtle nature. The idea of the state as being a mere instrument or tool of the ruling class neglects the fact that the state has a certain independence—a 'relative autonomy'. In the first instance, the state is—and is seen as such by Marx—a repressive agency. It is a specialised apparatus of coercion, a set of coercive institutions. These institutions are to a certain extent set over and above society.[13] Modern history must be seen as the process of the continued growth and the sophisticated development of those agencies of repression.

Hal Draper offers a useful summary definition of the Marxist theory of the state: 'The state is the institution, or complex of institutions, which bases itself on the availability of forcible coercion by special agencies of society in order to maintain the dominance of a ruling class, preserve the existing property relations from basic change, and keep all other classes in subjection.'[14]

The merit of this definition is that it focuses attention on two important ideas. The one idea is that the state consists of an increasingly complex apparatus of domination which has a certain life of its own and is separate from the sphere of civil society. The second idea is that nevertheless state power is not altogether divorced from society. The *raison d'être* of the state is to defend a particular social order. While it has a certain independence or autonomy, it is yet firmly tied to society in so far as it functions to 'preserve the existing property relations from basic change'.

Marx saw modern history as involving a process of continuous strengthening and reinforcement of state power. The specialised coercive state apparatus grew ever more complex and powerful. This development was typically revealed in France. Marx, indeed, supplied its most graphic illustrations in his writings on French politics. Drafting his text on the Paris Commune in *The Civil War in France*, he wrote of 'The centralised state machinery which, with its ubiquitous and complicated military, bureaucratic, clerical and judiciary organs, entoils the living civil society like a boa constrictor.'

The same text uses other metaphors to express the idea of the state as a deadweight on society, preventing the latter's free action and making genuine popular control and self-direction impossible. Marx refers to the state as 'this parasitical excrescence upon civil society', a 'deadening incubus'. The successive revolutions in France since 1789 had increased state power until, as he put it in his draft,

The state parasite received only its last development during the Second Empire. The governmental power with its standing army, its all-directing bureaucracy, its stultifying clergy and its servile tribunal hierarchy had grown so independent of society itself that a grotesquely mediocre adventurer with a hungry band of desperadoes behind him sufficed to wield it.

Only with the socialist revolution would the deadweight of the state be shaken off. In the short-lived Paris Commune of 1871 Marx found an anticipation of the public institutions appropriate to a socialist society. The Commune was 'a revolution not against this or that legitimate, constitutional, republican or imperialist form of state power. It was a revolution against the state itself.'[15] It replaced the bureaucratic state apparatus of the Second Empire. It abolished the standing army and police force. The aim was to have a system of government by 'municipal councillors, chosen by universal suffrage in the various wards of the town, responsible and revocable at short terms'.[16] They were paid workers' wages. It was, in other words, an approximation as nearly as possible to direct democracy. It was, as R.N. Hunt

puts it, 'democracy without professionals'.[17] The question
remains whether such a project of popular power is compatible
with a centrally planned collectivised economy.

While Marx submitted the might and power of the capitalist
state as prominently exhibited in Louis Bonaparte's empire to
a critical examination, he would at the same time, and with
respect to the same state, write that 'the state power is not
suspended in mid-air'. In writing that he revealed the other
side of the coin. Powerful as the state is and inclined to use that
power in independent ways, it is nevertheless linked to society:
to the system of class power which it serves to maintain. Above
all, the state is connected with the economically dominant
class. It is this association between state power and class power
that forms one basic tenet of the Marxist view of politics. We
shall have to consider how that connection is worked out and
how the balance between state power and class interest is
preserved. We shall also see by what means the state achieves
its purpose. Of course, it relies on its strength whenever it
shows its coercive power. But the state does not rely on
coercion alone.

4. DOMINANT CLASS AND GOVERNING CASTE

We have then to explain how the state, in the Marxist view, is
seen to function as an instrument in the interest of the ruling
class. The problem is to be discussed with special reference to
liberal-democratic systems. In the *Communist Manifesto* Marx
and Engels wrote that since the establishment of modern
industry and of the world market the bourgeoisie 'conquered
for itself, in the modern representative state, exclusive political
sway', so that 'the executive of the modern state is but a
committee for managing the common affairs of the whole
bourgeoisie'.[18] This is an oversimplification which Marx at
least would not have countenanced in his more mature years.
Of course, on the political scene which the authors of the
Manifesto had to face at the time, the direct influence of
industry and finance capital was far greater than in any of the
following democratic republics. In the July Monarchy of Louis
Philippe, France had one voter for every 170 inhabitants and

the voting right was restricted to 200-franc taxpayers.[19] It is clear from their other political writings that Marx and Engels did not think that the class character of the modern representative state gave the bourgeoisie *exclusive* political power. Democratic rights, and above all the franchise, which the Second and later the Third Republics granted, would in fact produce a 'pressure from below'.

The idea of the 'relative autonomy' of the state was anticipated by a distinction which Marx made between the 'dominant class' (*herrschende Klasse*) and a 'governing caste' (*regierende Kaste*). The holders of state power who staff the state machinery and form the government—what in an earlier chapter was called the state elite—are not normally the same people as those who control the means of production. In an article of 1855, one of five on British politics which he wrote for a German paper (*Neue Oder Zeitung*), Marx argued that 'The governing caste, which in England is by no means identical with the ruling class, will now be driven from one coalition to the next until it has given conclusive proof that it is no longer destined to govern.'[20]

It still remains true that the state, even in a liberal democracy, is a class state functioning to maintain the power of the dominant class. But if in this sense it is a 'committee' working for a purpose, the members of that committee have a certain freedom of action; they are not puppets responding to given directives. As Miliband says, the state may well act on behalf of the ruling class, but that is not to say it works at their behest. To understand the state as an immediately responsive instrument or tool of a class would be a very 'vulgar' form of Marxism. Miliband points out that the very notion of the state managing the common affairs of the whole bourgeoisie implies a process of selection.[21] The holders of state power have to decide which measures would in fact further the common interests of the property-owning class as distinct from the interests of a section or fraction of that class. Indeed, the state might decide on measures which are justified in the long-term interest of the capitalist order and its beneficiaries though in conflict with the immediate or short-term interests of the dominant class. The same point is made by Cohen when he writes: 'The capitalist state, legislator of the Factory Acts, is, then, the eye of the otherwise blind capitalist, the stabilizer of a system capitalist activity itself endangers.'[22]

The measures involved here represent concessions to the working class like a shortening of the working day, paid holidays and other acts of social legislation. Such measures, and others that may benefit the whole population, are felt as an immediate burden by industry, yet they stabilize the system. A large-scale example is the US New Deal of 1933. The government regulations it involved were denounced by some spokesmen for industry as 'creeping socialism'. Nevertheless, the action of the state was in the long-term interest of American capitalism enabling it to recover from the recession without in any way imperilling the basic system. Another example is the British welfare state, supported as it was by a wide consensus of political opinion. Its achievements, especially the National Health Service and the 1944 Education Act, were responses to popular pressure. There is, however, also considerable truth in seeing them as state-imposed changes involving immediate expenditure to be covered by taxation, yet necessary for the continued mass acceptance and legitimacy of the existing economic order.

There are, from the point of view of Marxist theory, two reasons why the state must have a relative autonomy, a sphere of its independent action. The first is that the state performs what Maguire calls a function of 'ruling-class cohesion'.[23] It does not represent the general interest of society; it maintains the general conditions necessary for the relatively smooth working of a system of class power. In order to represent a general capitalist interest it must not be bound closely to any one section of the ruling class. Furthermore, in order to protect a long-term capitalist interest it must be free to act in ways that transcend the immediate aims of the class as a whole. This implies the ability to impose concessions which might well be opposed but are, nevertheless, required for the survival of the ruling class. All this is implied in the concept of the state's autonomy.

Class cohesion means then the integration of often conflicting interests within the dominant class. Draper suggests that the capitalist class is more prone to internal divisions than any previous ruling class. Consequently the need for the state to function as a general representative of, yet acting independently from, the sectionally divided class, is even greater. As Draper puts it:

No other ruling class is so profusely criss-crossed internally with competing and conflicting interest groups, each at the other's throat—the dog-eat-dog pattern. Competing national groups (countries) are split by regional group interests, different industrial interests, antagonism within an industry, rivalry between producers of consumers' and producers' goods, light and heavy industry, and so on, aside from religious, political and other ideological differences...[24]

Secondly, the state in a liberal-democratic system must have some autonomy in order to preserve its legitimacy. If the state was seen to be too closely bound up with and dominated by one set of interests, it would not be able to maintain the belief that it represents the general interest and exists in order to serve the common good of society. But such a belief, which must be shared by the majority of its subjects, is essential for the smooth functioning of the state and its institutions. The state does not rely on coercion alone. In fact, under normal conditions its coercive aspect is masked, or deployed only against the minority which openly challenges its authority. The state can function effectively as the guardian of a class-divided society because the political sphere in a liberal-democratic system appears to be one in which all people are free and equal citizens. Their class position does not seem to matter. Whatever the inequalities of society, they count for nothing in the field of politics. The holders of political power must proclaim, and indeed may well sincerely believe, that they are neutral and impartial arbiters with respect to the various interests and pressures emanating from civil society. In other words, the state must appear to approximate to the ideal of a pluralist society. If it were incapable of ever acting on its own and always followed the lead of capital, the appearance would vanish at once. That it is merely appearance, and as such an illusion, is a basic tenet of all Marxist theories. In fact, the argument runs, even a reforming government's scope of action is limited by the socioeconomic structure of the system. Behind the open political scene, economic power asserts itself, perhaps by provoking a crisis in the fields of investment and employment, or through the mechanism of the stock exchange, affecting the national currency. In addition, resistance to such a government would emerge in the ranks of a political elite whose collective mind, as we have had occasion to note, is shaped by ideological factors though they may not be aware of the fact. Of even greater importance is the ideological conditioning of the masses. Ideology and a resulting consensus is thus seen as the second factor on which the state relies besides its repressive power. One might even say that coercion is suspended as long as the ideological function is effectively performed.[25] But what is that ideology?

5. THE STATE AND IDEOLOGY

The forces of production determine the social relations at a particular time; they determine the structure of society. That structure and the mode of production on which it is based are reflected in human minds. They take the form of ideas. The reflection might yield different pictures according to the standpoint from which the social reality is surveyed. Different classes might have different ideas. In actual fact, however, the dominant ideas of a society are the ideas of its ruling class. The explanation is that the ruling class dominates the field of education and learning. It also, normally, supervises the spread of ideas throughout society: 'The class which has the means of material production at its disposal, has control at the same time over the means of mental production.'[26]

Obviously people will be sympathetic to ideas which are convenient and confirm their advantageous position. Those who are the main beneficiaries of the existing order will want to maintain it. Nevertheless, it would be a mistake to assume that such systems of ideas—or ideologies—are consciously invented for the purpose they serve. They are transmitted by tradition from generation to generation as long as society develops in harmony with its productive powers. They are taken for eternal truths and unalterable conditions of human social life, sanctioned by God or imposed by nature. While they express the basic facts of a class-divided society, they also cover them up. In Cohen's words:

If the exploited were to see that they are exploited, they would resent their subjection and threaten social stability. And if the exploiters were to see that they exploit, the composure they need to rule confidently would be disturbed. Being social animals the exploiters have to feel that their behaviour is justifiable. When the feeling is difficult to reconcile with the truth, the truth must be hidden ... Illusion is therefore constitutive of class societies.[27]

Even in a situation when the old order is about to be overthrown, the defence of interest and privilege is conducted under the banner of ideas. The fight is made more ferocious because people think that they are not so much fighting for their material advantage but rather for what they believe to be the deepest meaning of their lives. The same applies to the attackers: 'For each new class which puts itself in the place of one ruling before it, is compelled to represent its interest as the common interest of all the members of society, that is expressed in ideal form: it has to give its ideas the form of universality, and represent them as the only rational, universally valid ones.'[28]

This ideological character of history, according to Marx, will only come to an end when, in a socialist society, there will be no classes. Meanwhile, however, the bourgeois ideology has a firm hold not merely in the ranks of the ruling class and its political and intellectual representatives, but also in the majority of the population. It is diffused through a variety of channels in state and civil society, and such diffusion is facilitated even futher by the commanding economic and social resources which the ruling class possesses. In the end even the working class takes the existing state of affairs for granted. As Marx wrote, 'the advance of capitalist production develops a working class which by education, tradition, habit, looks upon the conditions of that mode of production as self-evident laws of nature.'[29] This constitutes what the Italian Marxist, Gramsci, would later call 'the hegemony' of the bourgeoisie, a hegemony operating not solely in the political but equally or even more in the cultural field. This hegemony, Gramsci taught, must be eroded and dissolved before the socialist aspiration would have a chance of being fulfilled.[30]

If the ideology is to be acceptable and achieve its purpose it must somehow reflect the true nature of its society, but also the ideals which that society acknowledges as guiding its course. It cannot altogether be arbitrary. In his *Grundrisse* Marx, in the opening sections of the chapter on Capital, reviews the ideological superstructure of bourgeois society. His translator, in another place, suggests that Marx here is putting the argument 'into the mouth of an imaginary antagonist'.[31] The remark is quite correct as far as it goes, but more is implied. The theoretical picture which Marx here presents of the bourgeois society is at the same time the image of how that society appears to its members. It is therefore the ideology of that society. It is its existing reality expressed as an idea.

Liberté and *égalité* were the watchwords of the French Revolution. Within a limited range of their application, and on the surface of civil life, these ideals are realised in bourgeois society. This society is in a sense (in its own sense) a free and equal society. Its members meet as equals in the marketplace. This in itself is no mean achievement. We have to compare it with relations as they obtained in previous societies when one person by social convention was a slave, the other a free person; or the one as a lord confronted his serf. They could not meet as equals. Their social status was indelibly inscribed on their persons. Now a king as a customer counts as much as a worker. 'All distinction between the contracting parties is extinguished'—provided, we may add, they have the money.[32]

As people are equal so they are free. Brute force has been eliminated from the process of social action. The state of nature has been superseded. 'No one seizes hold of another's property by force. Each divests himself of his property voluntarily.'[33] There is freedom of contract. This is equally true of the worker who sells his labour as of the person who acquired money to spend for the satisfaction of his individual needs. Within such a society each of its members, provided they accept the conditions of the exchange system, are free to seek their own satisfaction. That is what later will be called the randomness of ends. The corresponding ethical theory is a utilitarian hedonism. Of course, it is true that the worker may or may not contract with that particular capitalist. The fact that under threat of starvation the worker is compelled to contract with some capitalist is conveniently overlooked.

The Marxist critique of this ideology emphasises the fact

that such freedom and equality as bourgeois society grants are available only within the limitations of the capitalist system and depend on its acceptance. Individuals have to subordinate their whole existence to the demands of the commodity system. The point is they that have no choice or freedom in this matter. In other words, they buy their rights, the very possibility of their existence, at the price of their complete alienation. As Cohen puts it: 'The rule of things is the price of bourgeois freedom.'[34]

Another aspect of the Marxist critique concerns the point that bourgeois freedom and equality are abstract concepts (in the sense in which Hegel speaks of 'abstract freedom'). The individual's range of action is limited at every step by the economic facts. As regards equality, all people, says Marx, are equal in the sense in which all physical bodies can be said to be equal in so far as they all have weight and occupy three dimensions in space. Once we go beyond that abstract quantitative determination and observe their qualitative properties, this semblance of equality disappears. In the same sense, an equality observable in the process of exchange applies to the surface process only, 'beneath which, however, in the depths, entirely different processes go on, in which this apparent individual equality and liberty disappear.'[35]

Later, in *Capital*, Marx described the ideology of the bourgeois society in a more satirical vein. It was 'in fact a very Eden of the innate rights of man. There alone rule Freedom, Equality, Property and Bentham'—Freedom and Equality in the sense we have just shown, 'Property because each disposes only of what is his own. And Bentham because each looks only to himself.'[36]

In *The German Ideology* Marx and Engels warned of the danger of abstracting the dominant ideology from its social context. As they put it:

If now in considering the course of history we detach the ideas of the ruling class from the ruling class itself and attribute them an independent existence, if we confine ourselves to saying that these or those ideas were dominant at a given time ...

then history would appear as nothing other than a history of ideas.[37] This was exemplified by Hegel, for whom the abstraction of the 'Idea' became, as he wrote, 'like the soul-conductor Mercury ... the leader of peoples and of the World'.[38] If, furthermore, the state is seen, as it was by Hegel, as the guardian of the 'Idea', this view could be adapted to Marxist theory; only what the state guards is the ideology. But the state is not a mythical or abstract entity. Its business is conducted by people who form the state elite, including the bureaucracy. They share the dominant ideology of society, which, according to Marxist theory, it is their task to defend and maintain.

In previous chapters there has been discussion of the role played by the political elite, the leading members of the civil service, the judiciary, the armed forces, and so on. They are not the elected representatives of the people; they are the functionaries of the state. The problem was raised above of whether their shared convictions and prejudices do not cast doubt on what was presupposed by pluralist theory—the neutrality of the state. The question is not one of the sincerity of their beliefs or desire to act in the best interest of society as they conceive it. Nevertheless, a certain uniformity of mental attitudes suggest that they provide an apt illustration of the Marxist concept of ideology.

In the introductory chapter above, reference was made to the analysis presented by Griffith of the British senior judiciary. It should be noted that he rejects as 'too broad' the Marxist view of the state as 'serving to protect and promote the interest of the ruling class', and of law as 'the will of that State which seems to stand outside and above society'. Nevertheless, he comes to the conclusion that as far as judges in Britain are concerned, 'their interpretation of what is in the public interest and therefore politically desirable is determined by the kind of people they are and the position they hold in our society; that this position is a part of established authority and so is necessarily conservative and illiberal.' From all this, Griffith continues,

flows that view of the public interest which is shown in judicial attitudes such as tenderness towards private property and dislike of trade unions, strong adherence to the maintenance of order, dislike for minority opinions, demonstrations and protests, indifference to the promotion of better race relations, support of governmental secrecy, concern for the preservation of the moral and social behaviour to which it is accustomed, and the rest.[39]

Griffith sees the senior judiciary as part of the governing group of society, unlikely to take decisions inimical to the power of that governing group. In his view, the idea of 'The Rule of Law' is not a total myth; judicial independence can provide defences for individuals against the power of the executive. Yet the way in which the Rule of Law is interpreted cannot be abstracted from the situation in which judges are recruited from a particular and relatively limited social background, and the function of the law is to help maintain a particular class-divided social structure. Thus certain judicial decisions, for example concerning the use of pickets, and the power of trade unions, are explicable in terms of this function of the law as safeguarding the existing social order.

6. THE AUTONOMOUS STATE

The argument so far was that if the state is to act successfully in the interest of the ruling class it needs a certain measure of 'relative autonomy'. This is especially true of a liberal-democratic system functioning in a capitalist context. It does not follow that the working class would have no influence whatsoever on the state and on the holders of political power. Marx thought that the capture of democratic rights was an indispensable factor on the road to the socialist emancipation of the working class. This applied in the first instance to that basic democratic right, the franchise, but also to other democratic rights such as the formation of political parties and trade unions or the holding of public meetings. Such rights were essential for the proletariat to win political power and achieve the transition from a capitalist to a socialist society. Once in possession of such rights the working class would be able to put some pressure on the capitalists and on the state. This did not mean that the state would cease to function as the instrument of the capitalist class, yet reforms might be achieved, for example a shortening of the working day, and labour organisations would be allowed to meet and act freely.

The point of the Marxist theory is that 'winning the battle of democracy' would eventually put the capitalists under pressure. However, under certain conditions the ruling class, while being exposed to such pressure from below, might come to abandon the democratic system. In a crisis situation they might call for a different state, a 'strong state' system of heightened autonomy. Such a state would frustrate the efforts of the working class by destroying or bypassing the democratic institutions built up under liberal-democratic rules. Marx saw such a development exemplified by the case of Louis Bonaparte's *coup d'état* of 2 December 1851. It was the abandonment of the democratic system by the bourgeoisie that provided the main theme of Marx's text *The Eighteenth Brumaire of Louis Bonaparte.* 'Its pervasive theme', as Draper notes, 'is the relations between the state power and the various social groups.' The importance of the text for Marxist theory is that it describes the circumstances under which the state assumes a heightened and intensified autonomy.[40]

Such an autonomy has two aspects. First, in this type of state, the bureaucratic and executive elements of the state become more powerful as compared with its democratic and representative elements. The army, police and bureaucracy take over power from representative assemblies. The latter become less significant, if indeed they survive at all. Certainly, in the case of Bonapartism in France, the army was a crucial pillar of the regime after Louis Napoleon had won its support which was instrumental in his *coup.*

The second aspect, beyond the strengthening of the executive at the expense of other elements of the state, is the intensification of state power as a whole over and above civil society. A specialised apparatus of coercion appears more prominent; it is separate from and opposed to society. The state becomes autonomous in an absolute sense with respect to civil society, even with respect to the ruling class. As Marx wrote: 'all classes, equally impotent and equally mute, fall on their knees before the rifle butt.'[41] That means that the dominant class too is politically subject to the state. Its control of the state is weakened, the state is much less the direct instrument of its power. All civil society comes under tutelage to a strong state. The ruling class switches its allegiance from its traditional representatives, parties or politicians that operate within the framework of parliamentary institutions. It now lends its support to a political leader of a quite different kind.

Marx argued that Bonaparte's assumption of state power could certainly not be explained by his personal qualities. This 'grotesque mediocrity' playing a hero's part was never a member of the traditional political class. In fact, he was an adventurer coming from nowhere. Under normal circumstances the property-owning classes would not have entrusted him with political power. His only political asset was his name as the nephew of the great Napoleon. He was elected President of the Republic in December 1848, largely through the support of the peasantry. They saw in him their protector, mainly the guarantor of the smallholdings which they had acquired as a result of the 1789 Revolution. His immediate social base was largely to be found in a *lumpenproletariat*, the dislocated and unemployed, all floating elements of society, whom he organised in the 'Society of 10th December'. His political bastion was the army where in his position of President and Commander-in-Chief he dispensed favours to make the army a kind of praetorian guard.

With all that, according to Marx's analysis, Bonaparte would not have succeeded had it not been for deeper reasons. The history of the Second Republic (1848–51) shows that the men wielding the power of the state used it to maintain 'order'. By this they meant proceeding against the workers who insisted on being employed (at least in the national workshops) and who also demanded that the most urgent social problems should be dealt with. It was to crush such aspirations that the insurrection of the June days in 1848 was most ferociously suppressed. The democrats of the 'Mountain', a parliamentary group by no means socialist, were driven into opposition. The power of the Republic was then divided between Bonaparte as President confronting the 'Party of Order'. Eventually, however, the property-owning classes lent their support to Bonaparte because in command of the army and with the help of his 'Society of 10th December', that crowd of rowdies, he seemed a better defender of what they understood by order than the parliamentary 'Party of Order'. He would put an end to the parliamentary regime which through its democratic rights and liberties gave the advantage to working and petty-bourgeois classes, thereby menacing bourgeois class rule. In Marx's words, the ruling class was prepared to accept that 'its political power must be broken in order to preserve its social power intact'.[42]

Bonaparte promptly destroyed the parliamentary system of the Second Republic. Under previous regimes, wrote Marx, the bureaucracy and the state in general 'was the instrument of the ruling class, however much it strove for power of its own. . . . Only under the second Bonaparte does the state seem to have made itself completely independent. As against civil society, the state machine has consolidated its position so thoroughly that the chief of the Society of December 10 suffices for its head. . .'[43]

In practice, this to all appearance completely independent position meant that the far greater weight of the state, notably its repressive and order-maintaining elements, pressed down on all society and on all its interests. It meant that even the property-owning classes knelt 'mute and powerless' in a condition of utter subjection. After the dissolution of the Party of Order they had no 'direct line' to the political power holders. The characteristic feature of Bonapartism, however, was not solely this intensification of state power. It was just as much the demagogic and plebiscitary direct approach to the masses. Marx, incidentally, notes the use by Bonaparte of the nationalist idea as a means of gaining popular support. The Empire, soon inaugurated by him after his overthrow of the Republic, 'professed to unite all classes by reviving for all the chimera of national glory'.[44] Since then all would-be dictators have resorted to similar methods, involving the destruction or bypassing of the representative assembly and of parties, indeed of all associations through which a genuine democratic participation is possible. They have all tried to stimulate and excite nationalist emotions. In France the state towered above all classes. It had achieved heightened autonomy.

'And yet the state power is not suspended in mid-air.' The specialised apparatus of coercion seemed to have grown enormously and to have taken on a life of its own; in a sense this was indeed the case. It was, as Draper puts it, a case of 'gigantism versus democracy'.[45] What Marx meant was that even in its independence the state defended and protected a system of class power. The property-owning classes (the bourgeoisie) believed they could not adequately protect their social and economic interests within the framework of a parliamentary system, not even by relying on their 'own' parliamentary party. They feared that universal suffrage and other democratic rights might assure the propertyless mass of victory. That is a fear we have seen arise in other places and at other times: the fear that the general franchise might destroy private property and lead to revolution. Capitalism under certain circumstances was felt to be incompatible with democracy.

Nevertheless, the state could not abolish classes nor altogether disregard the class structure of society. The peasants had not only elected Bonaparte as their protector but also, threatened as they were by pauperisation because their smallholdings were no longer viable economic units, they expected him to work miracles on their behalf. Bonaparte, however, soon to become the Emperor Napoleon III, needed the bourgeoisie in order to finance his foreign policy and the planned aggrandisement of his capital Paris. So he 'feels it his mission to safeguard bourgeois order'. 'Industry and trade are to prosper in hothouse fashion under the strong government.' Eventually, 'Bonaparte would like to appear as the patriarchal benefactor of all classes.'[46]

The conclusion must be that an executive-dominated state of the Bonapartist type still exhibits the two features which, in the Marxist view, characterise all states. It is a separate apparatus of domination with interests of its own, standing over and above civil society. At the same time this state machine is linked to the class structure of society. It props up and preserves the power of the ruling class. In the Bonapartist state the first feature was accentuated. As for the second feature, it involves a distinction between the political power of the dominant class, which was severely curtailed, and its economic and social power, which was very much kept in being. Even the Bonapartist state remained dependent on the material power of the owners of the productive resources.

Marx's writings on Bonapartism have received much attention, not least because they have provided a basis for the

Marxist analysis of later fascist and national-socialist regimes. These too are characterised by an enormous increase of executive and repressive agencies, partly incorporated in the state system, and by the destruction of all democratic institutions which are replaced by plebiscitary appeals to the masses. An important factor in the genesis of such regimes is also a general disillusion with the parliamentary system and a willingness of the property-owning classes to abandon their political power by deserting the parties which defend their interests—all this for fear of what they call 'anarchy' or of a socialist revolution. Of course, they do not resort lightly to the acceptance of a system of reinforced executive power. That system comes into being in conditions of deep crisis, not without 'costs' for the economically dominant class. All explanations of that kind, therefore, must not be over-simplified or interpreted in a mechanistic sense. There is nothing inevitable in 'playing the authoritarian card'.

The aim of this section has been to show, in fairly general and schematic terms, how Marx saw the state in a liberal-democratic system as linked to a structure of class domination. State power could not be understood in abstraction from class power even in a situation where the state seemed to develop a life of its own and completely dominate civil society.

7. MARX AND ENGELS ON REFORMS

As was already mentioned, Marx believed that the acquisition of democratic rights was a crucial stage in the class struggle waged by the workers against the ruling class. The most important of those rights was the vote. It would help the working-class movement in its task of 'winning the battle of democracy'. Unlike his anarchist critics, Marx insisted on political action as a necessary, if by no means sufficient, precondition for the socialist transformation of society. He considered the political organisation of the working class as an essential moment in the process of emancipation. In its course the workers would develop their class consciousness. The formation of political parties and their activity were vital factors in the revolutionary struggle. Through this struggle the working class would become ready to shake off its status of subjection to become itself the ruling class, prior to the disappearance of class distinctions altogether.

Obviously, as the workers' parties developed they would also become able to exert their pressure in the political field and to enforce at least a partial satisfaction of their economic and social demands. As Marx wrote, 'As to the limitation of the working day in England, as in all other countries, it has never been settled except by legislative interference. Without the working men's continuous pressure from without that interference would never have taken place.'[47]

Such reforms as limiting the length of the working day were to be striven for, not merely for humanitarian reasons, but because they would strengthen the force of the working-class movement and build up its morale. They would show the gains that could be made with the help of economic and political working-class organisations, thereby encouraging the latter's development.

Marx did not at all agree with the anarchists that the formation of political parties would imply integration and in fact a tacit acceptance of the existing system. The working class had to use all the opportunities for action open to it. A system of parliamentary democracy clearly offered more and better opportunities than an authoritarian system like Bonapartism. It meant the possibility of and relative freedom for the organisations of working-class politics, parties and trade unions. Democracy, therefore, must be defended whenever it came under attacks aiming at the establishment of strengthened state power, of heightened executive autonomy. Some examples of this comparatively positive attitude towards the existing political system are given in Engels' letters to Marx's son-in-law Paul Lafargue, on the occasion of the challenge delivered to the Third Republic by General Boulanger. The Boulangist movement, by exploiting social and nationalist grievances, aimed at overthrowing the parliamentary system and replacing it with a plebiscitary dictatorship led by the General. Lafargue, as a Marxist, was tempted to support the movement as being directed against a state form which upheld the power of the bourgeoisie. Engels, however, argued strongly against such a view. He emphasised the advantages of the parliamentary regime, imperfect though it might be, as compared with a 'strong' authoritarian state.[48]

With all that, whatever reforms and ameliorations in the workers' living standard could be achieved, they would not alter the basic economic system with its corresponding class structure. Marx was quite clear that a radical change of system was the ultimate goal. In the passage quoted before he continued by urging the workers to keep that ultimate goal firmly in their minds:

> The working class ought not to exaggerate to themselves the ultimate working of these everyday struggles. They ought not to forget ... that they are applying palliatives, not curing the malady.... Instead of the conservative motto, 'A fair day's wage for a fair day's work' they ought to inscribe on their banner the revolutionary watchword, 'Abolition of the wages system'![49]

As far as Marx is concerned it seems right to say that in his perspective the workers' movement should indeed seek improvements and reforms within the confines of capitalism, but that these reforms were to be stages on the way, or means for achieving the complete transformation of the system. Reforms were certainly not seen as ends in themselves; much less was it expected that they would make the existing system acceptable. They would strengthen the working-class movement without in the least weakening its revolutionary zeal.

The most powerful weapon in its struggle was, of course, the general franchise. In the capitalist system, the concentration of capital into fewer and fewer hands would inevitably lead to a polarisation of society. As it said in the *Manifesto*: 'Our epoch, the epoch of the bourgeoisie, possesses, however, this distinctive feature: it has simplified the class antagonisms. Society as a whole is more and more splitting up into two great hostile camps, into two great classes directly facing each other: Bourgeoisie and Proletariat.'[50]

Marx expected that the socialist movement would then be able to rely on the support of the vast majority of more or less propertyless people. Engels was even more optimistic in that respect. Marx was more circumspect: it was not enough to conquer by means of a parliamentary majority the political power positions. He warned that 'The working class cannot simply lay hold of the ready-made state machinery and wield it for its own purposes.'[51]

The socialist revolution would not repeat the mistake of the Prussian bourgeois revolution which Marx had criticised in his writings on the 1848 Revolution, when the liberal politicians with a majority in the National Assembly in Berlin tried to compromise with the state apparatus of the old feudal system.[52] The radical transformation of society could not be carried out within the framework of the old political institutions. New institutions would have to be created. What they would be like, we have already indicated when we mentioned the enthusiastic approval which Marx extended to the way the Paris Commune of 1871 organised its political life. Even if it could not be a blueprint, it provided crucial indications for the organisation of a future socialist society. To be sure, there would be no bureaucrats. Already in his early writings the young Marx had stigmatised bureaucracy: 'The bureaucrats are the Jesuits and theologians of the state. The bureaucracy is the religious republic.'[53] In any case, the emancipation of the workers must be the task of the working class itself.

One might wonder whether a watchword like this would not be vulnerable to the elitist criticism which Michels made when he stressed the danger of the bureaucratisation of a political movement and the separation of a leading group from the broad mass of followers. It could also be suggested that Marx perhaps underestimated the range of reforms which would be made available to the working class, partly as a result of their own efforts, partly as a result of the managers' discovery that it was good for business to keep their workers happy. From Marx's point of view such far-reaching reforms would have appeared as a mixed blessing: while there was no doubt that they benefited the workers they also integrated them into the system. Furthermore, it can be argued that the polarisation of capitalist society did not develop in the way Marx expected. While it remains true that the capitalists—in any case, those who matter—constitute only a minority, the vast majority of citizens do not confront them as a homogeneous class. The masses are diversified in their social composition; even within the working class there are sub-classes and groups which compete with each other, not to mention national rivalries and antagonisms. All these factors need not impair the validity of the Marxist analysis of social forces. They might, however, contribute to an understanding of why the actual development, at least in Western countries, followed a line different from the one which Marx anticipated, and why demands for reform did not develop into revolutionary politics, as he believed they would.

Marx did not live to witness the tremendous progress of the Social-Democratic Party in Germany after it had adopted a Marxist programme, but Engels was greatly impressed by it. In an introduction, written shortly before his death in 1895, to a new edition of Marx's text of 1848 *The Class Struggles in France*, Engels saluted the success due 'to the intelligent use which the German workers made of the universal franchise introduced in 1866'. They had transformed the franchise 'from a means of deception, which it was before, into an instrument of emancipation'. It appears that he was convinced that universal suffrage would not only produce reforms to improve the actual conditions of working-class life, but would eventually, in a slow but steady progress, lead to the final victory of the socialist movement. The state was already 'paralysed'. Rebellion in the old style, street fighting, was obsolete. 'It was found that the state institutions, in which the rule of the bourgeoisie is organised, offer the working class still further opportunities to fight these very state institutions.'[54] To a certain extent Engels' attitude here anticipates a later reformist movement led by Eduard Bernstein.

8. REFORM OR REVOLUTION?

The question has sometimes been raised why an oppressed and exploited working class in the Western countries has not attempted to overthrow capitalism by means of a violent revolution.[55] One would, of course, first have to decide whether the working class ever had such an opportunity. It might further be argued that the natural reluctance of people to risk their lives and, in addition, accept at least temporary material disadvantages, must be taken into consideration. These are issues which cannot be discussed here. Moreover, on occasions such as the Spartacus revolution in Germany after the First World War, the revolutionary enthusiasm of a vanguard was not spread equally among the working masses. The class as a whole did not appear as revolutionary as, according to Marxist texts, it ought to have been if it was to engineer the socialist transformation of society. Similar observations could be made in other places and at later times.

Some elements of an answer to the question have been indicated in the preceding section. They can be summarised under three headings. *Economically*, the fact is that an immiseration theory, which would apply to the working class as well as to the petty bourgeoisie or lower middle classes, has not been confirmed in modern society. In view of the chronic unemployment problem in contemporary Europe the words of the *Manifesto* still make sense, that the bourgeoisie 'is unfit to rule because it is incompetent to assure an existence to its slave within his slavery, because it cannot help letting him sink into such a state, that it has to feed him, instead of being fed by him.'[56] On the other hand, the capitalist system has over large periods 'assured an existence' to its 'slaves', i.e. the working class. There have been periods of economic growth which have resulted in rising living standards for the bulk of the population. Important reforms which were made rather suggest that Marx underrated the resilience of the capitalist system and its ability to accommodate itself to changing circumstances by achieving, at least to a certain extent, some accommodation and compromise in management–labour relations.

Socially, those economic changes have resulted, as noted above, in a diversification of the class structure whereby even the working class itself is divided in various ways. At the same time a certain bureaucratisation of social-democratic parties, especially in the German party, took place so that at least some party leaders became so accustomed to parliamentary institutions and procedures that they could hardly imagine activity transcending those institutions. The struggle for reforms led thus to results quite different from those Marx envisaged. Instead of a movement intended to strengthen the working class and weakening state power, the social-democratic movement was taking its place within the existing state. Its methods of campaigning for reforms had rather the effect of stabilising the existing socioeconomic system. This was in fact the point of Michels' criticism.

The third factor concerns the *ideological* conditioning of society. The point has been mentioned in discussing the ideology of the state. Individual groups and classes try to improve the conditions of their life but their efforts are kept within the limits of the given order which is accepted as natural and more or less unalterable. That is what Marcuse meant when he spoke of 'one-dimensional man': that people cannot even imagine transcending the plane on which they are kept in order to discover a new dimension of their social existence. It is part of what Gramsci understood by the term of bourgeois hegemony, seen as restricting the range of ideas, and hence that of action.[57]

In this connection it might also be suggested that Marx apparently underestimated the strength of national feelings and emotions. The claim of the *Manifesto* that 'the working men have no country' has not been confirmed by later historical developments. August 1914 already showed that the idea of defending the nation had a powerful hold over all classes. Patriotic feelings may well be compatible with socialist aspirations, but immediately at least they cut across an international solidarity which, Marx presumed, was an essential feature of the working-class movement.[58]

When all this is acknowledged and duly registered, we have still to remember that on Marxian terms a socialist revolution cannot happen at any time or whenever the occasion seems favourable. There is a certain rhythm in history which it is not possible to break up. The socioeconomic structure of a society will persist as long as all its latent potentialities can be developed within its framework: 'No social order ever perishes before all the productive forces for which there is room in it have developed; and new higher relations of production never appear before the material conditions of their existence have matured in the womb of the old society itself.'[59]

As far as the socialist revolution is concerned, it can only be successful when the bourgeois society has developed all its productive forces. That was after all the mission, the historic justification so to speak, of the bourgeoisie as a ruling class. The point is that there must be a material abundance available in order to implement the socialist programme. As Marx and Engels put it:

This development of productive forces ... is an absolutely necessary premise because without it want is merely made general, and with the destitution the struggle for necessities and all the old filthy business would necessarily be reproduced.[60]

Certain preconditions must therefore be met before the revolutionary transformation of society becomes a practical possibility. The economy must be sufficiently developed to produce enough goods for the overcoming of scarcity. A premature attempt would be condemned to failure; even if it succeeded at first, it could not be maintained and the old order would be re-established. This, however, must not be understood in terms of a Hegelian 'World Spirit' or 'History' itself personified working according to a fixed timetable to reach a predestined goal. There is nothing mechanical or automatic in the sequence of the historical epochs. Marx's theory of history is indeed frequently misinterpreted in such a way, despite explicit statements by Marx to the contrary. In an early work, written together with Engels, Marx declared that:

History does *nothing*, it 'possess *no* enormous wealth', it 'wages no battles'. It is *man*, real living man, who does all that, who possesses and fights; 'history' is not, as it were, a person apart, using man as a means to achieve its own aims; history is *nothing but* the activity of man pursuing his aims.[61]

As Marx also put it, 'Men make their own history'; it is human beings themselves, given the appropriate conditions, who must effect the transformation of society. When it comes to the question of the means to be used to achieve such a change, the answer is often couched in terms of two alternative means: Reform or Revolution. Yet this alternative is in a sense misleading. Reforms can be taken by definition to imply the retention of the existing system. Marx was quite consistent, therefore, if he rejected reforms as an ultimate end, while nevertheless welcoming reforms for reasons explained above. But there is another alternative: would the radical transformation to a socialist society, which we can call revolution, be effected on the whole in a peaceful way or would it require violence and the use of force?

There are really two questions which are often put together. The fundamental transformation from a capitalist to a socialist society would involve, in Marx's view, the abolition of private ownership of the means of production, their control by 'the associated producers', in other words the collectivisation of private property. This was what Marx understood by a socialist revolution. This is to be distinguished from the question of how, by what means, this revolution is to be achieved, whether through peaceful means, for example those of a parliamentary system, or necessarily by the use of force against a capitalist class determined to maintain its power and ownership of the productive resources. The nature and definition of what a socialist revolution is, in the Marxist perspective, is a separate question from that of the strategy and actions needed to achieve such a revolution.

As far as the latter question is concerned, it can be argued that Marx did not rule out as necessarily impossible a non-violent path to socialist society. This might be possible where democratic parliamentary institutions existed and furnished an opportunity for the majority demand for democracy and, as Marx thought would follow, socialism, to be effective. Marx did warn that such means of achieving the transition to socialism might provoke a backlash from the possessing classes. They might refuse to accept democracy if democratic politics seemed to threaten the end of their power.

Too often the question is treated in an abstract way. What were Marx's presuppositions for the socialist revolution to happen? They were, as has been pointed out, that the productive forces of capitalist society would be fully developed. But the hypothesis also was that the vast majority of the population would welcome the change. Accordingly, when he addressed the Hague Congress of the First International in 1872, Marx could say:

We know of the allowances we must make for the institutions, customs and traditions of the various countries; and we do not deny that there are countries such as America, England, and I would add Holland if I knew your institutions better, where the working people may achieve their goal by peaceful means.

His speech, however, continued:

If that is true, we must also recognise that in most of the continental countries it is force that will have to be the lever of our revolutions; it is force that we shall some day have to resort to in order to establish a reign of labour.[62]

In the same sense Engels, in his Foreword to *Capital*, written in 1886, said of Marx that he was 'a man whom that study led to the conclusion that, at least in Europe, England is the only country where the inevitable social revolution might be effected entirely by peaceful and legal means.' But Engels too added a warning: 'He certainly never forgot to add that he hardly expected the English ruling classes to submit, without a "pro-slavery rebellion", to this peaceful and legal revolution.'[63]

Marx thus appears to have thought it just possible that in England the dominant class would accept a democratic result that went against its fundamental convictions and prejudices and against its interests. In most other European countries, he held, it would be over-optimistic to expect such a favourable development. There, the state apparatus would have to be 'smashed'. Bearing in mind the later historical developments when fascist dictatorships arose in several of those countries, one could be inclined to think that there was substantial reason in Marx's view. The interpretation then is that force would have to be used, and an armed struggle would follow, in order to combat a counter-revolution, in other words the attempt to sabotage and reverse the revolutionary development.

The idea of a peaceful revolution, however, is not a contradiction in terms. The experience of history suggests that revolutions have not been violent in their early stages, in their 'honeymoon' period. Violence and fighting have arisen after the revolution itself. They developed out of attempts by groups and classes to mount a counter-revolution to crush the revolution and annul its achievements. This was the case with the democratic revolution of 1848 in France and February

1917 in Russia, and can also be said to be true of the October Revolution of 1917 in Russia.

It should also be noted that there is nothing in Marx's work of the party as a revolutionary vanguard (as Lenin viewed it), nor of the party as the repository and even the creator of an otherwise absent proletarian class consciousness. That was how the Hungarian Marxist Lukács saw it, but this was certainly a departure from Marx's views. Moreover, Marx nowhere envisaged a monolithic party with all other parties proscribed and eventually liquidated. If indeed the parliamentary system was to be replaced this was to prevent the representatives from dominating those whom they represented—the people. The representatives were to be delegates, kept under the strict control of the people. In this sense, as we shall see, the Paris Commune of 1871 could be called by Engels 'the dictatorship of the proletariat'.[64]

9. THE STATE IN POST-REVOLUTIONARY SOCIETY

Another frequent misunderstanding of Marx, by followers and opponents alike, suggests that on his view a successful revolution would immediately be followed by the establishment of a communist society; so the final purpose of history would be achieved at a stroke. Yet this was not what either Marx or Engels envisaged. There would indeed be a decisive event, namely the abolition of private property in the means of production. This change, however, would only open the way for a long development in the course of which 'circumstances and men' would develop, or, as Engels wrote in a letter: 'To my mind, the so-called "socialist society" is not anything immutable. Like all other social formations it should be conceived in a state of constant flux and change.'[65]

On several occasions Marx urged the workers to realise that even after the overthrow of the capitalist system they would have to struggle hard for many years before the vision of a communist society would come into sight. He even presumed that they were well aware of the fact that they had to face a bitter and protracted fight:

The working class did not expect miracles from the Commune. They have no ready-made utopias to introduce *par décret du peuple*. They know that in order to work out their own emancipation ... they will have to pass through long struggles, through a series of historic processes, transforming circumstances and men.[66]

To imagine that a fully-fledged communist society would immediately come into being after the overthrow of capitalism would be sheer utopia. From the point of view of our investigation two questions then arise: What will be the role of the state in the transitional period? What will the state be like under communism? The first question was briefly answered by Marx in his *Critique of the Gotha Programme*. The Gotha Programme was the draft unity programme of the German Social-Democratic Workers Party (later the SDP), formed when the party of Liebknecht and Bebel sunk its differences and united with the followers of Lassalle at the Gotha Congress of 1875. Marx stated in his critique that:

Between capitalist and communist society lies the period of the revolutionary transformation of the one into the other. Corresponding to this is also a political transition period in which the state can be nothing but the revolutionary dictatorship of the proletariat.[67]

The socialist revolution which Marx anticipated would in the end bring into being a classless society. It would be the first society, primitive communism excepted, in which there would be no private ownership of the means of production, hence no appropriation of the labour of a suppressed class by a ruling class. Since the state was viewed by Marx as an institution which arose in a class-divided society in order to protect and maintain the ruling class in its power, the revolutionary movement as it emancipated the working class would gradually reduce the scope and the functions of the state; it would tend towards the abolition of the state. This is the famous doctrine of the 'withering away' of the state. It distinguishes Marxist theory from the anarchist position because the anarchists demanded the immediate abolition of the state while Marx recognised that in the transitional period the proletariat would still need a state. Only, as Trotsky would later put it, what the proletariat needed was a dying state. From the moment the socialist victory was assured the state would enter into a process of decline.

This declining state would be the dictatorship of the proletariat. It would be the 'dictatorship' of the vast majority of the people and, therefore, it would be a form of genuine democracy. It would not be a state in the full sense of the term any longer, because it would dispense with that complex apparatus of domination characteristic of the modern state. A system of almost direct democracy would replace that apparatus. The purpose of the remaining organisation would be to develop and secure the achievements of the revolution. Gradually the cleavage between state and society would disappear.

What the dictatorship of the proletariat was to look like could be deduced from the actual organisation of the Paris Commune of 1871. Engels' statement that the Paris Commune *was* the dictatorship of the proletariat must be taken in a rather metaphorical sense. The Commune had nothing to do with Marxism, nor was it indeed a socialist movement. It was essentially the self-government of Paris in the aftermath of the Franco-Prussian war. What Marx saw in the Commune was the sharpest possible antithesis to the heightened executive power of the Bonapartist state which he had analysed in his *Eighteenth Brumaire.* Marx presented the Commune as an episode in which society had replaced that all-powerful state with a form of popular control. It restored to civil society the power of directing its own affairs. Society regained its initiative. It 'broke the modern state power'.

The features which most endeared the Commune to Marx were its prototype of an almost direct democracy, its anti-elitism, its decentralising organisation and the absence of bureaucracy. He emphasised the short-term revocability of representatives and the fact that they were paid workmen's wages. These were practices which prevented state administration and political activity becoming a specialized profession.

Marx himself never explicitly stated that the Commune was to be the model for post-revolutionary power organisation everywhere. Indeed in 1881 he wrote to Domela Nieuwenhuis that 'apart from the fact that it was merely the rising of a city under exceptional circumstances, the majority of the Commune was by no means socialist, nor could it be.'[68] It was, nevertheless, a participatory democracy 'without professionals'. The Commune was different from a system of parliamentary representation in that 'Instead of deciding once in three or six years which member of the ruling class was to misrepresent the people in parliament, universal suffrage was to serve the people, constituted in communes, as individual suffrage serves every other employer in the search for workmen and managers in his own business.'[69] One might suggest that the nearest thing to the Commune ever to be realised again was the short-lived soviet system in post-revolutionary Russia in 1917.

Depending on the extent to which the functions of the state are gradually absorbed by society, in other words, the more the state 'withers away', the more will people become free. 'Freedom consists in converting the state from an organ superimposed on society into one completely subordinate to it.' However, we are still here talking in terms of a transitional period and that is not surprising because the new communist society, as it is slowly born, 'is thus in every respect, economically, morally and intellectually, still stamped with the birthmarks of the old society from whose womb it emerges'. That is to be understood, as Marx expressly said, in two respects: It means that the economy, though no longer restricted by the capitalist demand for ever-growing profits, does not yet produce an abundance of everything that people want and desire. But it also means that the old ideas, mental habits and prejudices are still alive. So, for example, the principle of equal rewards for equal performance is still taken for granted as an overriding principle though it is a bourgeois principle. 'In a higher form of communist society ... the narrow horizon of bourgeois right will be crossed as society inscribes on its banner: From each according to his ability, to each according to his needs!'[70]

At that point a higher stage of morality, based on the enormous material advance which a socialised economy would achieve, would have been reached. It is that point where we can direct our sights towards the final stage of post-revolutionary society and we shall receive an answer to the second question, what the state would then be like. The answer is: There will be no state. That may remind us of the view held by that 'utopian' socialist, Saint-Simon, that 'the government of persons will give way to the administration of things'. The proposition, however, also reveals the idea that as an ultimate goal a reconciliation of the Marxist and of the anarchist positions can be envisaged. The emphasis, of course, must lie on the fact that this would be the ultimate stage of historic development. Marx was quite convinced that the state could not be 'abolished' as long as there existed classes which divided society. Only a classless society could eventually become a stateless society. Modern commentators have not missed the point: 'As Avineri aptly observes, while for anarchism the abolition of the state was a forcible political act, for Marx the supersession of the state was the final outcome of a protracted process of social and economic transformation.'[71]

Marx believed that under communism the economy would advance tremendously. There unfolds then the picture of a future humanity when human beings would no longer be the slaves of the machine: they would have become its masters. The antagonism of manual and intellectual labour would have disappeared. Unlike many of his later interpreters and commentators ('Western Marxists') Marx finds no evil in industrialisation. What he rejects as the source of all social evil is capitalist industrialism: 'Machinery does not lose its use value as soon as it ceases to be capital.'[72]

However, what we are invited to visualise is not a society of either robots or Marcusean worshippers of a free sensuality. The picture remains absolutely unbelievable, in fact sheer fantasy, if we forget that Marx expected to find in that new classless and stateless society a new type of human being. 'Free time—which is both idle time and time for higher activity—has naturally transformed its possessor into a different subject, and he enters the direct production process as this different subject.'[73] That was what Marx meant by saying that circumstances and people would change. Freedom would no longer be the freedom of free competition. The whole psychic structure, the purposes, the actions and reactions of humanity would be different. Here Marx, the scientific analyst of capitalist society who showed us how a gigantic superstructure of ideas and institutions rested on its economic base, anticipates an entirely different stage of human history.

For, while a socialist society would allow 'the artistic, scientific etc. development of the individuals in the time set free, and with the means created, for all of them',[74] it still is not the last stage in the evolution of the human race. As long as humanity has not completely conquered nature human freedom remains limited by necessity. 'In fact the realm of freedom actually begins only where labour which is determined by necessity and mundane considerations ceases; thus in the very nature of things it lies beyond the sphere of actual material production.'[75]

10. CONCLUDING REMARKS

It is obvious we cannot here offer a full assessment of Marxism as a socioeconomic theory of worldwide importance. We have more or less restricted ourselves to considering its political aspects. In this respect the Paris Commune was presented as the model of how, according to Marx's view, a future socialist society should be organised. The question must now be asked whether this model is compatible with a socialist society in an advanced stage of its industrial development. The main features of the Commune model were the abolition of a complex and ramified bureaucracy and also of the other coercive order-maintaining elements of the state. Furthermore, the model stressed the guiding ideas of decentralisation. While Marx insisted that the communal constitution, had it been extended over the whole of France, would not have broken up 'that unity of great nations which, if orginally brought about by political force, has now become a powerful coefficient of social production', the 'self-government of the producers' seems to have been envisaged on decentralised lines. But would not the system of a collectivised socialist economy require forms of centralisation and of a bureaucratic administration which would weaken, to say the least, the popular power so highly praised in *The Civil War in France*? Can popular control from below be maintained in a socialised economy? Such questions raise fundamental problems concerning the nature of a socialist society and its ability to dispense with bureaucracy. The course the Russian Revolution took seems not to be very encouraging in that respect, though the events happened there under very special and extreme conditions.

A second problem, which is of a more directly political nature, is raised by both elite theorists and anarchists, though they differ in their view of a possible solution. The Commune as Marx described and Lenin invoked it in *The State and Revolution* was indeed a 'democracy without professionals'. Yet in so far as it involved coercion it was a form of political power even though the coercion was not effected by military or bureaucratic means and was applicable only, theoretically speaking, against an ever-decreasing minority which tried to resist the new order. The direct responsibility and immediate revocability of all agents and officials of the Commune administration was supposed to prevent the emergence of a new political or bureaucratic elite. But would this in fact be the result? The elitist answer, say on the lines of Weber or Michels, would be that in spite of all counter-measures a controlling group or oligarchy would necessarily emerge. Weber argued that socialism with its collectivisation of the productive resources would intensify the pressures for the creation of a bureaucratic elite free from popular control. On his view 'the dictatorship of the official, not that of the worker' was 'on the advance'.[76]

The anarchists did not share the belief in the inevitability of an administrative elite, yet they argued that Marx perhaps too easily disposed of the problem of structures of power rising and becoming remote from the popular base. Bakunin suggested that in view of the tendencies of officials and powerholders to make themselves independent of the popular will, the precautionary measures proposed by Marx did not go far enough: 'What does raising the proletariat to the level of government mean? Surely the whole proletariat is not going to head the administration? There are about forty million Germans. Does it mean that all forty million will be members of the government?' Bakunin was deeply sceptical of the Marxist solution of the problem. He thought it would only 'conceal the despotism of a governing minority, all the more dangerous because it appears as a sham expression of the people's will.'[77]

As it happened, Marx commented derisively on this and other passages from Bakunin's book *Statism and Anarchy*, calling it 'democratic twaddle, political drivel'. His answer seems to be that everything depends on 'the economic foundation'. Writing about the functions to which people would be elected he wrote:

As soon as the functions have ceased to be political ones, there exists (1) no governmental function, (2) the distribution of the general functions has become a business matter, that gives no one domination, (3) election has nothing of its present political character.[78]

As against this both anarchists and elitists would argue that it might not be so easy to ensure that a reconstituted state did not rise again and the 'boa constrictor' state stifle society in all its pores, as Marx had put it. Perhaps Marx did underestimate the resilience not just of the capitalist state but of bureaucratic and statist tendencies altogether. Here too the analysis and discussion of the Soviet experience will be highly relevant.

The historical developments of the twentieth century have not borne out Marx's prognosis and expectations. A revolution was made in the name of Marxism in Russia, but there was no socialist revolution in the highly industrialised countries of Western Europe. While Marx believed that the working classes in those countries would become ever more radicalised and prone to revolutionary action, rather the opposite proved to be the case. The 'German model' prevailed. It was the social-democratic line which was classically represented by the German Social-Democratic Party in the period of the Second International from 1889 to 1914. It involved the perspective of large, well-organised socialist parties marching to victory along the electoral road, using the opportunities offered by the parliamentary system. In other words, this was the sort of perspective sketched out by Engels in his 1895 Preface. Certainly, Engels implied that if the ruling classes tried to rob the socialist movement of its victory by abandoning parliamentary methods, working-class violence in response would be the order of the day. Yet such an eventuality was likely to be postponed to an indefinite future. Kautsky, the leading theorist of social-democracy, did write in 1895 that it was utopian to think that 'the capitalist mode of production can be reformed within the framework of the existing state and by means of that state'. Yet ten years later, though he was greatly impressed by the events of the abortive Russian Revolution of 1905, he modified his views. 'But let the proletariat conquer political power', he then wrote, 'and you will see how parliamentarism will gain a new lease of life and will produce fruitful effects.' [79]

Taking a wider view we find, with all reservations that must be made in the case of such a generalised statement, that on the whole nearly all social-democratic parties in Western Europe adopted similar views and corresponding tactics. Everywhere party elites took the initiative. It also became clear that contrary to Marx's expectations the majority of the more or less propertyless people did not follow the lead of a socialist party. Even where such parties managed to secure a parliamentary majority, it did not mean the end of capitalism.

Marx's ideas, on the other hand, were restated by Lenin in the context of the Bolshevik Revolution of 1917. The Revolution, however, resulted in a state system where the state did not begin to 'wither away'. After the early months, it bore little resemblance to the organisation of the Paris Commune. Within the system a highly centralised party claimed a political monopoly.

It seems then that Kolakowski is right to say that 'The summer of 1914 was the beginning of a process whose consequences are still with us, and whose final outcome cannot be foreseen.' One may accept, he continues, the basic idea of a polarisation within Marxist politics 'leading to a state of affairs that still exists: on the one hand, reformist socialism bearing only a tenuous relation to Marxism and, on the other hand, the monopolisation of Marxism by Leninism and its derivatives.' [80] One can object that such a monopolisation has long been challenged. Nevertheless the fundamental division of Marxism between social democracy and Leninist communism cannot be denied, even though quite recently a new synthesis called Eurocommunism has been proposed. For a better understanding of the split, however, it will be necessary to discuss the ways in which Marxist politics were put into practice in Russia under conditions quite different from those Marx had envisaged.

NOTES

In this chapter, references are, wherever possible to the edition of Karl Marx and Frederick Engels, *Selected Works* in three volumes (Progress Publishers, Moscow, 1969) (abbreviated as *MESW*).

1. By 'Western Marxism' is meant theorists such as those of the Frankfurt School, emphasising the themes of culture and the importance of 'the superstructure'; see Perry Anderson, *Considerations on Western Marxism* (New Left Books, London, 1976), and J.G. Merquior, *Western Marxism* (Paladin, London, 1986).
2. F. Engels, Introduction to *Karl Marx, The Class Struggles in France 1848 to 1850, MESW* I, p. 190.
3. Engels, *Karl Marx, MESW* III, p. 85.
4. Marx and Engels, *The Communist Manifesto, MESW* I, p. 108.
5. R.H. Tawney, *Equality* (Allen and Unwin, London, 1964), p. 78.
6. Marx and Engels, *The Communist Manifesto, MESW* I, p. 111.
7. G.A. Cohen, *Karl Marx's Theory of History, A Defence* (Clarendon Press, Oxford, 1978), pp. 24–6.
8. See, for example, the section on 'Money', in Marx's *Economic and Philosophical Manuscripts*; Karl Marx, *Early Writings*, introduced by Lucio Colletti (Penguin Books, Harmondsworth, 1975), pp. 375–9.
9. Cohen, *Marx's Theory of History*, pp. 82–3.
10. See Karl Marx, *Wages, Price and Profit*: 'Besides this mere physical element, the value of labour is in every country determined by a traditional standard of life.' Marx further stated that 'the *value of labour* itself is not a fixed but a variable magnitude.' *MESW* II, p. 71–2.
11. Karl Marx, *Capital, A Critique of Political Economy*. Vol. I, *Capitalist Production* (Lawrence and Wishart, London, 1970), p. 171.
12. Marx and Engels, *The Communist Manifesto, MESW* I, p. 127.
13. This is how Engels describes the origin of the state: 'Society gives rise to certain common functions which it cannot dispense with. The persons appointed for this purpose form a new branch of the division of labour. This gives them particular interests, distinct, too, from the interests of those who empowered them; they make themselves independent of the latter and – the state is in being.' Engels to C. Schmidt, 27 October 1890, *MESW* III, p. 491.
14. Hal Draper, *Karl Marx's Theory of Revolution*, Vol. I: *State and Bureaucracy* (Monthly Review Press, New York and London, 1977), p. 251.
15. These quotations are all from Marx's First Draft of 'The Civil War in France', in Karl Marx, *The First International and After*, edited by David Fernbach (Penguin, Harmondsworth, 1974), pp. 246–9.
16. Karl Marx, *The Civil War in France, MESW* II, p. 220.
17. R.N. Hunt, *The Political Ideas of Marx and Engels*, Vol. II: *Classical Marxism 1850–1895* (Macmillan, London, 1984), p. 161.

18. Marx and Engels, *The Communist Manifesto, MESW* I, p. 110–11.
19. See Roger Magraw, *France 1815–1914, The Bourgeois Century* (Fontana, 1983), pp. 51 and 68.
20. Marx, 'Parties and Cliques', in Karl Marx, *Surveys from Exile*, edited by David Fernbach (Penguin, Harmondsworth, 1973), p. 279.
21. Ralph Miliband, *Marxism and Politics* (Oxford University Press, Oxford, 1977), pp. 74, 68.
22. Cohen, Marx's *Theory of History*, p. 295.
23. J.M. Maguire, *Marx's Theory of Politics* (Cambridge University Press, Cambridge, 1978), p. 23.
24. Draper, *Marx's Theory of Revolution* I, p. 322.
25. Maguire, *Marx's Theory of Politics*, p. 22.
26. Marx and Engels, *The German Ideology*, Chapter I, in *MESW* I, p. 47.
27. Cohen, *Marx's Theory of History*, p. 330, also p. 291, where Cohen notes: 'All classes are receptive to whatever ideas are likely to benefit them, and ruling classes are well placed to propagate ideologies.'
28. Marx and Engels, *The German Ideology*, Chapter I, in *MESW* I, p. 48.
29. Marx, *Capital* I, p. 737.
30. 'This hegemonic system of power was defined by the degree of consent it obtained from the popular masses which it dominated, and a consequent reduction in the scale of coercion needed to repress them': Perry Anderson, *Considerations on Western Marxism*, p. 79.
31. Martin Nicolaus, 'The Unknown Marx', in R. Blackburn (ed.) *Ideology in Social Science, Readings in Critical Social Theory* (Fontana, 1972), p. 318.
32. Karl Marx, *Grundrisse. Foundations of the Critique of Political Economy* (rough draft), translated by Martin Nicolaus (Penguin, Harmondsworth, 1973), p. 246.
33. Marx, *Grundrisse*, p. 243.
34. Cohen, *Marx's Theory of History*, p. 125.
35. Marx, *Grundrisse*, p. 247.
36. Marx, *Capital*, Vol. I, p. 176.
37. Marx and Engels, *The German Ideology*, Chapter I, *MESW* I, p. 48.
38. See Hegel, *Lectures on the Philosophy of History*, translated by J. Sibree (Dover Publications, New York, 1956), p. 8.
39. J.A.G. Griffith, *The Politics of the Judiciary*, 3rd edition (Fontana, 1985), p. 225.
40. Draper, *Marx's Theory of Revolution*, Vol. I, p. 386. Draper provides a very useful discussion of Bonapartism: see pp. 339–463.
41. Marx, *The Eighteenth Brumaire of Louis Bonaparte, MESW* I, p. 476.
42. Ibid., p. 436.
43. Ibid., p. 478.
44. Marx, *The Civil War in France, MESW* II, p. 219.
45. Draper, *Marx's Theory of Revolution*, Vol. I, p. 395.
46. Marx, *Eighteenth Brumaire, MESW* I, pp. 484, 486.
47. Marx, *Wages, Price and Profit, MESW* II, p. 73.
48. See Engels' letter to Lafargue, in F. Engels et P. Lafargue, *Correspondance-Textes recueillis, annotés et présentés par E. Bottigelli*, 3

vols. (Paris 1956–59), Vol. II.

49. Marx, *Wages, Price and Profit, MESW* II, p. 75.

50. Marx and Engels, *The Communist Manifesto, MESW* I, p. 104.

51. Marx, *The Civil War in France, MESW* II, p. 217.

52. See Marx's speech in his own defence at the trial of the Rhineland District Committee of Democrats, in Karl Marx, *The Revolutions of 1848*, edited by David Fernbach (Penguin, Harmondsworth, 1973), pp. 257–60.

53. Karl Marx, *Critique of Hegel's Doctrine of the State*, in *Marx, Early Writings*, introduced by Colletti, p. 107.

54. Engels, Introduction to *Marx, Class Struggles in France, MESW* I, pp. 194–96.

55. Most recently the question has been raised by Cohen, *Marx's Theory of History*, p. 244.

56. Marx and Engels, *Communist Manifesto, MESW* I, p. 119.

57. See H. Marcuse, *One-Dimensional Man. Studies in the Ideology of Advanced Industrial Society* (Routledge & Kegan Paul, London, 1968). On Gramsci, see D. McLellan, *Marxism after Marx, An Introduction* (Macmillan, London, 1979), pp. 175–95, and the references contained there.

58. On the large topic of Marxism and nationalism, see as an introduction H.B. Davis, *Nationalism and Socialism* (Monthly Review Press, New York, 1967); I. Cummins, *Marx, Engels and National Movements* (Croom Helm, London, 1980); M. Löwy, 'Marxism and the National Question', in R. Blackburn (ed.), *Revolution and Class Struggle. A Reader in Marxist Politics* (Fontana/Collins, 1977), pp. 136–60.

59. Marx, *Preface to a Contribution to the Critique of Political Economy, MESW* I, p. 504.

60. Marx and Engels, *German Ideology, MESW* I, p. 37.

61. Karl Marx and Frederick Engels, *The Holy Family*, in Karl Marx and Frederick Engels, *Collected Works*, Vol. 4 (Lawrence and Wishart, London, 1975), p. 93. The statement that 'Men make their own history' comes from *The Eighteenth Brumaire, MESW* I, p. 398.

62. Marx, speech to The Hague Congress (reporter's record), *MESW* II, p. 293.

63. Engels, Preface to the English edition of *Capital* (1886), in *Capital*, Vol. I, p. 6.

64. On the party, see Monty Johnstone, 'Marx and Engels and the Concept of the Party', in *The Socialist Register 1967*, edited by R. Miliband and J. Saville, pp. 121–58. On Lukács, see Georg Lukács, *History and Class Consciousness* (Merlin, London, 1971), and M. Löwy, *Georg Lukács – From Romanticism to Bolshevism* (New Left Books, London, 1979). Engels' comment on the Paris Commune comes from his 1891 Introduction to Marx's *The Civil War in France*; Engels wrote: 'Of late, the Social-Democratic philistine has once more been filled with wholesome terror at the words: Dictatorship of the Proletariat. Well and good, gentlemen, do you want to know what this dictatorship looks like? Look at the Paris Commune. That was the Dictatorship of the

Proletariat.' *MESW* II, p. 189.
65. Engels to Otto von Boenigk, 21 August 1890, *MESW* III, p. 485.
66. Marx, *Civil War in France, MESW* II, p. 224.
67. Marx, *Critique of the Gotha Programme, MESW* III, p. 26.
68. Marx to Domela Nieuwenhuis, 22 February 1881, in Marx and Engels, *Selected Correspondence* (Progress Publishers, Moscow, 1975), p. 318.
69. Marx, *Civil War in France, MESW* II, p. 221.
70. Marx, *Critique of the Gotha Programme, MESW* III, p. 25, p. 17, p. 19.
71. Merquior, *Western Marxism*, p. 54. Merquior refers here to S. Avineri, *The Social and Political Thought of Karl Marx* (Cambridge University Press, Cambridge, 1968), p. 208.
72. Marx, *Grundrisse*, p. 699.
73. Ibid., p. 712.
74. Ibid., p. 706.
75. Marx, *Capital,* Vol. III (Lawrence and Wishart, London, 1974), p. 820.
76. Max Weber, *Selections in Translation*, edited by W.G. Runciman (Cambridge University Press, Cambridge, 1978), p. 260.
77. Michael Bakunin, *Selected Writings*, edited and introduced by Arthur Lehning (Jonathan Cape, London, 1973), p. 268.
78. Marx, Conspectus of Bakunin's *Statism and Anarchy*, in Karl Marx, *The First International and After*, p. 336.
79. Quoted in Massimo Salvadori, *Karl Kautsky and the Socialist Revolution 1880–1938* (New Left Books, London, 1976), pp. 43, 93.
80. L. Kolakowski, *Main Currents of Marxism*, Vol. II, *The Golden Age* (Clarendon Press, Oxford, 1978), pp. 29–30.

4 Communism and Soviet-type Systems

1. INTRODUCTORY

This chapter is concerned with the nature of Soviet-type systems and with a critical examination of their power structure. By 'Soviet-type system' is primarily meant the political system of the USSR as it developed since the Bolshevik Revolution of 1917, but also that of the East European countries within the Soviet bloc. These systems have two basic features which distinguish them from liberal-democratic systems. They are ruled by a single party, the Communist Party. Secondly, they exist in a social context where the means of production have been collectivised. There is no private ownership of the means of production, private agricultural plots of varying size excepted. This collectivised economic infrastructure necessitates a planned economy. Economic decisions are not left to entrepreneurs, private individuals acting in response to market forces. They are taken by a group of leaders in whom political and economic power is vested. The fact of state ownership of the society's productive resources means that those at the summit of the party hierarchy also control the economy. They do not own, but they control, the economic resources. This control involves decisions on investment, output, price levels, employment and on all parts of an overall plan.

The nature of such a system must be explored with reference to the three theories of power presented in the earlier chapters. The chief reference point, however, for the discussion will be the Marxist theory. This is for the obvious reason that the origin of the Soviet state lies in a revolution made under the banner of Marxism and because the legitimising ideology of the system is couched in Marxist terminology. The claim is made that the system is socialist in the sense in which Marx understood the term. The present constitution of the USSR, adopted in 1977, states in its preamble: 'A developed socialist society has been built in the USSR', and that: 'The developed socialist society is an objectively necessary stage on the path to communism.' The Constitution's Article 1 of the chapter 'The Political System' further declares: 'The Union of Soviet Socialist Republics is a socialist all-people's state, expressing the will and interests of the workers, peasants and intelligentsia, the toilers of all the nations and nationalities of the country.'[1] Marxism (or what passes for such) is used to justify the power of the ruling group in the Soviet state. The first question to be examined is the revolutionary origin of the Soviet Union and the relation of the Bolshevik Revolution of 1917 to the revolutionary scenario as laid down by Marx and Engels.

The October Revolution was led by the Bolsheviks. Their party was in certain respects a party of a new type, an instrument for revolution created by Lenin and vindicated by him as the 'vanguard party'. Bolshevism is certainly a variant of Marxism as a strategy for world revolution. An understanding of the Bolshevik Party, of its theory as formulated by Lenin and of its development after the 1917 Revolution is essential for a correct assessment of Soviet-type systems. It should also be said that the Bolshevik Revolution occurred under circumstances which differed from those laid down by Marx and Engels as preconditions of a socialist revolution. The consequences of this for the politics of our time cannot be overestimated. The phenomenon of Stalinism and its significance will become intelligible only if seen in the context of a Marxist revolution being undertaken in the absence of a 'mature capitalism' on which basis alone, Marx thought, a socialist society could develop.

2. LENIN AND THE IDEA OF THE BOLSHEVIK PARTY

Lenin's chief contribution to Marxist politics lay in his creation of a party of a new type and in its theoretical justification. The origin of this party goes back to the split of 1903 in the Russian Social Democratic Labour Party at the Brussels and London Congress of that year. The party divided into two sections, one of Lenin's followers, the Bolsheviks (the majority), the other of those critical of Lenin, the Mensheviks (the minority). The exposition of Lenin's theory was given in his book *What is to be Done?*, published in 1902. This text is not Lenin's only pronouncement on the subject of the party. Indeed, at the 1903 Congress he argued that *What is to be Done?* was a polemical response to exaggerated views held by the 'Economists' whom he meant to criticise. He said on that occasion that '... the "Economists" have gone to one extreme. To straighten matters out somebody had to pull in the other direction, and that is what I have done.'[2]

Nevertheless it remains true that Lenin's text proposes certain ideas of fundamental importance for Bolshevik theory. Of these the most important, which have aroused most controversy, are the set of ideas concerning class consciousness. Lenin made a definite distinction between 'trade union consciousness' ('Economism') on the one hand, and 'social-democratic (or socialist) consciousness' on the other. By the former term he meant the awareness, on the part of the working class, of the need to improve conditions within the framework of the capitalist system. This would lead the workers to organise in trade unions, to press for better wages, for improved factory conditions, and for laws to secure such improvements. However, that was a different matter from social-democratic consciousness which involved the aspiration to a different type of social and political system, i.e. to a socialist system. It meant a perspective aiming at the overthrow of the existing capitalist system. It involved seeing the 'partial' struggles in a factory, or by a particular trade union, as part of a much wider struggle fought in opposition to the whole social order. Thus particular instances of class conflict had to be placed in the overall context of a general movement whose aim was the creation of a new type of society.

The crucial point for Lenin was not just the distinction between those two types of consciousness. He argued that left to their own devices the workers 'spontaneously' would merely attain a trade union consciousness. Socialism, he wrote, was a theory 'elaborated by educated representatives of the propertied classes, by intellectuals'. He further stated that 'the working class, exclusively by its own efforts, is able only to develop trade union consciousness'. In Lenin's view, such an assertion was valid not only for Russia, but was established by 'the history of all countries'.[3] Without theoretical and political guidance, the working class would remain subject to the powerful force of bourgeois ideology which was diffused through so many channels to become dominant. The latter could not be successfully challenged without a socialist consciousness, yet 'the spontaneous development of the working-class movement leads precisely to its subordination to bourgeois ideology'. For Lenin, 'trade unionism means the ideological enslavement of the workers by the bourgeoisie.'[4]

The fact that spontaneity was not enough made the party extremely important. Through the party the link between the spontaneous trade union activity of the workers and the socialist theory elaborated by intellectuals was established. Only by such means could a truly revolutionary movement develop, uniting mass action with theoretical awareness. The party would be an organisation of professional revolutionaries. It would coordinate all the limited local struggles and make them part of a coherent offensive against the existing order. The party was necessary to provide the theoretical perspective and to transcend the 'economism' of the workers. Socialist consciousness had to be 'introduced into the proletarian class struggle from without', as Lenin put it, quoting a phrase used by Kautsky.[5]

Another feature of the Bolshevik party is related to the conditions under which the struggle against the Tsarist autocracy had to be fought. Lenin insisted on the need for a centralised organisation working in secrecy. An open mass party was not possible in Russia. Lenin urged his fellow Social-Democrats not to be afraid of the accusation that they were creating a conspiratorial organisation. Complete inner-party democracy would require the two conditions of 'full publicity' and 'election to all offices'. Yet such '"broad democracy" in Party organisation, amidst the gloom of the autocracy and the domination of gendarme selection, is nothing more than a *useless and harmful toy*'. There must be no 'amateurishness'; Lenin maintained that 'a strong revolutionary organisation is absolutely necessary precisely for the purpose of giving stability to the movement, and of safeguarding it against the possibility of making thoughtless attacks.' A strong secretive centralised party was therefore prescribed.[6]

The organisational basis of the party on the lines of 'democratic centralism' was adopted in 1905 and agreed to by Mensheviks as well as by Bolsheviks. The principle of democratic centralism was intended to permit democratic debate within the party before a decision was taken. Yet once the policy had been fixed, there should be strict unity of action to implement it. In practice the politics of communist parties have been marked more by centralism than by inner-party democracy. We have already noted Lenin's argument that under the conditions of Tsarist autocracy open inner-party democracy was impossible. As for the Bolshevik Party, inner-party democracy after 1917 was short-lived. A crucial turning point came with the 'ban on factions' decided on at the 10th Party Congress of 1921 in the aftermath of the civil war at the time of the Kronstadt revolt. The ban on factions was intended as a temporary expedient, but it became a factor in the disappearance of inner-party democracy which accompanied Stalin's rise to power.

The reference to specific Russian conditions in Lenin's argument concerning the role of the party by no means exhausts the significance of *What is to be Done?*. The distinction between trade union consciousness based on spontaneity and social-democratic consciousness was part of a general theory of class consciousness held to be validated by 'the history of all countries'. Marx himself never made such a hard-and-fast distinction, though he expressed a similar idea when he criticised trade unions for 'limiting themselves to a guerilla war against the effects of the existing system, instead of simultaneously trying to change it...'[7] But such a distinction of aims was less significant for Marx than for Lenin. There was no suggestion in Marx that without a leading 'vanguard party' the working class would always remain at the 'economistic' level. Furthermore, Lenin's idea that the party was the necessary vehicle for bringing socialist consciousness to the working class 'from outside' seems to attribute a new vital role to the party. In the words of a recent commentator, 'Lenin exemplified a social-democratic praxis of a new type'. Henceforth the Bolshevik Party had a 'leading role' to play since without it there could be no revolutionary socialist politics. This view was to assume even greater significance once the party had taken power after the revolution: 'The Bolshevik seizure of power put the party permanently at the centre of socialist politics'.[8]

3. BOLSHEVISM AND THE OCTOBER REVOLUTION

In Marx's theory of socialist revolution socialism was seen as the heir to capitalism. A socialist society could come into being only on the basis of a mature capitalism. A socialist revolution could only be successful once capitalism had developed to its fullest extent the productive forces and thus created the material preconditions for a socialist society. In addition, Marx had envisaged the emergence of a politically mature and class-conscious working class which had developed its organisation and political activity. This working class would form the majority of the population. Capitalist development, on the other hand, would have come to such a point that the means of production were ever more concentrated and had become 'ripe' for socialisation.

It is clear that conditions in Russia in 1917 did not satisfy these requirements. Capitalism was far from mature in Russia; the proletariat did not represent the majority of the population. The Russian working class had relatively recently been formed. It had never had the chance to develop its political action and organisation through participation in a liberal-democratic system which obviously did not exist in Russia under the Tsars.

Nevertheless, the Bolsheviks managed successfully what was

claimed to be a Marxist socialist revolution. How then did Lenin justify this revolution and reconcile it with the tenets of the founders of Marxist theory? All Russian Marxists, Mensheviks as well as Bolsheviks, agreed that a socialist revolution in Russia could only be made after a bourgeois revolution had swept away the Tsarist autocracy. Such a bourgeois revolution would make the further development of capitalism possible and thus create the preconditions for socialism. The Russian Marxists adhered to that idea of the two revolutions, first the bourgeois and then the proletarian revolution. The difference between Mensheviks and Bolsheviks, apart from the question of party organisation, concerned the timespan which would separate the two revolutions. The Mensheviks insisted that in the bourgeois revolution the working class would play a secondary role to that of the liberal bourgeoisie. They further suggested that a protracted period of capitalist development would be required to lay the basis for a conversion to socialism. Against this, Lenin argued that because of the weakness and timidity of the Russian bourgeoisie, the task of the bourgeois democratic revolution would fall to a popular bloc of the workers and the peasantry. It would have to be a bourgeois revolution carried out against the bourgeoisie by those popular forces. They would, Lenin wrote in 1905, 'begin immediately ... to make the transition to the socialist revolution'. There would be no passive waiting for capitalism to develop fully. This formulation by Lenin was similar to Trotsky's theory of 'permanent revolution' emphasising the continuity between a bourgeois democratic and a socialist revolution. The leading role of the working class in the democratic revolution, Trotsky argued, would mean that there would be an immediate transition to the socialist revolution.[9]

When the Tsarist autocracy was overthrown in February 1917, Mensheviks and Bolsheviks agreed that this, according to the Marxist schema, was the bourgeois revolution. The situation from February to October was one of 'dual power', a division of power between the Provisional Government and the Soviets, the latter being councils of workers, peasants and soldiers, and as such organs of popular power. The majority of Bolsheviks critically supported the Provisional Government, not seeing a socialist revolution as an immediate possibility.

However, that changed with Lenin's return to Petrograd in April 1917. Neil Harding, among others, has convincingly shown the radical transformation which Lenin's political views underwent after August 1914, when all the social-democratic parties of Europe overwhelmingly accepted the war. Ideas of national defence and of national unity proved stronger than the idea of a socialist internationalism. Lenin vehemently rejected what he called 'socialist chauvinism', the unanimous acceptance of the idea of national defence.

After August 1914 Lenin held a strong belief that a socialist revolution on an international scale was imminent. He argued that given such a perspective the two prerequisites for a socialist revolution as demanded by Marx were indeed met: a mature capitalism centralised and ready for socialisation, and a class-conscious revolutionary working class. In September 1917 he proclaimed that all over Europe 'socialism is now gazing at us from all the windows of modern capitalism'. European capitalism had developed into its monopoly stage dominated by large cartels; the war had enormously stimulated state intervention. All this had brought Europe to 'the threshold of socialism, a rung on the ladder of history between which and the rung called socialism there are no intermediate rungs'.[10] The means of production were ripe for socialisation. The growing centralisation of the productive resources would facilitate their being run by ordinary workers without the need for a specialised and skilled administrative elite.

Equally the political requirements for a socialist revolution were met, again taking Europe as a whole. In Lenin's view the workers had been radicalised by the protracted sufferings and horrors which the war inflicted. They had been betrayed by their social-democratic leaders who in 1914 succumbed to patriotism and social chauvinism. The workers would respond to the new leadership of revolutionary communist parties urging them to turn 'imperialist war into a civil war'. Immediately after August 1914 Lenin broke with the Second International and called for the urgent creation of a new Communist International. This was to be a centralised organisation of parties, each of which would be organised on the Bolshevik lines of democratic centralism.

These were the theoretical considerations behind Lenin's famous *April Theses*. They proclaimed that the socialist revolution was now on the agenda in Russia. Support for the Provisional Government should cease. A revolutionary government based on the Soviets had to be created. It should be noted that these demands must be set in the context of the imminence of a revolution on a world, or at least European, scale. Socialist revolution in Russia, the weakest link in the capitalist chain, would be the signal for revolution in Europe. Only a socialist revolution in the advanced countries of the West could ensure the success of the Russian revolution. In April 1917 Lenin was quite at odds with his comrades and isolated within the Bolshevik Party. He converted the party to his views and it was with the expectation of an international socialist revolution that the Bolsheviks took power in October 1917.

4. THE REVOLUTIONARY STATE

Lenin's views had one important corollary regarding the state, i.e. the structure of power after the revolution. These views, put forward in *The State and Revolution*, were a restatement of Marx's analysis of the Paris Commune of 1871. Lenin argued that in a socialist revolution institutions of popular power like the Soviets were appropriate. He repeated the Marxist thesis that the revolutionary working class could not take over the existing machinery of the state. This had to be destroyed and replaced by a much more democratic system. Again, Harding has shown that behind Lenin's position lay certain assumptions concerning the maturity of capitalism on an international scale.[11]

In 1917 Lenin interpreted the idea of 'the dictatorship of the proletariat' in libertarian terms, akin to those in which Marx had written about the Paris Commune. The revolution would create a state system based on the Soviets, permitting a high degree of popular power and democratic participation. It would be a state that could immediately begin 'to wither away'. Lenin believed that the advanced stage of European capitalism made it possible for everyone to perform the tasks of administration and accounting required in a socialist society. Socialism would build on the progress which capitalism had made. Since everyone would be a bureaucrat no one would be one, meaning that there was no need for a specialised group of planners or administrators since every literate person could manage. Lenin envisaged a form of direct democracy with the maximum of initiative and participation from below.

This implied a vehement criticism of parliamentary democracy, again on the lines of Marx's Paris Commune text. Marx, it will be recalled, had written that 'instead of deciding once in three or six years which member of the ruling class was to misrepresent the people in Parliament, universal suffrage was to serve the people constituted in communes'.[12] Lenin likewise maintained that the October Revolution had brought into being a socialist, or proletarian, democracy formed by the Soviets. They were far more democratic than a parliamentary democracy. Parliament was 'given up to talk for the special purpose of fooling the "common people"'.[13] In his reply to Kautsky who criticised the Bolsheviks for taking power before the conditions were ripe, Lenin stated that 'Proletarian democracy is a million times more democratic than any bourgeois democracy; Soviet power is a million times more democratic than the most democratic bourgeois republic.' He added for good measure that 'to fail to see this one must either deliberately serve the bourgeoisie, or be politically as dead as a doornail, unable to see real life behind the dusty pages of bourgeois books...'[14]

Such was the justification behind the Bolsheviks' dissolution in January 1918 of the Constituent Assembly. The election date of 12 November 1917 had been fixed by the Provisional Government. After the October Revolution the Bolsheviks let the elections proceed and secured just under a quarter of the seats—175 out of 707.[15] The Assembly was closed down on the grounds that the soviet system was the appropriate form of state power in a socialist revolution. In addition, the Bolsheviks maintained that the Constituent Assembly did not accurately represent the wishes of the people because after the election the largest party, the SRs (Peasant Party) had split, most of their left-wingers allying themselves with the Bolsheviks.

The dissolution of the Constituent Assembly was criticised not only by moderate socialists like Kautsky. Rosa Luxemburg, a much more sympathetic critic, wrote in her pamphlet on the Russian Revolution that if the Bolshevik argument was correct and the Assembly 'reflected the position of the vanished past and not of the new state of affairs', the proper remedy would have been that 'without any delay new elections to a new Constituent Assembly should have been arranged'. Luxemburg agreed that 'every democratic institution has its limits and shortcomings', yet she concluded that 'the remedy which Trotsky and Lenin have found, the elimination of democracy as such, is worse than the disease which it is supposed to cure'. The closing down of a democratically elected institution dealt a blow to the 'source from which alone can come the correction of all the innate shortcomings of social institutions', namely the active and unlimited participation of the masses.[16]

The Bolshevik response to this charge, whether it came from Luxemburg or from the 'renegade' Kautsky, was to point out that the Constituent Assembly was a representative institution appropriate to a bourgeois democratic system. Its dissolution, therefore, did not matter. This response rested on an assumption that socialist revolution in the West would occur, complementing the Russian Revolution and providing the material base of advanced capitalism which was lacking in Russia. Yet as far as the Western working classes were concerned, their reaction did not conform to such an assumption:

The defeat suffered by the attempts made at proletarian revolution in Western Europe after the war of 1914–18 was due to a highly complex set of factors and circumstances; but from this diversity it is possible to select one incontestable fact which was of fundamental importance, namely, that the majority of the European working class, even where the crisis went furthest, as in Germany, continued to follow their traditional political and trade union organisations and not the new revolutionary party.[17]

The consequences of this failure of the revolution to spread to the West were enormous. The Bolsheviks had captured state power and had to 'go it alone' in a society lacking the material, social and cultural prerequisites for socialism. The vision of popular power, of a system more democratic than bourgeois democracy, as presented by Lenin in texts like *The State and Revolution*, could not be realised. Miliband points out that there were reasons for this other than those relating to the particular conditions of Russia in 1917. The dictatorship of the proletariat envisaged in terms of popular power on the Soviet model, 'even in the most favourable circumstances, is unrealisable without political mediation'.[18] Some institution would be needed to coordinate the Soviets, to provide a framework of political power in the post-revolutionary situation. Such political mediation was performed by the Bolshevik Party which soon became the only party in the state. Once this happened, the socialist democracy on the lines projected by Lenin could not be sustained.

In the aftermath of the Revolution, certain developments took place producing the basic features which Soviet-type systems have exhibited since their formation. These features involve the concentration of power in a single centralised, bureaucratic and relatively monolithic party. The party, in Soviet-type systems, oversees all aspects of social life. Initially, in the aftermath of the Bolshevik Revolution, the party was responsible for the creation 'from above' of the social and economic base necessary for a socialist society, a base which was lacking in the Russia of 1917. The developments which resulted in the 'leading role of the party' becoming institutionalised must now be briefly summarised.

After the October Revolution the promise of popular power and of the withering away of the state was not fulfilled. The Soviets lost out to the Bolshevik Party. Other political parties were banned and the Russian Communist Party (Bolsheviks), as the party was known from March 1918 on, became the sole ruling party. Within this party free discussion and democracy were eroded, notably after Lenin's death in 1924. They had vanished altogether by 1928/29 when Stalin, General Secretary since 1922, came to dominate the party. The Bolsheviks had come to power in a situation marked by scarcity. In a passage which Trotsky quoted in 1936, Marx and Engels had written that the 'estrangement' present in capitalist society could only be removed by means of 'a great increase in productive power, a high degree of its development'. Trotsky noted that this quotation 'provides an indispensable theoretical key to the wholly concrete difficulties and sicknesses of the Soviet regime'.[19] The withering away of the state, of its apparatus of coercion and specialised bureaucracy, could only begin in a society where scarcity had been overcome.

Lenin was clearly aware of the problem and in some notes on *Our Revolution* written in 1923 he addressed himself to it. The 'heroes of the Second International', he wrote, had repeatedly pronounced the 'incontrovertible proposition' that 'the development of the productive forces of Russia had not attained the level that makes socialism possible'. His response then was to say:

If a definite level of culture is required for the building of socialism..., why cannot we begin by first achieving the prerequisites for that definite level of culture in a revolutionary way, and *then*, with the aid of the workers' and peasants' government and the Soviet system, proceed to overtake the other nations?[20]

He went on to define those prerequisites as 'the expulsion of the land owners and the Russian capitalists'. This suggests that, in a sense, he was almost reversing the primacy of economics over politics which is at the heart of the Marxist view. The text can be read as implying that in the Russian case the revolutionary capture of political power preceded the necessary development of the economic base. In any case the process of 'overtaking the other nations', in other words industrialising the Soviet Union, could not take place under a system of decentralised popular power as sketched out in *The State and Revolution*. It required some form of central control for the purpose of a 'revolution from above'. This is what happened in the Soviet Union. It does not by any means follow that the horrors, purges and other aspects of Stalinism were unavoidable. What does follow is that the material conditions of Russia made it extremely difficult, not to say impossible, to realise the perspective of a participatory socialist democracy leading towards the withering away of the state. With such a perspective in mind, Lenin and the Bolsheviks had come to power.

It is noteworthy that *The State and Revolution* says very little about the role of a 'vanguard party'. The party recedes into the background.[21] The emphasis of the text, and also of Lenin's politics in the conjuncture of the October Revolution, lies very much on popular power and on the arming of the people. However, in the situation that developed after 1917 the party assumed a much larger role. As Claudin observes:

The effective workers' democracy of the model was short-circuited by the reality of a system of military, police, economic, administrative, juridical and ideological apparatuses which had escaped all popular control and were now the real power centres—in turn organised and controlled by the central apparatus of the single party.[22]

Two processes, in fact, took place. The first was that the dictatorship of the proletariat which in the 'honeymoon' period of the Revolution Lenin had identified with the mass of the working class came to be identified with the party. The party exercised that dictatorship in the name of a working class dwindling in size under conditions of civil war and because of the cooptation of some of its members to administrative posts. In 1920 Lenin announced that 'the Party, shall we say, absorbs the vanguard of the proletariat, and this vanguard exercises the dictatorship of the proletariat'.[23] Harding has argued that Lenin came to see the salvation of the revolution as depending on an ever smaller circle. The locus of the revolutionary vanguard shifted first from the whole body of the workers to the party. Then, faced with the problem of a growing bureaucracy and of careerism, Lenin saw the safety of the revolution entrusted to a party group, or section, in whom alone socialist virtue was to be found. He devised the Workers' and Peasants' Inspectorate (Rabkrin) as a means to prevent the degeneration of the revolution.[24] The point is that in conditions of civil war the party alone possessed the cohesion and force to run the country. So the vision of rule by the workers gave way to the rule of the party; dictatorship of the proletariat became the dictatorship of the party.

A second process was the increasing centralisation of the party. An important landmark in this process was the decisions taken at the 10th Party Congress of 1921. Faced with the Kronstadt revolt, the famous 'ban on factions' was passed together with the secret 'Point 7' which allowed expulsions from the Central Committee and even from the party.[25] The ban gave Stalin, who had become General Secretary in April 1922, the means to expel his opponents. Disputes within the party were still permissible and even for a while after Lenin's death the economic development of the USSR was still a matter for discussion. The Left Opposition under Trotsky's leadership argued for the priority of industrial development over the needs of agriculture. If industrial production was increased it would provide the goods the peasants needed and thus encourage them to produce more food. Against this, the Right, associated with Bukharin among others, stood for a continuation and extension of the New Economic Policy inaugurated in 1921. This policy was to let the prices of agricultural products rise and through market relations encourage the growth of agricultural production. This would in turn stimulate industrial production by creating an assured demand and, at the same time, provide much-needed food for the industrial workers.

Stalin, who in the meantime had brought his supporters into key positions, allied himself at first with the Right and secured the expulsion of Trotsky and the Left Opposition. Having accomplished that by 1927/28, he turned on the followers of Bukharin. With the first of the Five Year Plans, started in 1928, and the commitment to a rapid collectivisation of agriculture, he was able to purge the Right faction. He succeeded in completely destroying any vestiges of inner-party democracy. By 1929 the party had become an instrument of his power. He then proceeded to destroy it.

A further important point concerns the international aspect of Bolshevism. Already before Lenin's death, Bolshevism with its particular view of a disciplined party organised on the lines of democratic centralism came to be seen as the model to be followed by the revolutionary movement everywhere. In his pamphlet of 1918 attacking 'the renegade Kautsky', Lenin had stated that 'The mass of workers in all countries are realising more and more clearly every day that Bolshevism has indicated the right road for escape from the horrors of war and imperialism, that Bolshevism *can serve as a model of tactics for all*.'[26] Lenin believed that the creation of new communist parties everywhere, each organised on the model of the Bolshevik Party and forming part of a centralised International, would attract the workers throughout Europe. The Third (Communist) International was formed in Moscow in March 1919. What happened from the beginning, in a process later accelerated by Stalin, was the 'Bolshevisation' of the communist parties. This meant the imposition of a centralised structure on West European parties which had in many cases quite different traditions. Opposing members were expelled. Marxist politics came to be identified with one particular type of party organisation and with a centralised International in which the constituent parties were subject to control from above.

Stalinism may be called a 'revolution from above'. At an horrific cost, it achieved the forced industrialisation of the Soviet Union and the collectivisation of agriculture. Politically it involved the destruction of the Bolshevik Party which ceased to be an instrument of power in any meaningful sense. Stalinism meant unlimited power exercised by means of coercion and terror. It rested on the secret police, more generally on what R.C. Tucker calls a 'monstrously hypertrophied state power', poles removed from the commune-type state aspired to by Lenin in 1917. As Tucker describes it: 'Stalinism as revolution from above was a state-building process, the construction of a powerful, highly centralised, bureaucratic, military-industrial Soviet Russian state.'[27] It could be said that Stalinism had two aspects: the one was industrialisation from above, the other was the exercise of personal power in a 'hypertrophied' state system.

If the Soviet state was to survive, the Revolution had to create an industrial base. Stalinism was not the only way to achieve this. Its arbitrariness was in fact harmful and to a certain extent it obstructed the process of industrialisation. It is arguable that some sort of 'revolution from above' was un-avoidable and that it had to involve a certain measure of centralisation and coercion. What was by no means unavoidable was the terror, that essential feature of the Stalinist experience. The socialist project in our time has been deeply affected by that experience. The terror and the purges destroyed the Bolshevik Party, since they were responsible for the death of thousands of people who formed the old guard of the party, and also of many who had no connection with that group.[28] Stalinism itself was a highly contradictory phenomenon. It was in essence extremely anti-bureaucratic in the sense that the terror was arbitrary and a long way removed from any idea of bureaucratic routine. Nevertheless, the requirements of the centralised economy created a new bureaucratic apparatus and offered the opportunity for a new technologically trained elite to emerge.

5. ANALYSIS OF THE SOVIET SYSTEM: THE QUESTION OF BUREAUCRACY

What is the nature of the Soviet system, as it has developed since the Stalin period, and how is its power structure best conceptualised and understood? The different theories of politics (pluralist, elitist and Marxist) come to different conclusions concerning its nature and the possibilities of its further development. The three theories, however, agree on the need to give some account of its bureaucratic structure. This is not to say that bureaucracy is a specific feature peculiar to Soviet systems, though these are characterised by the existence of a bureaucratic apparatus, controlling the single party and the state. This bureaucracy derives its power from the fusion of economic and political power. In Western-type systems there is a separation between economic power stemming from ownership and control of the means of production, and political power derived from important positions in the state apparatus. These are separate hierarchies of power. As a result of the collectivisation of the means of production in Soviet-type systems the holders of political power (the elite of the party–state apparatus) also have economic power. They do not own but control the productive resources of society. In fact, the separation of the two kinds of power is somehow artificial. The political decisions are to a certain extent the economic decisions, about how much to invest, in what sectors of the economy, what to produce, the relative proportion of consumer and production goods, and so on. How do the different theoretical perspectives on politics view this feature of Soviet systems and what conclusions do they draw from it?

Within the Marxist tradition, very different answers have been given to such questions.[29] One of the earliest was given by Trotsky in his book *The Revolution Betrayed*, first published in 1936. Apart from its intrinsic merits, Trotsky's study can be taken as exemplary in raising certain crucial questions about this type of political and social system, from within a Marxist perspective.

The basis of Trotsky's analysis was the low level of Russian cultural and economic development at the time of the Revolution and afterwards. This was the origin of the rise to power of the Stalinist bureaucracy. Because of that backwardness some form of state was necessary; it was necessary to maintain order and to contain the struggle among people for necessities, a struggle that would last as long as scarcity persisted. The time for the state to begin withering away had not yet come. Yet, so Trotsky argued, such withering away was in classical Marxist theory the hallmark of a socialist society. One thing was certain: 'At the end of its second decade of existence, it [the Soviet state] has not only not died away, but not begun to die away.'[30]

Thus the Soviet system could not be described as socialist, let alone communist, if by the latter was meant the 'higher stage' when the state would totally 'wither away'. A state machine was necessary to overcome Russia's economic backwardness, to build up the productive forces needed to catch up with, and later outstrip, the level attained by capitalism. The economic development which capitalism had achieved over a long period of time had to be produced by other methods, through a policy of 'primitive socialist accumulation'.[31] This was what Trotsky meant when he wrote that 'the very essence of the present economic and cultural work in the Soviet Union' involved 'the application of socialist methods for the solution of pre-socialist problems'.[32]

Trotsky's argument was that the factors of economic backwardness explained why the state could not disappear. That was also how he accounted for the origin of the Soviet bureaucracy. The main point, however, was that the bureaucratic ruling group had outgrown its original function. It had created a system of inequality and privilege, politically 'expropriating' the workers: 'the wielding of power becomes the speciality of a definite social group', Trotsky wrote, 'which is the more impatient to solve its own "social problem", the higher its opinion of its own mission'. Arising out of a social necessity the bureaucratic group had 'far outgrown its socially necessary function and become an independent factor', a source of danger for the whole society. Its chief concern was to maintain its own power and privilege, its position of a ruling group separate from the rest of society, in the same way as any state apparatus, in the classical Marxist perspective, preserved its autonomy *vis-à-vis* civil society. Trotsky saw the Stalinist state as a type of Bonapartist state: 'The Stalin regime, rising above a politically atomised society, resting upon a police and officers' corps, and allowing of no control whatever, is obviously a variation of Bonapartism—a Bonapartism of a new type not before seen in history.' The analogy is important: in Marx's perspective Bonapartism was a strong state that arose when society could not govern itself and when for particular historical reasons a social class had to entrust power to a political group standing over and above society. To Trotsky it seemed that the problems of Soviet society gave rise to an autonomous state in which the bureaucracy held power. In Soviet society the workers, weakened in the aftermath of the Revolution, had been 'politically expropriated'.[33]

Trotsky thought that the Soviet Union was a society transitional between capitalism and socialism. There would either be a political revolution against the bureaucracy restoring true Soviet democracy on the basis of the collectivisation which constituted the great gain of the Bolshevik Revolution or, if the bureaucracy maintained itself in power, it would seek to restore private ownership of the means of production. This prophecy, of course, has not come true. The collectivist economic structure of the Soviet Union has not been abandoned. An important element in Trotsky's analysis is the argument that collective ownership of the productive resources is a necessary but not a sufficient condition for a socialist society. He analysed the concentration of power in the hands of a bureaucracy which had destroyed any element of democracy within the party, let alone outside it. The Soviet Union was marked by the monopolisation of the running of its affairs by a group under Stalin's direct command.

More recently this aspect of Trotsky's analysis has been taken up by other writers within the Marxist tradition. R. Bahro in *The Alternative in Eastern Europe* sees the chief feature of Soviet systems in their total exclusion of the workers from the running of society. He argues that these systems are marked by the dominance of a politico-bureaucratic group which keeps to itself the right to take all decisions affecting society. Society is denied the right to manage itself; there prevails 'subalternity', implying the rigid distinction between those who command (the party–state elite) and those who obey—the mass of the producers. This concentration of power in the hand of a self-appointing and self-perpetuating group is the chief feature of 'real existing socialism', by which he means Eastern European socialism. It is not the vision of socialism held out by Marx and Engels.[34]

There are, on the other hand, those who dismiss such a perspective of the 'self-government of the producers' and of a society free from bureaucracy as a utopian prospect. In his recent book *The Economics of Feasible Socialism* Alec Nove deals with some problems concerning the extent to which it will be possible in a socialist (or any other) society to dispense with forms of hierarchy and subordination. Nove argues that 'some hierarchy and subordination are inescapable in organising production'. He poses the question:

How can the workers rule, how can they be 'organised as the ruling class', what can all this mean in practice, in the face of the objective need for hierarchy which Bahro so explicitly recognises.... Again and again the same problem arises: what does rule by the workers, or the dictatorship of the proletariat mean? What could it mean?[35]

Nove further asks whether the division of labour could ever be eliminated and how it would be possible to manage without a controlling group, especially in the context of an advanced planned economy. Such an economy may, indeed will, require specialisation and a hierarchy of control and subordination. This may make, in Nove's view, ideas of the direct rule of the associated producers very difficult, if not impossible, to realise.

6. THE ROLE OF THE PARTY

Soviet-type systems are characterised by being single-party systems. In this type of state the Communist Party controls the state apparatus, indeed it is fused with the state apparatus. The single party controls the collectivised economy and maintains control over all aspects of social life. Furthermore, the party is centralised and controlled from the top.

The internal organisation of the party is based on democratic centralism which formally involves four principles:

a   Election of all leading party bodies, from the lowest to the highest.
b   Periodic accountability of party organs to their respective party organisations.
c   Strict party discipline and the subordination of the minority to the majority.
d   Decisions of higher bodies are absolutely binding on lower bodies and on party members.[36]

As Tiersky notes, these principles are supplemented by two futher items not included in the formal rules. The first is the ban on factions: 'The crucial unwritten rule of democratic centralism is that its entire structure is erected on the prohibition of factions and factional behaviour.'[37] The ban has remained in force, though some commentators argue that ruling communist parties are by no means totally monolithic but exhibit at least a degree of 'pluralism'.

A second feature is *nomenklatura*, a list of appointments. It means that the elections to all leading party bodies are conducted on the basis of approved lists which provide for each post or office a candidate screened in advance and approved by the higher party authorities. In the words of a recent study, 'the primary meaning of the word *nomenklatura* is 1) list of key positions, appointments to which are made by the higher authorities of the party; and 2) lists of persons appointed to these positions or held in reserve for them.'[38]

Indeed this recent account views the *nomenklatura* as a relatively homogeneous class, a privileged group commanding and exploiting the mass of the population through the power stemming from its control of key positions in the party and state hierarchy.[39] Elections are in fact ratifications of people chosen by the higher party elite. The *nomenklatura* system was established by the 9th Party Congress of December 1919, as Geoffrey Hosking notes:

The Ninth Party Congress recommended party committees at all levels to keep lists of employees suitable for particular kinds of work and for promotion within their field. Such lists, coordinated and extended by the Secretariat, became the nucleus of the *nomenklatura* sytem of appointments, not just in the party, but in all walks of life.[40]

The *nomenklatura* system has been regarded as of crucial importance for maintaining both the centralisation of the party and, no less importantly, the control of this centralised party over other social organisations. Control from above prevents genuine election or effective democratic supervision from below. Again, as Hosking says:

Through this by now highly developed and sophisticated *nomenklatura* system of patronage, this Central Committee [of the Communist Party of the Soviet Union] supervised in principle every single appointment of any importance in any walk of life, delegating these powers to lower-tier party organisations for appointments lower down the hierarchy.[41]

He further writes that 'If there is a "ruling class" in the Soviet Union then its kernel is to be found in the *nomenklatura* posts at the disposal of each party committee, and in the people selected to fill them'. This controlling group is not a ruling class in the Marxist sense of a group owning the means of production, though the *nomenklatura* appointees certainly control those resources. The chief point is that there exists within the system a single centralised, though not totally monolithic, party. In this party, appointments at all levels are made from the top down and elections are a formality. The party's apparatus controls the economic life, the planning system, of society. Civil society has no, or very limited, autonomy from this bureaucratic apparatus.

7. NON-MARXIST THEORIES OF SOVIET SYSTEMS

Non-Marxist theories exhibit no less a variety of perspectives on the power structure of Soviet systems than the Marxist theories. For a time the concept of 'totalitarianism' was claimed in Western political science to be an appropriate paradigm for the conceptualisation of Soviet-type systems. Definitions of the term 'totalitarianism' differ. In general the idea can be taken to refer to the aspiration to total control of all aspects of life by those who hold political power. In the words of F. Neumann, the distinguishing characteristics of totalitarianism, 'the most repressive of political systems', are 'the destruction of the line between state and society and the total politicisation of society by the device of the monolithic party'.[42] There is no 'private' sphere; all institutions become transmission belts intended to promote the same ideas and spread the same beliefs. Dissenters, unless they keep their opinions strictly to themselves, are not tolerated. At the same time, the masses are expected to manifest actively their participation in the system and to show on official occasions their enthusiastic support.

In certain important respects the Soviet Union does fit this model, though a certain latitude of tolerance may be noticed in some of the Eastern European states which otherwise conform to the system. Still, Trotsky in describing what he called 'the Soviet Thermidor' wrote in 1936 that 'the Soviet state has acquired a totalitarian-bureaucratic character'.[43] The hyphenated epithet, however, may direct our attention to the fundamental difference between the Soviet and certain other, i.e. fascist, systems which are often equally subsumed under the same heading of totalitarianism. Although in each case the aim is the total politicisation of all aspects of social life, the attempt to place both types on the same level means neglecting the differences in their historic origin, economic context and in their *raison d'être*.

A number of arguments have been raised against the validity of the totalitarian model as applied to Soviet-type systems. A.H. Brown suggests that this model exaggerates 'the success of the official socialisation effort *vis-à-vis* Soviet society'.[44] Interpretations of Soviet politics based on the concept of totalitarianism present a picture of an almost totally monolithic and united Communist Party, and a population totally indoctrinated, 'internalising' the party ideology. Such interpretations fail to account for the conflicts over policy which certainly do occur in Soviet systems, and for pressure for change from below the level of the top leadership, and even from outside the party. The politics of some East European countries could not be understood without taking such factors into account; they suggest a much less rigid picture than do accounts based on the concept of totalitarianism.

It must also not be forgotten that since Stalin's death the Soviet state has undergone a development which is by no means completed. The terror and purges of the Stalin era are no longer characteristics of the system. Some analysts suggest that the totalitarian model no longer applies in so far as a bureaucratic elite rather prefers a quiet life to the perpetual mobilisation of the masses. In this perspective, the present Soviet systems would be examples of 'directed' society and better characterised by a certain 'petrification' than by the instability of Stalinism.[45] The 'ruling class', or bureaucratic elite, was no less affected by that unpredictability than the broad masses. It has learned in the meantime how not to be dominated by a single personality nor by an arrogant secret police. In this respect one may speak of a 'post-totalitarian' society.[46]

There has been discussion too about a degree of 'pluralism' within the party and outside it. Clearly, Soviet-type systems are not pluralistic in the sense in which the term has been used in this book to mean a range of political parties, of groups and associations, openly competing with one another and pressurising the power-holders, with each group having its autonomy and separate organisation. Yet it is argued that the achievement in the USSR of an advanced modern economy has led to the development of a range of interests which find expression at the upper levels of the party. The Communist Party is then seen as much less monolithic than the totalitarian model would suggest. Some people in its upper echelons are more responsive to some interests than to others; clearly the party apparatus has interests of its own, as have the military, the heavy industry lobby and again the consumer goods industry.[47] The Soviet historian Roy Medvedev, in his book *On Socialist Democracy* discusses three ideological trends within the CPSU: neo-Stalinist, moderate conservatives and those like himself whom he refers to as 'party democrats'. Medvedev admitted that the last of those three were the weakest group and almost completely unrepresented in the highest party organs. By 'party democrats' he meant those who called for 'wide freedom for party members to criticise and discuss any matter, including the activity of the highest party organs'.[48]

In the same vein a Western student of the Soviet Union distinguishes between 'Reformers' and 'Conservatives'; there have been 'sustained struggles between reformist and conservative groups inside the high political establishment, including the party itself'.[49] Finally, Jerry Hough suggests the idea of 'institutional pluralism'—institutional in the sense that the pluralism is strictly confined within the limits and apparatus of the party. Groups can have no substantial degree of independent existence outside the party. Nevertheless, in Hough's view, 'In the Soviet Union too, there is unmistakable evidence for the existence of factional and bureaucratic-occupational interest group activity.'[50] Whatever the degree of pluralism within the party, these views taken together do suggest that the totalitarian model of the party as the utterly monolithic instrument of a dictatorial leader does not now apply to Soviet-type systems. That model is too crude to explain adequately the nature of the contemporary Soviet system.

Supporters of an elite theory of society see the Soviet system as marked by the concentration of power in the hands of a bureaucratic elite. The elitist point of view with respect to socialist or collectivist systems is best expressed by Weber's famous phrase of 'the dictatorship of the official'. Weber argued that socialism must reinforce the power of bureaucracy. In a capitalist system there were two separate bureaucratic hierarchies, the governmental one and one for private industry. However, he wrote, 'If private capitalism were abolished, the state bureaucracy would rule *alone*. Where now the bureaucracies of government and private industry can at least in principle counterbalance each other and hold the other in check, they would then be forged together in a single hierarchy.'[51]

The Italian elitist Mosca, in his critique of collectivism, painted much the same picture: 'Communist and collectivist

societies would beyond any doubt be managed by officials ...
Under collectivism everyone will have to kowtow to the men in
the government. They alone can dispense favour, bread, the joy
or sorrow of life. One single crushing, all-embracing, all-
engrossing tyranny will weigh upon all.'[52]

In a sense the Marxist analyses of Soviet-type systems which
we have examined also point to the dominance of a
commanding group which combines political domination with
economic control. On the basis of a collectivised economy it
recreates the domination of the state over society, which a fully
socialist system would have removed. This view, however,
differs from the Weber and Mosca analysis in so far as it does
not see bureaucratic dictatorship as an unavoidable feature of
a collectivised economy. It rather speaks of a 'bureaucratic
distortion' which could be removed.

8. CONCLUSION

We have seen that some recent writers, such as Nove, have
raised the question of how realistic the ideas of reducing the
role of the bureaucracy and realising 'the rule of the associated
producers' are in the context of a complex planned economy.
In other words, how relevant are the perspectives of the
'withering away of the state', or the ideas presented by Marx in
The Civil War in France and restated (though never completely
realised) by Lenin in *The State and Revolution*? This is Nove's
view:

If thousands, or even millions, of interconnected and interdependent
decisions must be taken, to ensure production and delivery of the items
which society needs—and this must be preceded by some operationally
meaningful set of decisions about what is needed—elaborate administrative
machinery is required to ensure the necessary responsibilities and
coordination.[53]

Two points can be made by way of conclusion, as partial
answers to this problem, and as indicating crucial tensions
within Soviet-type systems. First, however conceptualised, the
power structure of such systems involves a small group of a
politico-bureaucratic kind, holding both economic and

political power and effectively disposing over the affairs of society. Bahro is right to talk of 'subalternity' as a feature of these societies. Because of the collectivist economic structure of these systems, one of the chief concerns of their ruling elite is the management, planning and development of the economy. This is true of the USSR now as it was in the Stalinist period of forced industrialisation. Yet there seems agreement in a variety of critical discussions of Soviet-type systems that many of their problems stem from the lack of any effective degree of political democratisation. Such is the sharp separation of the controlling group at the top from the 'collective worker' at the bottom that the 'associated producers' have limited influence. As W. Brus says, genuine social ownership is to be distinguished from state or public ownership: 'the basic criterion of socialisation of the means of production therefore, in our understanding, is the criterion of democratism.'[54] Society must have effective disposition over the economic resources it owns, and for that purpose there would have to be the possibility of greater control 'from below'. Economic and other decisions would not be monopolised by the upper echelons of a party controlled from the top. Three changes would be required in the system: (1) changes within the party, allowing for factions and inner-party discussion; (2) economic decentralisation allowing greater autonomy to particular enterprises at lower levels of the planning system; (3) a greater degree of autonomy for 'civil society'. Institutions and associations would have to develop their independence to be free from party control.

This last point forms the second item for the discussion of the tensions in Soviet-type systems. It can be said that oppositional movements in Eastern Europe (though not in the Soviet Union) since the Second World War have all expressed the demand for groups and associations which would not be mere 'transmission belts' for party commands, but which would be free from party control. This is what is meant by the idea of civil society having some 'space' or autonomy. The demands in Hungary and Poland in 1956 were for independent workers' councils; such were the demands of the 'revisionists' in those countries in the period of de-Stalinisation inaugurated by Khrushchev's 'Secret Speech' of 1956. The councils would not only bargain with the state over questions of pay and working conditions but also play an effective part in industrial management.[55] In Czechoslovakia the April 1968 Action Programme of the party developed an incipient pluralism: 'people should have the right to organise themselves in groups and express their opinions.'[56] Then again, the demands of Solidarity in Poland were for trade unions which would genuinely represent the interests of the workers and not be controlled by the party. The Gdansk Agreement signed on 31 August 1980 confirmed the recognition of free unions which would be independent from the party. It was stated that the existing unions had not 'answered the hopes and aspirations of the workers'.[57] In all these cases the demands for reform came up against the orthodoxy of Soviet-type systems under the form of 'the leading role of the party'. In all these cases too the calls for reform met with no success. They were crushed by Soviet intervention or, in the case of Poland in 1981, by an 'internal' military *coup*. Nevertheless, the claim for an area of group life free from the grip of the party is unlikely to disappear. There will remain challenges to the monopoly of power held by the chief party organs.

To conclude then, there are two main problems which in their present form Soviet systems have to face: a degree of democratisation inside and outside the party and, as part of outside democratisation, the granting to groups and associations, including trade unions, a certain amount of autonomy and independence from the single party.

NOTES

1. Aryeh L. Unger, *Constitutional Developments in the USSR: A Guide to the Soviet Constitution* (London, Methuen, 1980), pp. 233–4.
2. Quoted in Marcel Liebman, *Leninism under Lenin* (Merlin Press, London, 1980), p. 31.
3. V.I. Lenin, *Collected Works*, Vol. 5 (Lawrence and Wishart, London, 1961), p. 375.
4. Ibid., p. 384.
5. Ibid.,
6. Ibid., pp. 477, 479, 476.

7. Marx, *Wages, Price and Profit*, in Karl Marx and Frederick Engels, *Selected Works* (Progress Publishers, Moscow, 1969), Vol. II, p. 75.
8. Ronald Tiersky, *Ordinary Stalinism: Democratic centralism and the question of communist political development* (Allen and Unwin, London, 1985), p. 48.
9. E.H. Carr, *The Bolshevik Revolution 1917–1923* (Macmillan, London, 1950), Vol. I, pp. 68, 69 ff. for Trotsky's position.
10. Neil Harding, *Lenin's Political Thought*, Vol. II, (Macmillan, London, 1981), p. 75.
11. See Harding, *Lenin's Political Thought*, II, Chapter 6.
12. Marx, *The Civil War in France, MESW* II, p. 221.
13. Lenin, *The State and Revolution*, in Lenin, *Selected Works* in one volume (Lawrence and Wishart, London, 1969), p. 296. (Hereafter referred to as Lenin, *SW*.)
14. Lenin, *The Proletarian Revolution and the Renegade Kautsky* (Progress Publishers, Moscow, 1976), p. 24.
15. Carr, *Bolshevik Revolution*, I, p. 120.
16. Rosa Luxemburg, *The Russian Revolution*, introduction by B.D. Wolfe (University of Michigan Press, Ann Arbor, 1961), pp. 59–62.
17. Fernando Claudin, *The Communist Movement, from Comintern to Cominform* (Penguin, Harmondsworth, 1975), p. 56.
18. R. Miliband, 'The State and Revolution', in Ralph Miliband, *Class Power and State Power* (Verso, London, 1983), p. 162.
19. Leon Trotsky, *The Revolution Betrayed. What is the Soviet Union and Where is it going?* (Pathfinder Press, New York, 1970), p. 56.
20. Lenin, *Our Revolution*, in Lenin, *SW*, pp. 696–9.
21. As noted by Miliband, 'The State and Revolution', in *Class Power and State Power*, p. 159.
22. Fernando Claudin, *Eurocommunism and Socialism* (New Left Books, London, 1978), p. 78.
23. Quoted in Harding, *Lenin's Political Thought*, II, p. 276.
24. Ibid., pp. 303–8.
25. See Carr, *Bolshevik Revolution* I, p. 207.
26. Lenin, *Proletarian Revolution and the Renegade Kautsky*, p. 69 (italics in original).
27. R.C. Tucker, 'Stalinism as revolution from above', in R.C. Tucker (ed.), *Stalinism: Essays in historical interpretation* (Norton, New York, 1977), p. 95.
28. See R. Medvedev, *Let History Judge: The Origins and Consequences of Stalinism* (Spokesman Books, Nottingham, 1976).
29. See P. Bellis, *Marxism and the USSR: The Theory of Proletarian Dictatorship and the Marxist analysis of Soviet society* (Macmillan, London, 1979).
30. Trotsky, *The Revolution Betrayed*, p. 51
31. On this, see Isaac Deutscher, *The Prophet Unarmed, Trotsky: 1921–1929* (Oxford University Press, Oxford, 1970), pp. 43 ff. Trotsky used the term in 1922 to argue the need for the Soviet government to build up an investment fund for the necessary industrialisation of the Soviet Union.

As Deutscher notes, Trotsky's view was that 'The nation's accumulation fund could be increased either at the expense of the earnings of private business and farming or of the nation's wages bill.' In the history of capitalism, the investment fund necessary for industrialisation had been built up by a series of 'extra-economic' measures, like plunder of colonies, over centuries. In the Soviet case, such accumulation had to be carried out by the state, at breakneck speed.

32. Trotsky, *Revolution Betrayed*, p. 57.
33. Ibid., p. 102, 113, 278.
34. R. Bahro, *The Alternative in Eastern Europe*, translated by David Fernbach (New Left Books, London, 1978).
35. A. Nove, *The Economics of Feasible Socialism* (Allen and Unwin, London, 1983), pp. 50, 57.
36. Tiersky, *Ordinary Stalinism*, p. 44.
37. Ibid., p. 66.
38. Michael Voslensky, *Nomenklatura: anatomy of the Soviet ruling class*, translated by Eric Mosbacher (Bodley Head, London, 1984), p. 75.
39. Ibid., p. 118.
40. Geoffrey Hosking, *A History of the Soviet Union* (Fontana Press/Collins, London, 1985), p. 89.
41. Hosking, *History of the Soviet Union*, pp. 375, 380.
42. F. Neumann, *The Democratic and the Authoritarian State* (The Free Press, Glencoe, 1957), p. 245.
43. Trotsky, *Revolution Betrayed*, p. 108.
44. A.H. Brown, 'Political Power and the Soviet State', in N. Harding (ed.), *The State in Socialist Society* (Macmillan, London, 1984), p. 56.
45. For a discussion of the question of 'petrification', see Jerry F. Hough, 'The Soviet System: Petrification or Pluralism', in J.F. Hough, *The Soviet Union and Social Science Theory* (Harvard University Press, Cambridge, Mass., 1977), pp. 19–49.
46. Hosking, *History of the Soviet Union*, p. 463.
47. See H.G. Skilling and F. Griffiths (eds.), *Interest Groups in Soviet Politics* (Princeton University Press, Princeton, N.J., 1971). For an analysis of Khrushchev's fall from power in 1964 in terms of an interest group approach, see C.A. Linden, *Khrushchev and the Soviet Leadership 1957–1964* (Johns Hopkins University Press, Baltimore, 1966).
48. Roy Medvedev, *On Socialist Democracy*, translated and edited by Ellen de Kadt (Macmillan, London, 1975), p. 60.
49. S.F. Cohen, 'The Friends and Foes of Change: Reformism and Conservatism in the Soviet Union', in S.F. Cohen, A. Rabinowitch and R. Sharlet (eds.), *The Soviet Union since Stalin* (Macmillan, London, 1980), p. 14.
50. J. Hough and M. Fainsod, *How the Soviet Union is Governed* (Harvard University Press, Cambridge, Mass., 1980), p. 536.
51. Quoted (from Weber's series of articles on 'Parliament and Government in a Reconstructed Germany') in David Beetham, *Max*

Weber and The Theory of Modern Politics (Polity Press, Cambridge, 1985), p. 83.
52. G. Mosca, *The Ruling Class* (McGraw-Hill, New York, 1939), pp. 284–5.
53. Nove, *Economics of Feasible Socialism*, p. 34. See also P. Rutland, *The Myth of the Plan. Lessons of Soviet planning experience* (Hutchinson, London, 1985).
54. W. Brus, *Socialist Ownership and Political Systems*, translated by R.A. Clarke (Routledge and Kegan Paul, London, 1975), p. 30.
55. L. Kolakowski, *Main Currents of Marxism*, Vol. III, *The Breakdown* (Clarendon Press, Oxford, 1978), p. 459.
56. Hosking, *History of the Soviet Union*, p. 369.
57. *Le Monde*, 2 August 1980.

5 Fascist Movements and the Fascist State

1. FASCISM AND AUTHORITARIANISM

This chapter deals with the nature of the fascist or national-socialist state. It also tries to explore the conditions under which such a form of state comes into existence. In general terms it can be said that the fascist state is a form of dictatorial authoritarianism, if this term is taken to refer to a system in which state power is not restricted by any pluralist checks and controls. Historically, fascist systems emerged in situations of a liberal-democratic society in deep crisis. Such crisis had many dimensions—political, social and economic, all contributing to a general crisis of legitimacy of the liberal-democratic order. The most significant examples of fascism (Italy, Germany) appeared when that order seemed unable to meet severe social and economic challenges after the First World War. Then fascist mass movements developed, voicing their opposition to the parliamentary system and their intention of replacing it with a dictatorial regime.

The nature of this fascist dictatorship must be specified more closely. The most important aspect of the fascist movement is its mass base. This is true both of the situation preceding the fascist seizure of power and of the period after the regime has been established. An important distinction is to be drawn between those authoritarian systems which do not seek to mobilise the masses, and the fascist variety of authoritarianism. Mass involvement of a pseudo-democratic kind is a defining characteristic of fascism. This involvement is structured and controlled by a mass party. After its seizure of power this party destroys all other parties in its attempt to maintain the mass basis on which the fascist system rests. The means by which this purpose is achieved are terror and the intense use of propaganda.

Dictatorial systems which do not aim at mass involvement will here be labelled simply as *authoritarian*, and contrasted with *fascist* systems. The latter are defined by the existence of a mass movement drawn from various social groups and controlled by a monopolistic party. It is also the case that the pillars of authoritarian regimes are the elements of the traditional state apparatus, chiefly the military and the bureaucracy. It is through these institutions that the power of the authoritarian state is exercised; they form the basis of the regime. By contrast, the key political institution for fascist regimes is the mass party as the instrument of the dictatorial ('Caesaristic') leader, totally controlled by him. Before the movement is successful, the mass following is used as a 'battering ram' against the representative institutions of the liberal-democratic state. Once victory is achieved and those institutions are overthrown, the party becomes the pivot of the fascist regime. It acts as a potent rival to the traditional state apparatus of bureaucracy, military and police. In the *authoritarian* system this apparatus holds the monopoly of political power, but in the *fascist* system it is challenged by those who seek to achieve the supremacy of the party. The party is seen as the agent of the fascist or national-socialist 'revolution' and as the means of propagandising the masses. Through propaganda and coercion the party enforces the mass adulation of the dictatorial leader, affording him a token of pseudo-democratic legitimation.

In authoritarian systems, as long as people do not interfere in political matters nor overtly oppose the system, they are left alone. Fascist regimes, by contrast, require popular participation. The masses have to play their part; mass acclamation of the leader and of the system is demanded. The principle of 'who is not with us is against us' is applied. Hence the rallies, parades, demonstrations and other manifestations of popular enthusiasm. These are essential features of a fascist system, and are organised by the party.

Authoritarian systems include military dictatorships and

regimes of clerical conservatism, both of which are marked by the absence of a mass party as an instrument of the regime. Such systems are not one-party systems, but rather 'no-party systems'.[1] Therein lies their weakness, because under modern conditions it is difficult to exclude the people from political life. 'The dictator', as Franz Neumann points out, 'is therefore compelled to seek mass support and, having obtained it, to practice the ritual of democracy even if its substance is withheld.'[2] Neumann contrasts this with 'simple dictatorship' where 'the dictator may exercise his power through absolute control of the traditional means of coercion only, i.e. the army, police, bureaucracy and judiciary'.[3] This is what has here been called authoritarian rule, exemplified by such instances as Chile under the domination of General Pinochet; Greece under the military rule of the Colonels after their *coup* in 1967; Spain under Franco. In this last case, while a mass fascist party, the Falange, did exist, it did not seriously challenge the exercise of power by the traditional elements of the state.[4]

Some authoritarian regimes have at times created a political party to give themselves a façade of democratic popular participation. Even the autocratic Shah of Iran once authorised the formation of a political party for that purpose.[5] Yet the thrust of such systems is to seek to prevent mass involvement and to maintain politics as the sole preserve of a political elite. In this sense such twentieth-century authoritarian regimes can be seen as the heirs to pre-democratic traditional autocracies which attempted to ignore or beat back the tide of democracy, like the regimes of Prussia, Austria-Hungary, and Russia in nineteenth-century Europe. However, twentieth-century authoritarian dictatorships use far more violence in their repression than the comparatively easy-going regime, say, of Metternich in pre-1848 Austria. The fact that such regimes as Pinochet's Chile or Argentina under military rule are not fascist does not mean that they are any less repressive, though they may not aim at the total control of society nor require the mobilisation of the masses which is characteristic of the fascist system.

It should be added that the mass party is a necessary but not a sufficient condition of a fascist regime. Plebiscitary or populist dictatorships, like Peronism, are characterised by the presence of such a 'Caesaristic' party securing popular backing for a dictatorial leader. Yet fascist regimes, as we shall see, go further in that they manifest a totalitarian aspiration to control all aspects of social life, so that no sphere of human existence is 'private'.

2. THE MOBILISATION OF THE MASSES

Since the existence of a mass movement is a vital part of the fascist phenomenon, it is necessary to discuss in more detail the nature and composition of that mass movement. Fascism will be discussed here with chief reference to the movements and regimes of fascist Italy and national-socialist Germany. The term fascism will thus be used to cover both systems, though there were significant differences between them. Indeed some authors, such as the Italian historian de Felice, argue that these differences, particularly in the ideology of fascism and Nazism, were substantial, and make comparison problematic.[6]

Speaking now of both Italian fascism and German Nazism, it can be said that fascist movements were not composed of a single class. Fascism involved a heterogeneous cross-class mass consisting of various large groups in opposition to the institutions and values of the liberal-democratic state. Fascism developed in societies where democratic and parliamentary institutions had weak legitimacy. Moreover, in both Italy and Germany support for the liberal-democratic state was further eroded by its apparent inability to cope with the difficult social and economic problems of the post-First World War era. The crucial problems, notably in Germany, were the high level of unemployment and rapid inflation which completely devalued the currency. As a result large sections of the middle class and of the petty bourgeoisie lost their savings and were often financially ruined. On the other hand, as in Italy in 1919–20 (the 'Biennio Rosso' or 'Red Two Years'), there was a widespread fear of a proletarian revolution on the Bolshevik model. It was felt that the democratic system might be too weak to resist that challenge.

Under such conditions fascist leaders commanded parties

which sought to gain support from the diverse mass of the disaffected. The aim of such leaders was to destroy liberal-democratic institutions and have them replaced by a dictatorial order with the fascist party dominant. The complexity of the fascist phenomenon stems from the heterogeneity of the various groups on which it drew for support to build up the mass movement which eventually brought it to power. What those groups had in common was their dissatisfaction with the existing state of affairs, which was blamed on the democratic system. This dissatisfaction was fully exploited by the fascist leaders.

The varied nature of the fascist movement was realised at an early stage by at least some analyses of fascism. Writing in 1928 the Italian communist Togliatti stressed 'the complexity of the fascist phenomenon'. Fascism 'was not simply capitalist reaction'; it embraced a variety of elements. These included capitalist interests, but also involved the petty bourgeoisie, i.e. those intermediate groups of small-scale property owners in town and country. Such petty bourgeois elements were mobilised by *déclassés*, ex-officers, unemployed professionals, students, who led the fascist movement in an organisation structured on military lines, with its own para-military forces 'which claimed the ability to take on the regular armed forces of the state with some probability of success'.[7]

Even before Togliatti's analysis, an Italian socialist, Zibordi, had discussed the specific characteristics of Italian fascism's mass base. Writing in 1922, the year of Mussolini's March on Rome, Zibordi broke the fascist movement down into three components. These three elements were:

- a counter-revolution of the bourgeoisie proper in response to a red revolution which only threatened but never took place.
- a revolution, or rather an upheaval, of the middle classes, the disoriented, the deprived and the discontented.
- a military revolution.[8]

This analysis was very similar to that of the Austro-Marxist Otto Bauer writing in 1936, and thus covering German National-Socialism as well as Italian fascism. Bauer too saw fascism originating in militaristic and nationalistic groups of ex-combatants unable to adjust to civilian life. These groups, violently hostile to both democracy and socialism, got the support of other disaffected and dislocated elements, students and *déclassés*, all of them at odds with democratic ideas and middle-class bourgeois society.[9]

However, as both Zibordi and Bauer recognised, such military groups on their own could not constitute the mass base of fascism. This was furnished in large part by the intermediary stratum of the petty bourgeoisie, who formed the bulk of the movement. They were particularly affected by the post-war economic crisis. They feared proletarianisation intensely and were therefore responsive to the anti-socialist appeal of fascism. At the same time they were hostile to big business and hence receptive to a strand of anti-capitalism which was to be found in the programme of fascist parties. For example, the NSDAP (National-Socialist German Workers Party) spoke in its 1920 programme of 'the nationalization of all businesses which have been formed into corporations (trusts)'.[10] Such intermediary groups rallied to the demagogic promises of a 'third way', a national socialism that would look after all groups in the nation, hostile to international socialism (usually equated with Bolshevism) as well as to 'finance capital' and, in theory at least, opposed to the power of big business. Such were the arguments which, on many occasions supported by terroristic acts and by intimidation, swelled the ranks of the movement. In Germany, the use of anti-Semitism provided a means of identifying a scapegoat which could be blamed for the problems of the petty bourgeoisie. Blaming 'Jewish capital' was also a suitable way of preventing the anti-capitalist strand in National-Socialism from attacking capital in general.

To these two elements (ex-combatants and nationalists on the one, petty bourgeoisie on the other hand) the analysis of Zibordi and Bauer added a third factor. This was the support of some sections of large-scale industry and the cooperation of members of the state elite and politicians previously loyal to the parliamentary system. The argument advanced here was that economically dominant groups and some of their allies saw in the fascist movement a suitable instrument to hold down working-class political parties (whether social-democratic or communist) and trade unions. Such parties and institutions were seen either as presenting a revolutionary challenge to the capitalist system, or, in the case of social-democratic parties and unions, as defending working-class interests, wages and factory conditions within the limits of the system. In either case capitalists and managers saw them as infringing on their own economic and social power, particularly in a situation of capitalist crisis and profit erosion. The dominant classes would then rather support the fascist movement. This switch of support away from the parties operating within the parliamentary system in favour of fascism in an attempt to defend capitalist privileges and interests, was not made without some reluctance. The demagogic rhetoric of fascist leaders was not highly appreciated by traditional conservatives, nor was it apparent at the time to what a limited extent the anti-capitalist points in the fascist programme would be implemented.

In fact, once fascism was in power those who had supported it found that it was far more than a pliant tool of capitalist interests. The instrument dominated the user. The fascist state is a system of heightened state autonomy. It is what Poulantzas calls an *'exceptional state* corresponding to the needs of a political crisis'. Poulantzas also notes that 'the relative autonomy of the exceptional state from the dominant classes and fractions is particularly important and significant'.[11] These 'dominant classes and fractions' certainly assisted fascist movements in coming to power. But after its installation the fascist state came to control those who had opened the way to the fascist takeover. It is true that once in power fascist regimes disappointed the hopes of those activists and intransigents in the party ranks, some of whom wanted a 'second revolution' which had an anti-capitalist component. Nevertheless, if *those* hopes were not satisfied, neither can the fascist state be seen in crude terms as directed by capitalist interests. As Marx said of Bonapartism, all classes knelt beneath the rifle butt. This was true of fascism, although the fascist state dominated a society in which capitalist property and private ownership of the means of production were maintained.

The above-mentioned accounts of Zibordi and Bauer

(among others) thus emphasised one central feature of the fascist movement, the varied nature of the social groups and classes on which it drew for support. A further characteristic of fascism was the adulation of the plebiscitary leader by the mass. Fascism as a type of mass movement involves the 'leadership principle' (*Führerprinzip*). This is a distortion of the democratic principle or idea. In the theory and practice of fascism, the leader seeks and receives mass backing, unlike a traditional autocracy which does not aim at mass legitimacy. Yet the fascist leader (Duce, Führer) was in no way accountable to the mass, nor did he represent it in any democratic sense. The leader led, and the mass followed; the mass was not seen as a collection of rational individuals or organised groups, seeking to have their interests furthered and wishes carried out. This would imply a form of democratic politics in which a leader could be removed for not truly representing the wishes or interests of the people. Yet fascism explicitly rejected democracy; in the words of Mussolini, 'After socialism, fascism attacks the whole complex of democratic ideologies and rejects them both in their theoretical premises and in their applications or practical manifestations.'[12]

The fascist idea of the mass and the leader was different. The mass or people had no autonomy, but was there just to give a pseudo-democratic legitimacy to the leader. The people was a sounding-board to echo and applaud the thoughts and wishes of the leader, who 'represented' the true will of the people, nation or race. There is here an irrational perversion of democratic ideas of popular sovereignty. Fascism involved the destruction of all forms of genuine democratic politics. The task of the mass was to obey the commands of the leader and give him mass support. As Mussolini put it again, 'If democracy means not to relegate the people to the periphery of the state, then fascism could be defined as an "organised, centralised, authoritarian democracy".'[13] The mass was mobilised by the fascist party, which itself had no inner-party democracy, and was not intended as a policy-making body. Fascist leaders in power curbed the pretensions of those who saw in the party a body for deciding policy and carrying on the fascist revolution. However, this raises the issue of whether fascism can in any genuine sense be called a 'revolutionary' movement.

3. FASCISM AS 'PSEUDO-REVOLUTION'

One of the difficult questions in the study of fascism is to decide on the revolutionary nature of the movement and the state form which it brought into being. Clearly, fascism must be demarcated from conservatism. Conservative parties follow the politics of tradition. They seek to 'conserve' the existing order of society by working within its state institutions and structures of power. Their aims do not preclude change, but such change is of a gradual kind accepting the limits and constraints of the given situation: 'Politics is the art of the possible.' Fascist movements, by contrast, proclaimed their contempt for the existing state of affairs. Their ideology utterly rejected the liberal-democratic system. They intended to destroy its institutions, as indeed they did. Moreover, the personnel of the movement, especially the leaders, was quite different from the political elite of liberal or conservative parties working within the parliamentary framework. Neither Mussolini nor Hitler had the characteristics of traditional bourgeois politicians. They were *déclassé* demagogues. Fascist movements were radically hostile to a bourgeois society born out of the struggles and traditions of 1789. They harnessed an activist energy in opposition to the established order.

These factors might lead one to conclude that fascism was a revolutionary movement. The fascist seizure of power led to the annihilation of liberal-democracy and to the attempt to create a totalitarian system. Yet fascism can also be seen with much justification as a defence of the existing system of private property against the presumed threat of a socialist revolution, or even against the pressure of social-democratic reforms. This was one element in the situation leading to the fascist seizure of power. It involved the connivance of some sections of the traditional political elite which became what Linz calls a 'semi-loyal opposition', opening the way to power for the 'disloyal opposition' of the fascist movement.[14]

Fascism may most accurately be termed a pseudo-revolution. It tried, with considerable success, to win over the masses by offering them the spectacle or outward appearance of a true revolution. The masses were to be persuaded that this was their revolution, a revolution undertaken in their interest and for their benefit. The latent revolutionary energies were to be used and diverted into the substitute revolution. Revolutionary slogans were used to stir up the emotions, but those slogans were 'myths' in Sorel's sense of the word, images which offered some picture of a future society and which appealed to popular sentiments. If, especially in the German case, hopes were raised that the power of capitalist ownership was to be broken, they were soon disappointed. After the Nazi seizure of power those who expected and called for a 'second revolution' to follow the first were liquidated in the Night of the Long Knives in June 1934. There followed what was called 'the winding up of the revolution'.[15]

Not only was there no socialist achievement, but the actual living conditions of the German working class deteriorated in the first years of the Nazi regime as real wages declined. It was true that later on, under conditions of labour shortage, wages rose, but they had to be earned by longer hours and harder work. The 'intense stress and a crippling work tempo' even threatened industrial productive capacity. In the end, older workers who could still remember the time when they were politically organised resigned themselves to the fact that they had to work hard for low wages under whatever regime was in power.[16]

The tension between the apparently revolutionary nature of fascism and its functions of objectively preserving the capitalist system against the socialist challenge reveals the inherent contradiction of the movement. Its ambiguity resulted from the many different social strata and conflicting interests to which appeal was made, but even more from the fact that no real solution for the problems of society was offered. In order to make the plethora of promises credible, scapegoats had to be created against which 'crusades' were led. The targets for these 'crusades' were international socialism in the form of Bolshevism and Jewish capitalism. Both were made responsible for all the evils of the times, in particular for the sorry plight of the petty bourgeoisie and for the unemployment afflicting the working class. The pictures set up for the imagination of the masses were not the likenesses of any actual living beings; they were stereotypes abstractly constructed: the sub-human Russian Bolshevik and the greedy

Jew as caricatured in Streicher's *Stürmer*. Anti-Semitism, as Kershaw notes, proved useful 'in giving ideological purpose to the "enforcement agency" of the regime—the SS-Gestapo-SD organization'. Besides, it somehow synthesised the two-pronged attack on the scapegoats by associating the Jews with both Bolshevism and plutocracy.[17]

A vision of national renewal and regeneration was conjured up, together with the myth of an eternal fight which Lyttelton sees as the essence of a fascist 'ideology of permanent conflict'. This was transposed on to the international plane.[18] The nation, or the race, was seen as locked in violent conflict with other nations or races, ennobling men who had to face the ordeal of a heroic struggle. Hence Mussolini's praise of war: 'Above all, Fascism ... believes neither in the possibility nor in the utility of perpetual peace.... War alone brings up to their highest tension all human energies and puts the stamp of nobility upon the peoples who have the courage to meet it.'[19]

Fascism has been defined as an 'anti-movement'. It 'defines itself by the things against which it stands'.[20] As early as 1921 the Italian Marxist Gramsci described Italian fascism as 'the anti-party' which 'has opened its gates to all applicants; has with its promise of impunity enabled a formless multitude to cover over the savage outpourings of passions, hatred and desires, with a varnish of vague and nebulous political ideas'.[21] Linz summarises 'the basic anti-dimensions of fascism' as 'anti-Marxist, anti-communist, anti-proletarian but also anti-liberal, anti-parliamentarian and, in a very special sense, anti-conservative and anti-bourgeois'.[22] This by no means exhausts the list. Linz adds, among other things, 'anti-Semitism, anti-capitalism, anti-internationalism and anti-cosmopolitanism'. Against that stands, in a positive sense, the myth of the nation. This is precisely the myth as Sorel described it: a body of images which cannot be proved either true or false. They 'enclose with them all the strongest inclinations of a people, of a party or of a class, inclinations which recur to the mind with the insistence of instincts in all the circumstances of life.'[23]

Sorel was a socialist, indeed for a while he considered himself a follower of Marx. He believed that he could improve on Marx by substituting for the latter's scientific method his own mythical approach. The myth was for Sorel an instrument to release action. Its details were of little importance; it was quite possible that nothing it contained would ever come true. That did not matter. 'The myth must be judged as a means of acting on the present.' In this sense Mussolini could well say that nowhere had he learnt as much as from Sorel's writings. What he did learn was how to work the psychological mechanism. His phraseology would stimulate the emotions and drive the masses into action. But it was action for action's sake. It was the negation that did not bring forth a new synthesis. History was seen as the playground for the 'strong men' of the century. The romanticism of a belief that personality could be stronger than fate and impose on reality the myth it had created led to an arrogant contempt for the facts: it found its psychological counterpart in Mussolini's *vivere pericolosamente*—to live dangerously.

This now reveals the nature of the ultimate 'anti' of the fascist movement. It was a movement against reason itself. It denied the rational presuppositions of political action. What was called 'the revolt against reason' found its consummation or final apotheosis in the fascist phenomenon. That was why fascism turned against the European tradition which was derived from the great revolutions in England and France and which found its philosophical formulation in the Enlightenment. From this source issued the three great streams of political thought: liberalism, democracy and socialism. They were all ideas based on rational arguments. Fascism, which denied the sovereign right of the individual in its liberal interpretation, equally rejected the democratic belief in popular sovereignty expressed through representative parliamentary institutions. 'Now we are beginning to bring the century of democracy to trial,' wrote Mussolini. 'The chief epithet of democracy is *all*, a word which completely filled the 19th century. The time has come to say: the *few* and the *elite*.'[24]

Finally, fascism repudiated socialism. While it promised the masses social justice, it destroyed the organisations which effectively served such a purpose. Comparing Nazism with Italian fascism, Alfred Rosenberg, the ideologue of the National-Socialist movement, wrote: 'Like National-Socialism, fascism had realised that there could be no compromise with Marxism as an international organisation, rather that this international movement had to be overcome and its organisation extirpated.'[25]

Yet even in its defiance fascism could not completely ignore the European tradition, though it perverted it. Its dictatorial rule backed by the acclamation of the masses it called 'true' democracy. It pretended to be a revolutionary movement, offering its own brand of what was claimed to be 'national' socialism.

4. THE NATURE OF THE FASCIST STATE

It is important to distinguish clearly between fascism in the period before its seizure of power and fascism as a regime once it had captured state power. The crucial dates are Mussolini's March on Rome on 30 October 1922 and 30 January 1933 when Hitler became Chancellor. In its gestation period fascism was a mass movement appealing to and involving different social groups, some containing a revolutionary anti-capitalist element. The mass movement was structured and led by the party. After the conquest of power the party certainly remained important both as a propaganda agency and an instrument of terror. Nevertheless, its position changed significantly.

The expectations of that section of the fascist movement which hoped for a 'Second Revolution' were not satisfied. There were those in the fascist ranks who hoped that the capture of political power would be merely the prelude to a more thorough-going fascist or national-socialist revolution. In Italy the fascist movement had always aimed, only too successfully, at terrorising the workers, both urban and rural. Yet there were those, like Farinacci, who expected a *seconda ondata* (second wave) which would not just sweep away the liberal-democratic system but totally revolutionise—in a fascist sense, of course—society. Such hopes were not realised, as it became clear in the years after 1922 that Mussolini was prepared to come to some accommodation with the conservative forces of the monarchy and the Vatican. This went against the wishes of those whom Lyttelton calls the 'radical intransigents' within the fascist party, some of whom 'opposed the subordination of the movement to State authority, and attacked Parliament and the spirit of compromise.... They also attacked Fascism for following a reactionary policy, hostile to the interests of the working class and the petty bourgeoisie.'[26] We shall deal in the next section with the implications of this for the relationship of party and state in the fascist and National-Socialist systems. As far as Germany is concerned, we have already mentioned the fate that befell Röhm and his SA comrades. The Night of Long knives also led to the murder of Gregor Strasser, one of the leaders of the left of the Nazi party. This 'was a clear signal that the socialist left within the NSDAP and NSBO [the Nazi factory cell organisation] was also to be put down.'[27]

Furthermore, in neither the Italian case nor even in Germany did the party achieve clear-cut dominance over the traditional state apparatus, although in Italy Mussolini created the fascist Grand Council and the Militia in December 1922 in an attempt to 'fascisticise' the state.[28] Nevertheless in both Italy and Germany the traditional state apparatus continued to exist and to function, albeit purged of its democratic elements and subject to challenge and interference from the party and from the arbitrary decisions of the leader.

The only positive idea in the fascist programme in Italy was corporatism as embodied in the Law of Corporation of April 1926. Corporatism was based on the idea of the state as the controlling agency, the highest arbiter in all social conflicts. Individual or class interests had to be subordinated to the interest of the community and of the nation. While the Law of Corporation put an end to independent trade union activity, it was supposed to ensure the peaceful collaboration of management and workforce. There would be no strikes. All were 'producers'. In fact, the results showed 'how little the interests of the working class or the views of the fascist left weighed in the balance against the arguments of the industrialists'.[29]

In this respect it is possible to interpret fascism as a movement of capitalist reaction against the challenge of socialism. Yet it would be a mistake to regard the fascist state as nothing but a device of the bourgeoisie to buttress up the capitalist system. It is quite true that big business organisations like the Italian *Confederazione dell' Industria* welcomed the fascist movement and invited it to the seats of power because they believed that was the surest way to 'restore order'. Yet they soon found that they had conjured up a force far stronger than they meant to use for their purpose. The fascist state not only destroyed working-class organisations; it controlled and subordinated all classes, workers and capitalists alike. It was a strong state indeed that completely dominated society. It forced even the economically dominant class to follow a course which they would not have voluntarily chosen. The analogy with the Bonapartist state, as Marx described it, is striking. The fascist state too would eventually lead to its own destruction by way of a national catastrophe.

K.D. Bracher has usefully summarised the three stages by which Nazi rule was established; they can be considered as exemplifying the nature of the fascist state and its opposition to liberal democracy. First, the massive intensification of executive power by means of presidential rule; second, the liquidation of the constitutional pluralist state and its replacement by a one-party system; third, the institutionalisation of a 'total leader state' controlled by the single party which would seek to dominate the state apparatus, thereby establishing the totalitarian system.[30]

In the German case the first of these three stages was reached even before Hitler's seizure of power, for which it paved the way. Rule by presidential decree undermined parliamentary power. It resulted in the strengthening of the executive power and in the weakening of liberal-democratic institutions. Governments like that of Brüning eroded the legitimacy of those institutions. They confined political decisions to an elite, notably to the President (Hindenburg), and removed them from public control and parliamentary scrutiny. Once the fascist party took power its first task was the destruction of all forms of pluralism. This corresponds to the second of Bracher's three stages.

In the Italian case the same process had been accomplished over a longer period. Four years elapsed between the March on Rome in 1922 and the banning of all non-fascist parties in 1926. The institutions of liberal democracy still functioned for a while after the seizure of power. A decisive point was reached with the assassination of Matteotti in 1924 when the non-fascist parties failed to react energetically to the event. In November 1925 the opposition press was suppressed. In October 1926 the fascist Council of Ministers drafted a series of emergency laws designed to eliminate the last vestiges of a democratic system. In November Gramsci, leader of the Communist Party, was arrested and confined to prison until his death in 1937.[31] Thus the fascist state revealed itself as entirely different from any form of liberal democracy.

It was a fateful error of the German Communist Party not to recognise this fundamental difference. The theory of 'social fascism' equated the social-democrats with the fascists, thereby undermining all common working-class action. Such a theory overlooked the fact that the fascist destruction of liberal-democratic institutions was fatal to *all* socialist and communist parties and trade unions. When Trotsky later wrote that 'Fascism has for its basic and only task the razing to their foundations of all institutions of proletarian democracy', it may be doubted whether this was its *only* task, but it certainly was one of its first and most important objectives.[32]

The same assault on democratic institutions was made in Germany with greater rapidity and more drastically. It started immediately after Hitler had become Chancellor and was well under way by the time of the last parliamentary elections of the Weimar Republic held on 5 March 1933. In those elections, held under conditions of intimidation and violence, the NSDAP got 43.9 per cent of the vote. The period between January and March had been used to crush the parties of the Left. The burning of the Reichstag on 27 February led to the arrest of KPD (Communist Party) deputies and officials. It led to the passing of the Emergency Decree 'For the Protection of People and State' which 'ended all the basic rights of the Weimar Constitution'. It allowed summary arrest by the police of all persons suspected of treasonable activities or intentions. The decree was 'not followed up by any written guidelines' and this allowed Goering as Reichs Commissioner 'to give an extraordinarily wide interpretation to the decree from the outset'.[33]

The actions against the KPD were the first in a series that led to 'the end of the parties' in Germany and to the establishment of the NSDAP as the only party. The abolition of political parties proceeded apace after the March elections, starting with the Left but eventually affecting all parties, even the Nationalist Party (DNVP) which in the election had been the allies of the Nazis. The SPD was banned in June; a directive of Goering asserted that 'the Social Democratic Party of Germany is to be regarded as an organisation hostile to the state and people, particularly after its action in recent days and weeks.'[34]

The process did not stop there. On 27 June 1933 the Nationalist Party—the Deutschnationale Front, successor to the DNVP—dissolved itself, its members for the most part joining the NSDAP. Finally, the only remaining party—the Centre—ceased to exist on 5 July. The end of political parties, those key institutions of a pluralist system, was signalled by a law of 14 July 1933, 'The Law against the Establishment of New Parties'. It declared that the NSDAP was Germany's only legal party and threatened to punish any attempt 'to maintain the organisation of any other party' or 'to form a new political party'.[35]

A crucial act in this liquidation of the democratic constitutional state was the Enabling Act of 23 March 1933. This effectively deprived the Reichstag of its power, thus enabling Hitler to be free from parliamentary control and no longer dependent on presidential decrees. The act was passed by the Reichstag in the absence of the KPD deputies and against the opposition of the SPD. It concentrated power in the hands of Hitler's government. The Nazi party now attempted to take over and control the administrative apparatus in the Reich and in the federal states. The Reichstag still existed, but was no longer a democratic institution. It was used by Hitler as a legislative medium in the same way as the referendum was used as a means to claim mass support and legitimacy. On 12 November 1933 a plebiscite was held to approve Germany's departure from the League of Nations. There were at the same time legislative elections. Only one list of candidates, the 'Führer List', was available. Justified fears that abstention or rejection of the list would be met with reprisals ensured that 95 per cent of the electorate voted for the list. Here too the Nazi regime showed its concern for mass backing and pseudo-democratic legitimacy, distinguishing itself from authoritarianism or 'simple dictatorship'. Hitler insisted, when setting up a Reichs Ministry of Information and Propaganda, that the regime could not tolerate political apathy.[36] The party functioned as a propaganda and mobilising agency preventing any withdrawal into a private sphere. Any barrier to the controlling activity of the party had to be removed. This was called *Gleichschaltung* – the forced coordination of all social institutions, causing them to lose any autonomy they might have had.

5. PARTY AND STATE IN FASCIST REGIMES

The relationship between party (or movement) and state is one of the key problems in fascist systems. As long as the movement was on the march and fighting to achieve power the problem was not acute. The party was everything, the mobilising force in the struggle. The members of the movement viewed the state apparatus—army, police, bureaucracy—as an adversary to be won over or conquered. After the seizure of power, however, a new situation developed. The fascist movement, or rather its leaders, had assumed responsibility for the administration of the country, and for that purpose it was necessary that the military–bureaucratic apparatus should continue to function. There was thus conflict and tension between the two authorities of party and state, though the ultimate decision in all matters rested with the leader. This conflict was also characterised by the different methods used by each camp. The party movement as a fighting organisation was determined that the masses should follow. For that purpose persuasion through propaganda was carried out, but where persuasion failed it was replaced by force and the exercise of terror. Violence and often brutality were the order of the day, carried out by the Italian *squadristi*, or the Nazi stormtroopers. Decisions were taken arbitrarily, in an *ad hoc* fashion by local fascist leaders and militants. This contrasted with the use of force by the state bureaucracy, which employed force only against cases of open disobedience and resistance. Where force was used it was employed to a greater extent according to rules and precedents, and was less subject to the arbitrary decisions of the local fascist groups and leaders 'at the base'.

In Italy, after the crisis caused by the murder of Matteotti and the ensuring secession of the non-fascist parties from parliament had been overcome, there were many convinced fascists who thought that it was time to begin a process of 'normalisation'. The previous line of fascist party politics and tactics, based on a large extent on violence, should be changed. For Mussolini 'The idea of the "totalitarian state" served in fact to emphasize the necessity for a *single* hierarchy in which State authority would be supreme and the party would be subordinate.'[37] This idea was not shared by Farinacci who in February 1925 had become general secretary of the party. With him the 'intransigents' now opposed the 'revisionists'. Not content with the fact that the institutions of the liberal-democratic state were to be swept away, Farinacci's fight was, so to speak, for the soul of the Italian people. As long as the mental attitude of the people had not yet completely changed to conform to the fascist ideal, the party, even if not supreme, should still survey the activities of the political leaders at every step. Totalitarianism, then, meant something quite different: 'Farinacci and his supporters rested their case on a typically totalitarian conception of continuous struggle, or permanent revolution.'[38] The state was viewed with suspicion. As one of the 'intransigents' wrote, 'A Fascist revolution which settled down quietly in the State would be a revolution that has finished.... A revolution which may be fully victorious at home but is opposed and undermined abroad cannot be defended and sustained unless the revolutionary temperature is constantly kept high.' The civil service was suspected of Freemasonry. Officials were now forbidden to be members of secret societies. More important, they were threatened with dismissal whenever they showed their 'incompatibility with the general political directives of the Government'.[39] The tendency was to promote fascist party members to higher posts in the administration. In the lower echelons of state service and local government the majority were convinced fascists. But still the party encouraged violence, and the *squadristi* continued with their terroristic methods.

Mussolini had been in favour of the attack on the state bureaucracy, but he came to worry that the violent behaviour of his followers might damage the image of the fascist movement abroad and impair the prestige of his regime. Moreover he saw the leaders of the party as possible competitors in the attempt to establish his leadership. His bid, after all, was for personal dictatorship. He wanted to achieve the position of being the sole ruler. There began the process of what Lyttelton calls 'the defeat of the party'. From 1926 onwards Mussolini consolidated his rule by strengthening the old administrative apparatus rather than by destroying it and creating something new.[40] On 30 April 1926 Farinacci was removed from his post of general secretary and replaced by A. Turati, who in turn was succeeded by Starace. The independence of the party was broken. The revisionists had won over the intransigents. The supremacy of the state was maintained.

In Germany the national-socialist movement wished to express the dynamism of a 'new order'; it claimed to be superior to the state apparatus. This supposed superiority was constitutionally secured by the 'Law Securing the Unity of Party and State' of 1 December 1933. The law asserted that the party was 'the representative of the German state idea and indissolubly linked to the state'. It has been noted that the law 'proved itself to be extremely problematic'; 'it did not establish an *institutional* and *constitutional* but only a vague theoretical supremacy of the party over the state'.[41]

K.D. Bracher speaks of the 'dualism' between 'a dynamic-revolutionary political movement' and, on the other hand, a 'regimented authoritarian state order'.[42] It seems that in theory the movement stood 'higher' than the state. Such, in any case, was the opinion of Röhm, SA leader, who considered the SA a force separate from the state. Broszat notes that, especially in Bavaria, 'the claim of the NSDAP, SA and SS, to supremacy over the state administration was resolutely pressed after 9 March [1933], if in different ways.'[43] Such 'different ways' included unofficial SA Commissioners who furthered the national-socialist revolution by challenging and putting pressure on the state authorities in Bavaria and elsewhere.

However, it seems clear that in the actual practice of the

regime the Nazi party never achieved the primacy to which it aspired. 'Political importance resided not in the party but rather in high-ranking party officials who used their position as a stepping stone to the usurpation of public office and functions of state.'[44] There was thus a split power structure, a dualism between the party and the traditional administrative apparatus. The link between and above the 'jurisdictionary thicket of party organs and state machinery' (Broszat) was the figure of the leader. The radicals who wanted to see the party sweep away the existing administrative order were pushed aside in the early days of the Nazi system when the 'revolution from below' had ended. The movement left the traditional state machine basically intact. On 6 July 1933 Hitler declared: 'The Party has now become the state, all power belongs to the Reich authority.'[45] What he meant was the subordination of the party to the state leadership.

The function of the party after the seizure of power was to act as a mass organisation to extend the state's power and to whip up support for government policy through propaganda and intimidation. Broszat cites an extremely interesting (anonymous) report on an address given by Hitler to assembled *Gauleiters* in Berlin (2 February 1934). There Hitler said that the essential tasks of the party were '1. To make the people receptive to the projected government measures. 2. To help carrying out throughout the nation the measures ordered by the government. 3. To support the government in every possible way.'[46] The document quoted Hitler as emphasising that 'those who maintained that the revolution had not ended were fools'. According to Broszat, 'little headway was made in remodelling the inner structures of the conservative state bureaucracy' in Nazi Germany, though the 'old ministerial bureaucracy was increasingly bypassed and politically neutralised' by inroads from the Nazi party.[47]

Generally it may be concluded that the party, fascist or national-socialist, never achieved the total political ascendancy to which it aspired. One might venture to explain the power of resistance or inertia of the traditional state apparatus by the fact that a truly new political organisation could only have arisen on the basis of a transformation of the socioeconomic structure of society. Such was the historic case of the French Revolution, for example, but no corresponding attempt was ever made by the so-called fascist 'revolutions'. We have tried to characterise them as 'anti-movements', defined by what they opposed. This was reflected in fascist ideology, in what Lyttelton calls its 'vagueness' and 'open-ended character'. Both fascism and national-socialism were movements based on the personality of their leaders, who reduced the masses of their followers to the status of mere crowds. What was essential to fascism was the constant stirring up and manipulation of the masses by a demagogic leader: 'The closest bond between Hitler and Mussolini was their belief that the road to power lay through the mastery of collective psychology, the manipulation of mass passions; they were both disciples of Gustave Le Bon and his "psychology of the crowd".'[48]

Nevertheless, if the fascist parties failed politically in their bid for total and unrivalled power, it is impossible to overrate their importance as an element in fascist regimes. The chief reason for this is that the party was the vehicle for an attempted totalitarian remoulding of human nature. The propaganda mission was central to the role of the fascist or Nazi party, both before and after the seizure of power. These parties got hold of the whole person, enveloping him or her, in a literal sense, from the cradle to the grave: from Hitler Youth or Balilla, the fascist youth organisation which 'soon became a powerful instrument for the totalitarian regimentation of youth', through the occupational associations like the DAF (German Labour Front) to fascist cultural associations like Dopo Lavoro and 'Kraft durch Freude'.[49] Had such regimes lasted, they might well have succeeded in their aspiration to achieve total control and the remoulding of human minds. This leads on to the question of totalitarianism as a feature of fascist systems of power.

6. *GLEICHSCHALTUNG* (TOTAL COORDINATION)

We have distinguished the traditional authoritarian system from the fascist state. The latter emerges with the coming to power of a mass movement. The masses are won by means of manipulation and of force. Traditional authoritarian systems lack this aspect of mass mobilisation. They seek to exclude the masses, while fascist systems depend on popular acclamation.

Such acclamation and the support of the masses were not enough to satisfy the fascist state. Its ultimate aim was the total control of all aspects of social life. A totalitarian system is described by F. Neumann as involving 'the destruction of the line between state and society and the total politicisation of society by the device of the monopolistic party'.[50] The abolition of the political institutions of the liberal-democratic state is a necessary prelude.

Gleichschaltung (total coordination) in Germany meant that any institution, pressure group or social organisation in 'civil society' was to be deprived of its independence. All such groups would be destroyed if necessary, to prevent their survival as autonomous representatives of social interests. They would be replaced by associations structured and controlled by the Nazi party. In the political field that meant the prohibition of alternative parties and the end of *Länder* or federal autonomy. Socially, action was taken to abolish the trade unions. After 2 May 1933 they no longer existed. Their place was taken by the German Labour Front (DAF) completely under the control of the party. Those who expected the DAF to advance the interests of the working class were disappointed. The 'Law for the Ordering of National Labour' of 20 January 1934 put the DAF firmly in a subordinate position, and made no concessions to anti-capitalist aspirations within the party. By 1934/35 when the employment record or work book was introduced for all workers and employees, the Nazi state had obtained the complete control and direction of labour. No independent labour organisation was left.[51]

The same thing had happened in Italy some ten years earlier. We have already mentioned the suppression of the non-fascist unions under the corporatist system.

During 1923 the destruction of the non-Fascist unions continued.... The Fascist unions relied on the well-tried methods of intimidation. To the brutality of the squads there was now added state pressure: Prefects might confiscate the funds of a union or co-operative, or hand over their offices to the Fascist union.[52]

This process of total coordination was an essential feature of the fascist system, and was by no means restricted to the economic sphere. The attempt was made to control all aspects of social life. The chief instrument of such control was the party with its paramilitary forces. The fascist state did not shrink from intrusion into private life. A case in point was the racial legislation in the Third Reich—the Nuremberg Laws. Another instance was the attempted regulation of marital life: the demand for the production of a 'master race', in any case for the production of more children. In Italy a tax was imposed on the unmarried, and education from the earliest age was attuned to the requirements of a 'heroic life' in the service of Mussolini. The sphere of cultural production was also subjected to totalitarian control in Germany; so-called 'degenerate art' (Expressionism, Cubism, etc.) was not tolerated. Books by Jewish authors were burned.

A separate chapter would be required to deal adequately with the relationship of fascism and religion. In Italy, Mussolini had made his peace with the Vatican, and the Curia looked quite favourably on his regime because they saw in him the protagonist in the crusade against Bolshevism. A similar confidence in Hitler as crusader against the 'godless' Bolsheviks bolstered morale in Germany, particularly in the Catholic regions like Bavaria, and even more so in war-time. It compensated for the many grievances, government regimentation, food shortages, hard work and so on. More radical sections in the Nazi party rejected any compromise with the Church. As they resented the Jewish origin of Christianity they tried to replace it by a belief system more suitable for Aryan supermen. At times the party showed itself quite hostile to the Church, but then it had to reckon with protests from the side of the population. Kershaw reports a characteristic incident when *Gauleiter* Wagner (in his capacity as Minister of Education in Bavaria) ordered the removal of all crucifixes from schoolrooms. Resentment and angry protests grew strong. People complained that while a 'crusade against Bolsheviks' was on they had to suffer from 'Bolshevism' at home. In the end the Ministry capitulated and the crucifixes were restored.[53]

7. CONCLUSION

Many discussions use the term 'totalitarian' to describe the fascist state. Franz Neumann distinguishes five features characteristic of a totalitarian dictatorship. Such a system is different from an authoritarian state where, as has been shown, the important institutions are those of a traditional bureaucracy. It also means more than mere Caesaristic dictatorship such as Bonapartism, or populist Peronism in more modern times, for these leave the private sphere intact. Totalitarian dictatorship, on the other hand, attempts 'the total politicisation of society'.[54]

The five features Neumann considers essential are:

1. 'The transition from a state based upon the rule of law (the German *Rechtsstaat*) to a police state.' The latter term here refers to a system of arbitrary and unrestricted power.
2. 'The transition from the diffusion of power in liberal states to the concentration of power in the totalitarian regime', i.e. the rejection of pluralism.
3. The existence of a monopolistic party. While trying to control both state and society it performs the pseudo-democratic rituals to gain mass legitimation.
4. Society is 'totally permeated by political power'. As society loses all independence the individual becomes atomised and as such more easily subject to control and manipulation. What Neumann calls 'synchronisation' is but another word for *Gleichschaltung*.
5. Finally, a totalitarian society uses terror 'as a permanent threat against the individual'. The regime, of course, also uses propaganda and manipulation in order to obtain at least the appearance of legitimacy.

How then, from the point of view of the three theoretical perspectives which we have discussed, would fascism be interpreted and judged?

In the pluralist perspective a totalitarian society, of which the fascist state would be an instance, is seen as the antithesis of pluralism. It is a 'monist' or unitarian society as opposed to one characterised by the 'cross-cutting cleavages' and multiple group affiliations of pluralism. Instead of diffusing it concentrates power.

Some versions of pluralism use a 'mass society theory' to explain the rise of fascism. It is argued that group membership would constitute a barrier against fascism.[55] Fascism is seen as a movement which recruits those marginalised people who are not members of any group. People who are safely involved in one or preferably more sub-groups of the wider society will not be 'free-floating', and hence not available for mobilisation by an extremist demagogic leader. The antidote to totalitarianism is group membership.

The problem with this sort of explanation is that much of Nazi support did in fact come from people who were enrolled in pressure groups and associations of various kinds. The Nazis built up their power by infiltrating and taking over a range of pressure groups, notably those which organised the discontented middle strata of town and country.[56] Nevertheless, the pluralist perspective has the merit of emphasising as a central feature of fascism its destruction of group autonomy and its rejection of pluralist group competition.

The relationship of elite theory and fascism is more complicated. Elitism formed part of the fascist ideology. It was used to justify the anti-democratic stance of fascism. The Italian fascists adopted some of Pareto's ideas on the subject of elite circulation. They invoked the need for a vigorous new elite to replace a decadent bourgeois elite weakened by humanitarian ideas.[57] The new elite (by which they meant themselves) would use a combination of coercion and manipulation to win power. The limits of the elitist approach are to be found in the fact that the structural analysis of society is neglected, meaning the question *why* the fascist elite could come to replace the existing liberal-democratic elite.

For example, one could trace out the steps by which a part of the political elite of the Weimar Republic came to behave increasingly as a 'semi-loyal opposition'.[58] Such an explanation in terms of the errors of the ruling elite could well be accommodated within the parameters of elite theory. However, sufficient account is then not taken of the wider structural factors of an economic and social crisis, or the fear of a socialist revolution, that is to say, of all the elements which are indispensable for a proper understanding of the fascist phenomenon.

Explanations of a Marxist type are stronger, in so far as they reveal the economic and social factors contributing to the crisis out of which fascism emerged. The link between Marx's writings on Bonapartism and later Marxist analyses of fascism is that both seek to show how the property-owning classes were prepared to abandon parliamentary democracy in favour of a movement from which they expected protection against a socialist attack. It would be a simplistic and very crude version of such views to present fascism as nothing but the direct tool and instrument of capitalism. This error was not committed by subtler Marxist analyses, some of an early date.[59] These analyses rightly emphasise two crucial features: first, the mass character and the heterogeneous nature of the fascist movement; secondly, the way in which the fascist state subjected all classes to its rule, capitalists as well as workers, though it maintained the private ownership of society's productive resources, and in that sense it remained a capitalist state.

Finally, it should be said that while fascism has been discussed with almost exclusive reference to the cases of Italy and Germany in the inter-war period, it should not be seen as of purely historic and academic interest. Similar movements could arise where a liberal-democratic regime faces intractable economic and social problems under two conditions. The first condition is a mass base, though not necessarily of the petty bourgeoisie as was the case with 'classical' fascism. This mass base could be mobilised by a demagogic leader against some scapegoat or target which is blamed for poor social conditions like unemployment, or for economic failure and decline. The second condition is that there are moves towards a 'strong state' which gradually erodes democratic rights, strengthening the executive and repressive elements of the state at the expense of its representative and power-restraining elements.[60] The experience of the Weimar Republic shows how such erosion of democratic rights can weaken the legitimacy of the liberal-democratic order.

The conclusion is that fascism might remain a possibility in a liberal-democratic system whenever the above conditions are given. A mass-based authoritarianism with a totalitarian drive—which is what fascism is—could develop in contemporary democracies shaken by severe economic problems, like unemployment, which successive governments seem unable or unwilling to tackle. Such authoritarianism might use slogans and symbols quite different from those used by the fascist movements of the inter-war period. However, it seems that a powerful xenophobic nationalism is usually one element in such anti-democratic movements of the extreme Right. One may thus conclude that the fascist brand of authoritarianism is a possible outcome where liberal-democratic systems are in a situation of crisis, and where demagogic leaders stir up a mass movement through slogans, offering pseudo-solutions to social and economic problems.

NOTES

1. See S.P. Huntingdon and C.H. Moore, *Authoritarian Politics in the Modern World: the dynamics of established one-party systems* (Basic Books, New York and London, 1970); S.P. Huntingdon, *Political Order in Changing Societies* (Yale University Press, New Haven and London, 1968), p. 403 ff.
2. Franz Neumann, *The Democratic and the Authoritarian State* (The Free Press, New York, 1957), p. 249.
3. Neumann, *Democratic and Authoritarian State*, p. 235.
4. For discussion of these regimes, see Nicos Poulantzas, *The Crisis of the Dictatorships: Portugal, Greece, Spain* (New Left Books, London, 1976).
5. Huntingdon, *Political Order in Changing Societies*, p. 406.
6. See R. de Felice, *Fascism. An Informal Introduction to its Theory and Practice* (Transaction Books, New Brunswick, N.J., 1977), p. 55 ff.
7. P. Togliatti, 'The Contradictions of Fascism in Power', in David Beetham, *Marxists in Face of Fascism. Writings by Marxists on Fascism from the inter-war period* (Manchester University Press, Manchester, 1983), p. 138.
8. G. Zibordi, 'Towards a Definition of Fascism', in Beetham, *Marxists in Face of Fascism*, p. 88.
9. O. Bauer, 'Fascism', in T.B. Bottomore and P. Goode (eds.), *Austro-Marxism* (Clarendon Press, Oxford, 1978), pp. 167–86.
10. *Documents on Nazism, 1919–1945*, edited by Jeremy Noakes and Geoffrey Pridham (Jonathan Cape, London, 1974), p. 38. The programme also called for 'the abolition of incomes unearned by work'.
11. Nicos Poulantzas, *Fascism and Dictatorship. The Third International and*

the Problem of Fascism (New Left Books, London, 1974), pp. 310, 313.

12. B. Mussolini, 'The Doctrine of Fascism', in A. Lyttelton (ed.), *Italian Fascisms from Pareto to Gentile* (Jonathan Cape, London, 1973), p. 49.

13. Lyttelton (ed.), *Italian Fascisms*, p. 50.

14. J.J. Linz, *The Breakdown of Democratic Regimes: Crisis, Breakdown and Reequilibration* (Johns Hopkins University Press, Baltimore and London, 1978), p. 27 ff.

15. K.D. Bracher, *The German Dictatorship. The Origins, Structure and Effects of National Socialism* (Penguin, Harmondsworth, 1973), p. 290.

16. Ian Kershaw, *Popular Opinion and Political Dissent in the Third Reich: Bavaria 1933-1945* (Clarendon Press, Oxford, 1983), pp. 99 and 314.

17. Kershaw, *Popular Opinion in the Third Reich*, p. 276.

18. Lyttelton (ed.), *Italian Fascisms*, p. 12.

19. Mussolini, 'The Doctrine of Fascism', in Lyttelton (ed.), *Italian Fascisms*, p. 47.

20. J. Linz, 'Some Notes Toward a Comparative Study of Fascism in Sociological Historical Perspective', in W. Laqueur (ed.), *Fascism: A Reader's Guide. Analyses, Interpretations, Bibliography* (Penguin, Harmondsworth, 1979), p. 29.

21. A. Gramsci, 'On Fascism', in Beetham, *Marxists in Face of Fascism*, p. 84.

22. J. Linz, 'Notes Toward a Comparative Study of Fascism', in Laqueur (ed.), *Fascism: A Reader's Guide*, p. 29.

23. Georges Sorel, *Reflections on Violence* (Collier Books, New York, 1950), pp. 125 and 135.

24. Mussolini, 'Which Way is the World Going?', in Lyttelton (ed.), *Italian Fascisms*, p. 66.

25. Alfred Rosenberg, 'The Folkish (*Völkisch*) Idea of State', in B.M. Lane and L.J. Rupp (eds.), *Nazi Ideology before 1933, a documentation* (Manchester University Press, Manchester, 1978), p. 62.

26. A. Lyttelton, *The Seizure of Power. Fascism in Italy 1919-1929* (Weidenfeld and Nicolson, London, 1973), p. 177.

27. Martin Broszat, *The Hitler State. The foundation and development of the internal structure of the Third Reich* (Longman, London, 1981), p. 149.

28. Lyttelton, *Seizure of Power*, pp. 104-105.

29. Ibid., p. 309.

30. Bracher, *German Dictatorship*, pp. 266-7.

31. See Lyttelton, *Seizure of Power*, Chapter 10, for the Matteotti crisis; and Giuseppe Fiori, *Antonio Gramsci. Life of a Revolutionary* (New Left Books, London, 1970), p. 217 ff.

32. Trotsky, *The Struggle Against Fascism in Germany* (Penguin, Harmondsworth, 1975), p. 129.

33. Broszat, *Hitler State*, p. 72.

34. Ibid., p. 86.

35. Ibid., p. 90-1. On the ending of the parties in Germany, see E. Matthias and R. Morsey (eds.), *Das Ende der Parteien 1933* (Droste Verlag, Düsseldorf, 1960).

36. Broszat, *Hitler State*, p. 79.

37. Lyttelton, *Seizure of Power*, p. 269.
38. Ibid., pp. 288, and 293 for following quote.
39. Ibid., p. 277.
40. Lyttelton, 'Italian Fascism', in Laqueur (ed.), *Fascism, A Reader's Guide*, p. 95.
41. Broszat, *Hitler State*, p. 208.
42. Bracher, *German Dictatorship*, p. 292.
43. Broszat, *Hitler State*, p. 196.
44. Hans Mommsen, 'National Socialism: Continuity and Change', in Laqueur (ed.), *Fascism, A Reader's Guide*, p. 171.
45. Broszat, *Hitler State*, p. 204.
46. Ibid., p. 209.
47. Ibid., p. 258.
48. Lyttelton, *Seizure of Power*, p. 364.
49. Ibid., p. 409, for reference to Balilla. See also A.L. Unger, *The Totalitarian Party. Party and People in Nazi Germany and Soviet Russia* (Cambridge University Press, Cambridge, 1974), Chapter 6.
50. Neumann, *Democratic and Authoritarian State*, p. 245.
51. Broszat, *Hitler State*, p. 147-8.
52. Lyttelton, *Seizure of Power*, p. 231.
53. Kershaw, *Popular Opinion in the Third Reich*, pp. 340-57.
54. Neumann, *Democratic and Authoritarian State*, p. 244 f.
55. See, for example, W.A. Kornhauser, *The Politics of Mass Society* (Routledge, London, 1960).
56. Bracher, *German Dictatorship*, pp. 195 ff.
57. See, for example, the exchange of letters between Pareto and the Italian Nationalist Prezzolini, in Lyttelton (ed.), *Italian Fascisms*, pp. 129-33.
58. See J.J. Linz and A. Stepan (eds.), *The Breakdown of Democratic Regimes: Europe* (Johns Hopkins University Press, Baltimore and London, 1978), Chapter 2.
59. For instance the analyses of Zibordi and Togliatti, both in Beetham, *Marxists in Face of Fascism*.
60. See R. Miliband, *Capitalist Democracy in Britain* (Oxford University Press, Oxford, 1982), Chapter 6, for a discussion of this.

6 Conservative Perspectives on Politics and the State

1. THE POLITICS OF IMPERFECTION

This book is concerned with different theories of the nature and role of the state, and with the distribution of power in various types of political system. The final two chapters present two contrasting perspectives on the purpose of the state and on the nature of politics in general. Each of these perspectives—the conservative view and the anarchist view—leads to certain conclusions concerning the distribution of power as it is and as it ought to be. They each have implications for the nature and the limits of political action.

The best way to introduce conservative perspectives may be to start with the view of human nature which underlies them. This view has important implications for the conservative theory of politics. It has been called 'the politics of imperfection'.[1] In certain varieties this view has a religious basis, bound up with ideas of original sin. However, whether religious or not, the idea is that human beings will be unable to create social order through their own spontaneous efforts. Because of inherent qualities of greed and selfishness, people will need what Burke, the founder of the political theory of conservatism, called a 'power out of themselves' to restrain them.[2] This power is the state, the backbone of the social order and authority, the guarantor of a social hierarchy. The state plays a central role in conservative thought.[3] It is seen as the crucial institution necessary to prevent society from dissolving into disorder and chaos.

Furthermore, there are forms of inequality and privilege

216

which are viewed by conservative thinkers as ineradicable and necessary elements of any society. 'Inequality of function, role and power is as necessary to the social order as a whole as to the family.'[4] The forms of inequality may change, new types of wealth and power may emerge, but what remains constant is the fact of inequality and privilege as such. Without a hierarchical structure no society can survive. Anarchy will result from the vain attempt to achieve an egalitarian society; 'levelling' leads to disastrous consequences. This is the reason why state power is essential. In the traditional conservative perspective, social order is not, and can never be, achieved spontaneously by the free play of individual activities as is claimed by the defenders of the liberal and indeed also of the anarchist view. Social order has to be maintained through the strong leadership of those who hold positions of political responsibility. This is not to say that the state is the *only* agency which maintains social order. Conservatives stress the importance of tradition, custom, and of a network of long-standing groups and associations, all prerequisites of social order.

In the conservative view, therefore, the inherent imperfections of human nature make a 'strong state' necessary. It is needed to control the anti-social impulses of the individual. As Burke puts it:

Society requires not only that the passions of individuals should be subjected, but that even in the mass and body as well as in the individuals, the inclinations of men should frequently be thwarted, their will controlled, and their passions brought into subjection. This can only be done *by a power out of themselves*; and not, in the exercise of its function, subject to that will and to those passions which it is its office to bridle and subdue.[5]

This power, the state, is the lynchpin of social order. The idea of a 'strong state' is not meant to suggest that the conservative view, like the fascist view, aims at an all-powerful totalitarian state which is essentially arbitrary in its operation, knowing no legal or moral restraint. On the contrary, the conservative view of politics can equally be named 'the politics of tradition'. The state, and society in general, must operate with respect to traditions and customs, accepting such rights of the individual and of groups as are acknowledged in that particular society. The conservative perspective works within the limits of the given order, accepting what is, developing forms of political action within the structural framework of existing institutions. The revolutionary opposition to the institutions of the liberal-democratic state manifested by fascist movements and revealing an 'activist' character is quite different from the 'limited style of politics' characteristic of conservatism.[6] The latter seeks to preserve and develop existing institutions for the purpose of defending the 'natural' gradations of wealth and power. This means a defence of tradition and an emphasis on continuity. In this respect, as also in others, conservatism is fundamentally opposed to fascism.

2. TRADITION AND CONTINUITY

The state, then, is central to the conservative view of politics. First, it preserves the existing hierarchy, that system of inequalities which is inseparable from an ordered society. The task of defending that order need not rule out change altogether, although such change will be of an incremental and evolutionary type. As Karl Mannheim writes in his essay *Conservative Thought*, conservatism must be distinguished from an unthinking static traditionalism. The latter is defined by Mannheim as 'a tendency to cling to vegetative patterns, the old way of life...'[7] Conservative politics, on the other hand, has often involved changes which were seen as necessary for the preservation of the social order.

Second, the role of the state is seen as upholding tradition and continuity. These are key values in the conservative perspective. It has often been remarked that conservatism as an explicit theory of politics emerged as a reaction to the French Revolution.[8] It was the product of a particular moment in European history. In 1789 the existing order had been radically challenged. Liberals and democrats demanded the reconstruction of society, a reconstruction to be guided by universal rationally-based laws. The Revolution in which the privileges and age-old traditions of the *ancien régime* were swept away was the final outcome of the Enlightenment tradition. The conservative response was classically enunciated by Burke in his *Reflections on the French Revolution* of 1790. There he put forward a defence of the old order, exalting the values of tradition and historic continuity. Political institutions and social arrangements were valuable, Burke asserted, because they had lasted a long time. They encapsulated a fuller and higher wisdom than any rational individual could ever attain. Tradition was also a better guide to action and a more valid criterion for judging political institutions than were abstract general rules and theories which neglected customs, conventions and traditions.

Traditionalism found expression in Burke's defence of what he called 'prejudice and prescription'. 'We are afraid', he wrote, 'to put men to live and trade each on his own private stock of reason; because we suspect that this stock in each man is small, and that the individuals would do better to avail themselves of the general bank and capital of nations, and of ages.'[9]

As Nisbet explains, by 'prejudice' Burke meant 'a distillation of a whole way of knowing, of understanding, and of feeling; a way he saw as being in total contrast to the ways of thought which flourished in the French Enlightenment and then, momentously, in the Revolution.'[10] As against a radical rationalism, conservatives have always defended tradition as a better guide for human conduct. In their view the existing political system is seen as the product of past history and tradition. This means that it is worthy of defence and preservation. It continues the past and embodies a collective wisdom built up over generations.

Here again it is the state which preserves this continuity and acts in its defence. Thus acceptance of the institutional structure of the state becomes all the more important. Again in Burke's words:

By this unprincipled facility of changing the state as often, and as much, and in as many ways as there are floating fancies or fashions, the whole chain and continuity of the commonwealth would be broken. No one generation could link up with the other. Men would become little better than flies of the summer.[11]

The state, he continued, was 'a partnership in all science, a partnership in all art; a partnership in every virtue, and in all

perfection'. It was 'a partnership not only between those who
are living, but between those who are living, those who are
dead, and those who are to be born.'[12] The state, then, is not
only the basis of authority and hierarchy. It is the guarantor of
the cross-generational continuity which is the source of the
highest political wisdom and from which springs social order.

At the same time Burke recognised that society was a very
complex organism with many interdependent functions.
Therefore, 'it is with infinite caution that any man ought to
venture upon pulling down an edifice which has answered in
any tolerable degree for ages the common purposes of society,
or on building it up again, without having models and patterns
of approved utility before his eyes.'[13]

Abstract reason was not a suitable instrument to be used for
such tasks. This applied both to the reason of the individual
and the reason embodied in general declarations and maxims,
such as 'The Declaration of the Rights of Man and of the
Citizen' of 1789. The conservative idea of politics thus involves
an emphasis on 'the concrete', on circumstances, on what is
the case, facts seen as superior to theory and to abstract
principles and universal statements: 'One of the most essential
characteristics of this conservative way of life and thought
seems to be the way in which it clings to the immediate, the
actual, the *concrete*.'[14]

This distrust of rationalism has often been accompanied by
suspicion of the values of an individualism which was deemed
destructive of social cohesion.[15] Conservative thought
emphasises the social whole over and above the rights of
individuals. As Mannheim explains: 'The concept of the social
organism is developed by the conservatives to counter the
liberal-bourgeois belief in the universal applicability of all
political and social innovations.'[16] Each social organism has
its special characteristics and traditions. This also implies the
idea of a whole, or an aggregate, which is something more than
the sum of its parts. 'The state or nation is not to be
understood as the sum of its individual members, but the
individuals are to be understood only as parts of the wider
whole.'[17] Individual rights, therefore, must be subordinate to
the needs of the whole. This antithesis of individualism versus
the demands of the national whole has at times been expressed

very sharply, though not by Burke, but rather by late nineteenth-century politicians. They argued that if need be the rights of the individual must be sacrificed for the sake of the national institutions. For example, at the time of the Dreyfus affair in France anti-Dreyfusards like the writer Maurice Barrès declared that even if Dreyfus were innocent (which they doubted) the fact was of secondary importance to the need to maintain the prestige of the army, the latter being indispensable for national safety. In this case conservative thought assumed a specially intense and abrasive form.

3. INEQUALITY IN AN AGE OF DEMOCRACY

In conservative thought, then, the state holds society together. It represents the tradition and the continuities which have existed across generations. Equally important is the defence of inequality and privilege. The state secures the inegalitarian order which is the prerequisite for a stable society. This has been freely admitted by exponents of conservative perspectives, who have pointed out what they regard as the dangerous effects of equality. As is stated in a recent account of the theory and practice of British Conservatism: 'This is the essence of the Conservative Party's role—to formulate a policy that conserves a hierarchy of wealth and power and to make this intelligible and reasonable to a democracy.'[18] The same authors provide a definition of conservatism when they state that 'Conservatism may be deemed the intellectual justification of inequalities in society and the preservation of the privileges that such inequalities entail.'[19] This is indeed correct in so far as since Burke's *Reflections* conservative writers have set themselves against the challenge of democracy and egalitarianism which has dominated political life from the French Revolution onwards.

For Burke the chief enemy was egalitarianism with its twin aspects of democracy in the political sphere and the challenge to the rights of property in the social sphere. He denied the natural rights theory according to which everyone had an inherent right to a share 'of power, authority, and direction ... in the management of the state'.[20] As for property, Burke wrote that 'the characteristic essence of property, formed out of the combined principles of its acquisition and conservation, is to be *unequal*. The great masses therefore which excite envy, and tempt rapacity, must be put out of the possibility of danger.'[21] While he admitted that in the partnership of society 'all men have equal rights', those equal rights were not to equal things.[22]

The interesting question is how a political philosophy which set itself the task of opposing the sweeping challenge of egalitarianism has been able to mount such a successful resistance to it. Nisbet argues that 'There is an inexpugnable element of feudalism in the conservative theory of authority.'[23] Certainly, the underlying idea is of a God-given natural order, a 'Great Chain of Being' stretching from the lowest to the highest with each element 'knowing its place'. But how is it that such an assumption has survived in the modern world? An answer to the question involves an assessment of the conservative attitude to democracy.

Since Burke's day conservatives have insisted on the dangers of democracy and the threat which egalitarianism in the political field poses to the stability of society. It has also been a major theme of conservative thought that political affairs are best handled by an elite, an aristocracy well versed in and trained for the task of government. Politics, wrote Burke, was not an abstract science, but a matter of experience. It was one of his charges against the leaders of the Third Estate in France in 1789 that 'of any practical experience in the state, not one man was to be found. The best were only men of theory.'[24] Conservative thought joins with elite theory in its insistence on the need for an elite group of skilled political leaders. Democracy with its egalitarian tendencies is seen as threatening the formation of such an elite. Traditional conservatism stresses more than elite theory the stable character of the leading group. Yet both theories regard the running of society's affair by a small minority as a necessary condition of ordered social existence. Lord Salisbury makes the point: 'Every community has natural leaders to whom, if they are not misled by the insane passion for equality, they will instinctively defer.'[25] In his eyes political equality was not only folly, but a chimera or impossible fancy. Political leadership had to be exercised by an aristocracy, though Salisbury seemed to suggest that it need not always be an aristocracy of birth, but rather one of wealth and talent: 'Always wealth, in some countries birth, in all intellectual power and culture mark out the men to whom in a healthy state of feeling, a community looks to undertake its government.'[26] Similarly the English conservative, Lecky, wrote in *Democracy and Liberty* (1896) in an explicitly elitist vein: 'In every field of human enterprise, in all the competitions of life, by the inexorable law of Nature, superiority lies with the few and not with the many, and success can only be attained by placing the guiding and controlling power mainly in their hands.'[27]

Such views of a natural hierarchy, whether expressed by Burke or by later conservatives, led to obvious conclusions concerning the dangers of democracy. If a 'swinish multitude' (Burke) entered politics and gained the right to choose political leaders, the natural hierarchy would be overturned. The structure of wealth and privilege would be menaced; political democracy would lead to social levelling. The state would become the instrument of redistribution and spoilation. To quote once more Salisbury: 'Whenever democracy has prevailed, the power of the state has been used in some form or other to plunder the well-do-do classes for the benefit of the poor.' An extension of the suffrage would mean that 'two day labourers shall outvote Rothschild.' Salisbury realised the difficulty of beating back the tide of democratic advance; he suggested that the task of the Conservative Party was to

promote, more efficiently perhaps in opposition than in office, the great work of arresting the march of Democracy, until the lessons which America and France are teaching every year with increased force shall have exploded the delusion that, in the minds of so many, confounds democracy with freedom.[28]

We have previously quoted Pitt's argument against an extension of the franchise as well as the warnings of the Duke of Wellington and of Disraeli concerning the dangers inherent in democracy. Such an unenthusiastic attitude towards democracy is not absent from contemporary advocates of the conservative view. In a recent study of *The Meaning of Conservatism*, Roger Scruton writes: 'In politics, the conservative attitude seeks above all for government, and regards no citizen as possessed of a natural right that transcends his obligation to be ruled.' As for democracy, it 'corresponds neither to the natural nor to the supernatural yearnings of the normal citizen'; thus democracy 'can be discarded without detriment to the civil well-being as the conservative conceives it'.[29]

Given this attitude, the question posed above seems all the more urgent: how has such an anti-democratic set of ideas survived in the post-1789 age throughout two centuries of democratic pressure? Indeed, not only has conservatism survived, but it remains a most powerful force gaining support precisely through that universal suffrage which it initally suspected as subversive of the established order. Part of the answer lies in its adaptability, its rejection of abstract principles; in other words, in a strand of pragmatism that is an important part of the conservative way of life. Such pragmatism has been more strongly manifested in British than in Continental conservatism. It has inspired a willingness to make concessions and be flexible when some degree of change seemed unavoidable. One could cite Disraeli's extension of the suffrage in 1867 (the Second Reform Bill) and his concern with the 'elevation of the condition of the people' expressed in his famous Crystal Palace speech of 1872. This suggests a distinction between conservatism and an unthinking 'reactionism', the latter implying an insistence to preserve the existing order unchanged at all costs. The pragmatic flexibility of conservatism will be explained further with reference to conservative views of political change.

4. 'PIECEMEAL TINKERING' VERSUS 'HOLISTIC PLANNING'

Conservatism in theory and practice offers a critique of revolutionary change, and a defence of gradual pragmatic adjustment. Like many other conservative themes, this attitude too has its origin in Burke's writings. He castigated the revolutionaries of 1789 for their wish totally to remodel society on the basis of abstract theories. Instead, Burke argued, they should have built on what was already there and remedied the defects. 'Is it then true', Burke asked rhetorically, 'that the French government was such as to be incapable or undeserving of reform; so that it was of absolute necessity the whole fabric should be at once pulled down, and the area cleared for the erection of a theoretic experimental edifice in its place?'[30] The French system, he admitted, was not perfect, there were abuses which should have been remedied. Yet he accused the revolutionaries of acting as if they 'had never been moulded into civil society, and had everything to begin anew'.[31] Instead of a policy of piecemeal amelioration, they chose wholesale reconstruction which would lead to the disasters and horrors of a revolutionary movement. Thus in the conservative view, reform of particular defects is to be preferred to a change of the whole system. In Mannheim's words: 'Progressive reformism tends to tackle the system as a whole, while conservative reformism tackles particular details.'[32]

This is precisely what the philosopher Karl Popper recommends as 'piecemeal tinkering' in contrast to 'holistic planning' which he condemns. The latter, Popper argues, as it tries to remodel the whole of society all at once, remains helpless in the face of side-effects which every such reconstruction will inevitably produce. The proper 'scientific' method is rather one of trial and error where small faults can immediately be adjusted and errors of judgement remedied.[33] Accordingly the conservative critique asserts that revolutionary wholesale attempts at social transformation are doomed to failure. They will produce catastrophic results. The social order is complex, an organic whole, which is itself the product of a long process of historical evolution. Hence any proposed solutions, such as new constitutions based on abstract ideas, are inadequate. As Burke put it: 'The nature of man is intricate; the objects of society are of the greatest possible complexity; and therefore no simple disposition or direction of power can be suitable either to man's nature or to the quality of his affairs.'[34]

Another aspect of the conservative critique is derived from the fact that even a revolution cannot effect a complete break with the past. Every political action, revolutionary though it may be, takes place in a particular context with assumptions and institutions inherited from the past. The actors themselves are affected by that heritage; if they ignore the fact they do so at their peril. The implication is that the post-revolutionary era will still have some links with pre-revolutionary society. Such was de Tocqueville's argument in his study of *The Ancien Régime and the French Revolution*.[35] He showed how certain features like centralisation and authoritarianism survived the revolutionary turmoil. No completely new beginning was made. A case in point in modern times would be Lenin's awareness, shortly before his death, of the difficulties posed by bureaucratic traditions and a 'Great-Russian chauvinism' inherited from the old order. The Russian Revolution, like all previous revolutions, found it had to confront attitudes and problems deeply rooted in national traditions which could not be swept aside even after the capture of political power.

It could be said that in this recognition of the weight of the past lies one of the strengths of the conservative view of politics. It implies a realisation of the importance of history and the traditions of any particular society. These create a context and impose constraints on any kind of political action which aims at the radical transformation of society. Revolutionary transformation is rejected by conservatives in favour of preserving the framework of the existing order. This does not altogether preclude change. Indeed, the practice of conservative politics, particularly in Britain, shows many examples of conservative leaders taking the initiative to effect such changes. The purpose of the change is the preservation of an inegalitarian society. The price of the preservation is a degree of flexibility in response to what are seen as irreversible tendencies. So, for example, if Peel in 1846 had not prevailed on the Conservative Party (or at least a section of it) to acquiesce in the repeal of the Corn Laws, the party could not have made the adjustment from a predominantly agrarian society to an industrial one. It would have become politically irrelevant.[36] In this sense, Nigel Harris is right in his study of British Conservatism to argue that 'the political—as opposed to electoral—success of the party turns upon its ability to continue to recruit rising groups within society and represent them politically.'[37] The ability to recognise which are the most important interests in society at a particular time and hence to opt for the crucial changes is indeed vital. A further instance would be Disraeli's extension of the suffrage in 1867. Such a move, made despite his distrust of democracy, must be seen as taking the steam out of a potentially revolutionary demand for suffrage reform.

In the practice of conservative leadership, especially in the British case, two elements have been important: a form of state paternalism and the appeal to patriotism and to nationalist sentiments. The conservative tradition has not been at all averse to state action of a paternalistic kind, conceiving the state as an agency of social reform for the purpose of cementing social cohesion. This can also be seen in Britain in the acceptance during the period since 1945 of the welfare state by conservative leaders like Macmillan (the late Lord Stockton) and Butler. There has been no objection to state interference in order to mitigate discontent and prevent social grievances building up. Nowadays such an attitude is rather ascribed to the 'wet' element of the British Conservative Party.

Lord Hugh Cecil in his study of *Conservatism* (published in 1912) identified three factors basic to a conservative perspective:

1. Distrust of the unknown and love of the familiar.
2. Defence of Church and monarchy, based on a reverence for religion and for authority.
3. Imperialism, which he defined as 'a feeling for the greatness of the country and for that unity which makes it great'. He also observed that 'Conservatisim comes also to be identified with measures of social improvement designed to raise the condition of the poor.'[38]

It can thus be said that British conservatism has been flexible in securing social cohesion in two respects: first, with respect to the ruling group. It did not remain tied to the landed aristocracy, but adapted itself to changes in the economic structure of society. Secondly, British conservatism has also shown adaptability with respect to lower-class groups. In order to secure their loyalty it has at times made gestures to 'raise the condition of the poor' i.e. to take measures which preserve inequality all the more effectively by making concessions to those at the bottom of the hierarchy.

It should also be noted that the identification of the British Conservative party with the theme of 'one nation' and the emphasis on patriotic feelings have helped to strengthen its popular support. Both Disraeli and Cecil referred to imperialism as one basic element in conservatism. The idea that conservatives represent national unity as opposed to the divisive tendencies of the socialist class struggle has often been exploited in conservative ideology. Balfour, as Prime Minister, condemned the 'abominable creed' of class war. It prevented, he said, the cooperation which 'was and must be at the base of every species of success'.[39]

5. THE NEW RIGHT

Recent years have seen the emergence of a 'New Right' which differs in important respects from the conservatism we have tried to sketch out. Politically such a 'New Right' has found expression in Mrs Thatcher's government in 1979 and, in the USA, in the Presidency of Mr Reagan.

Traditional conservatism sees the state as the bastion of an established hierarchical order. It is somewhat distrustful of individual action which is suspect as potentially threatening social unity. The 'New Right', on the other hand, owes as much to liberal as to conservative traditions. It is averse to state interference, particularly in the economic sphere, and rather encourages individual efforts. The intellectual sources of such ideas are associated with the work of F.A. Hayek, the Austrian economist, who has long argued that any extension of the range of state activity is inimical to liberty. It makes the citizen subservient to an ever more powerful state, leading to a socialist collectivism along a *Road to Serfdom*—to quote the title of Hayek's most popular book. Two ideas are predominant in the theory and practice of the 'New Right': first, a free-market theory implying the 'rolling back' of the frontiers of the state. The second idea has sometimes been called 'authoritarian populism'.

The free-market theory is basically derived from the liberal tradition. It holds that the state impedes individual initiative, the only source of social prosperity. The danger, as Hayek points out, is of a state which interferes with the rights of individual persons and takes decisions which they should take for themselves: 'Thus the welfare state becomes a household state in which a paternalistic power controls most of the income of the community and allocates it to individuals in the form and quantities which it thinks they need or deserve.' This also implies reservations with respect to the welfare activities which the state undertakes. While Hayek concedes that people should be given 'security against severe physical privation, the assurance of a given minimum of sustenance for all', he strongly opposes 'the desire to use the power of government to ensure a more even or more just distribution of goods'.[40]

'Authoritarian populism', on the other hand—to use S. Hall's term—differs from the traditional conservative attitude which tried to prevent the involvement of the masses in politics. It means that a more direct appeal is now made to those same masses, taking into account their prejudices, for example, on trade unionism or immigration issues. Thereby a climate of opinion is created, favourable to conservative forces at the expense of the Left. In accordance with such an approach greater emphasis is laid on the role of the leader. On occasion patriotic feelings are roused to cover up internal divisions.[41]

If such are the chief differences between 'old' and 'new' Right in the theory and practical application of the conservative idea, there is yet a third theme which links the modern with the traditional version and which can be considered the major theme of conservatism in general. This is the theme of authority and power, both vested in a strong state, albeit in one operating under the rule of law. A recent exposition of conservative thought suggests: 'It is through an idea of authority that the conservative experiences the political world.' The power of the state is seen in Scruton's perspective as the crucial means for maintaining the 'life of the social organism'. The justification of that power is not that it achieves any particular end. Scruton seems to come near to saying it is sufficient justification that state power maintains a traditional existing system of authority and allegiance:

For the conservative, power will not be able to mask itself as subordinate to some clear justifying aim—it is not the means to 'social justice', or 'equality', or 'freedom'. It is power to command and coerce those who would otherwise reform or destroy, and its justification must be found within itself, in an idea of legitimacy or established right.

This appears to imply that the existing order, such as it is, must be defended by state action under all circumstances: 'Conservatism presupposes the existence of a social organism. Its politics is concerned with sustaining the life of that organism, through sickness and health, change and decay.'[42] The justification for this seems to be that the 'social organism' represents an accumulation of tradition and prejudice in the Burkean sense. The political conclusion of this modern conservative perspective comes close to proscribing any form of opposition as subversive: 'The conservative believes in the power of the state as necessary, and will seek to establish and enforce that power in the face of every influence that opposes it.' True, that power should be 'clothed in constitution, operating always through an adequate system of law', but it might be objected that the existence of an 'adequate system of law' is quite compatible with a system of repressive authority, such as in South Africa.[43]

In the same way as Burke defended the values of tradition, hierarchy and authority, Scruton as a modern-day conservative reiterates such views. Democracy cannot be the basis for the legitimacy of government: 'No conservative, then, is likely to think that democracy is an essential axiom of his politics.' Scruton correctly observes that Burke did not see 'total franchise' as a necessary part of the constitution, 'or as having anything to do with the legitimacy of rule'. For his part Scruton goes so far as to state: 'It is quite possible that even now the constitutional essence of our country would remain unaffected were the franchise to be confined to people of position, education, wealth or power—to those, in other words, with a self-conscious interest in the fortunes of the nation.' What he also defends, again in a way Burke would approve, is the need to resist the 'contagion of democracy' by having power invested in institutions like the House of Lords which are 'partially immune to democratic pressure'. Their autonomy 'has lent to British political life its admirable mixture of continuity and flux, so conserving national unity through decades of European unrest'.[44]

6. CONCLUSION

Given this area of agreement on the importance of state authority and its function of preserving the existing structure of society, the differences between the traditional and the 'New Right' versions of conservatism seem less substantial than might have appeared at first sight. The latter version arose, in Britain at least, in the context of a critical examination of the post-1945 welfare state. The critique included as one of its themes the activity of the state, particularly in its wealth-redistributing effects, small though these were. All this drew on liberal ideas. There are thus discernible differences of opinion between the two types of conservative thought on the merits of a free-market economy, which is treated much more favourably by contemporary conservative thought than by the traditional more 'organicist' type of conservatism. Even these differences, however, should not be exaggerated. As has been pointed out by commentators as different as Nisbet on the one hand and C.B. Macpherson on the other, Burke was 'an apostle of *laissez-faire*' (Nisbet); 'central to Burke's political theory were his bourgeois assumptions about the actual and desirable economic order' (Macpherson), assumptions chiefly set out in his text of 1795, *Thoughts and Details on Scarcity.* Freeman observes that 'Burke was committed to both extreme *laissez-faire* and extremely strict enforcement of law and order.'[45]

The distinctive strength of the conservative view is that it recognizes the importance of history, the weight of the past and its traditions conditioning the expectations and the conduct of people. This recognition is not the property of the conservative view alone, but there it is most clearly articulated. Emphasis is given to the fact that the present and the possibilities it opens up for action cannot be understood without reference to the past from which the present emerges.

The two central aspects of conservatism have been shown to be first, its critique of revolutionary change and its recommendation of limited reforms when unavoidable; second, its defence of authority and of a social hierarchy.

On the first point it may be suggested that the prescriptions for Burkean (or Popperian) piecemeal adjustments are not always applicable. Burke blamed the French revolutionaries for neglecting the remedy of gradual improvements. The historical fact is that reforms of the *ancien régime* were indeed often attempted (for the last time by the Swiss banker Necker shortly before the Revolution) but that these could not be successful until the class structure of French society was radically changed. As regards the authority of the state being used to maintain the stability of the existing system, the conservative argument seems often to become a defence of vested interest and privilege. The conservative view of politics fails to offer a convincing justification of an inegalitarian order to those who are at the bottom of the hierarchy and find themselves systematically excluded from effective involvement in the affairs of society.

How does the conservative view of politics fit into the three schemes of power we have been discussing?

A convincing case can be made that conservatism implies a form of pluralism. This is also the opinion of Nisbet who writes of a 'feudal-conservative structure of political authority' in Burke and other conservative thinkers. The individual is seen as rooted in a plurality of traditional authorities and groups. The monarchy, the Church, government, industry, would all constitute such groups. Conservative pluralism, however, would show a specific character in so far as the groups are set in a hierarchical order.[46]

Conservatism also shares some common ground with elite theory. Both emphasise an inherent inequality in society, and the inevitability of a leading elite. The conservative view tends rather to pay attention to a traditional elite whose members have acquired over generations a political knowledge which cannot be formulated in explicit rules.

Obviously conservatism stands in sharpest contrast to any form of socialism. This is partly a matter of *Weltanschauung*, fundamentally opposed ways of viewing the world, which as such is not the object of the present analysis. In a more technical sense it could be said that conservatism utterly rejects the 'constructivist' attitude of socialism. Traditional conservatism opposed the notion of a rational reconstruction of the whole social order. Some of the more liberalism-based forms of contemporary conservatism tend to accept the Hayekian model of a 'spontaneous social order', i.e. of society as a self-regulating system, though this seems incompatible with the traditional conservative emphasis on the state.[47] Marxists might reply to this by pointing out that Marx certainly was not a victim of the 'constructivist fallacy'. He did not submit (as the utopian socialists did) a rational plan 'from outside' for the improvement of society, nor enjoin what ought to be done. He merely believed he could analyse the tendencies in the existing order which, unless counteracted, would lead to certain developments and the emergence of a new form of society.

NOTES

1. See A. Quinton, *The Politics of Imperfection* (Faber, London, 1978); N. O'Sullivan, *Conservatism* (Dent, London, 1976).
2. Edmund Burke, *Reflections on the Revolution in France*, edited by C.C. O'Brien (Penguin Books, Harmondsworth, 1968), p. 151.
3. Thus the perspective on conservatism developed in this chapter differs from a recent statement of 'a conservative philosophy of politics', in which the author tells us in the introduction that 'The state is also omitted; I do not believe that it matters very much how we treat the word 'state' and what we believe the nature of the state to be.' Lincoln Allison, *Right Principles, A conservative philosophy of politics* (Blackwell, Oxford, 1984), p. 4.
4. Robert Nisbet, *Conservatism: Dream and Reality* (Open University Press, Milton Keynes, 1986), p. 51.
5. Burke, *Reflections*, p. 151 (italics in original).
6. O'Sullivan, *Conservatism*, pp. 12 ff.
7. Karl Mannheim, 'Conservative Thought', in *Essays on Sociology and Social Psychology* (Routledge and Kegan Paul, London, 1953), p. 95.
8. Nisbet, *Conservatism*, p. 1; Mannheim, 'Conservative Thought', p. 79.
9. Burke, *Reflections*, p. 183.
10. Nisbet, *Conservatism*, p. 29.
11. Burke, *Reflections*, p. 193.
12. Ibid., pp. 194–5.
13. Ibid., p. 152.
14. Mannheim, 'Conservative Thought', p. 102.
15. See S. Lukes, *Individualism* (Blackwell, Oxford, 1973), pp. 3 ff.

16. Mannheim, 'Conservative Thought', p. 118.
17. Mannheim, 'Conservative Thought', p. 118.
18. P. Norton and A. Aughey, *Conservatives and Conservatism* (Maurice Temple Smith, London, 1981), p. 47.
19. Norton and Aughey, *Conservatives and Conservatism*, p. 47.
20. Burke, *Reflections*, p. 150.
21. Ibid., p. 140.
22. Ibid., p. 150.
23. Nisbet, *Conservatism*, p. 35.
24. Burke, *Reflections*, p. 128.
25. P.S. Buck (ed.), *How Conservatives Think* (Pelican, Harmondsworth, 1975), p. 117.
26. Ibid.
27. Ibid., p. 94.
28. Ibid., pp. 104–6.
29. Roger Scruton, *The Meaning of Conservatism* (Penguin Books, Harmondsworth, 1980), p. 16.
30. Burke, *Reflections*, p. 230.
31. Ibid., p. 122.
32. Mannheim, 'Conservative Thought', p. 103.
33. Karl Popper, *The Poverty of Historicism* (Routledge & Kegan Paul, London, 1957).
34. Burke, *Reflections*, pp. 152–3.
35. A. de Tocqueville, *The Ancien Régime and the French Revolution*, translated by Stuart Gilbert (Collins, The Fontana Library, 1966), p. 61.
36. See Robert Blake, *The Conservative Party from Peel to Thatcher* (Fontana, London, 1985), Chapter II. On p. 57 Blake notes that the repeal of the Corn Laws 'was not a straight division of landed gentry against the rest. It was a division between those who considered that the retention of the Corn Laws was an essential bulwark of the order of society in which they believed and those who considered that the Irish famine and the Anti-Corn Law League had made retention even more dangerous to that order than abandonment.'
37. N. Harris, *Competition and the Corporate Society. British Conservatives, The State and Industry, 1945–1964* (Methuen, London, 1972), pp. 263–264.
38. Buck, *How Conservatives Think*, p. 131.
39. Ibid., p. 128.
40. F. Hayek, *The Constitution of Liberty* (Routledge and Kegan Paul, London, 1960), pp. 259–61.
41. S. Hall, in S. Hall and M. Jacques (eds.), *The Politics of Thatcherism* (Lawrence and Wishart, London, 1983), pp. 19–40.
42. Scruton, *Meaning of Conservatism*, pp. 19, 25.
43. Ibid., p. 33.
44. Ibid., pp. 54, 58.
45. Nisbet, *Conservatism*, p. 58; C.B. Macpherson, *Burke* (Oxford University Press, Oxford, 1980), p. 52; Michael Freeman, 'Edmund

Burke and the Sociology of Revolution', *Political Studies* XXV (4), December 1977, pp. 459–73, p. 464.

46. Nisbet, *Conservatism*, p. 48 ff.
47. John Gray, *Hayek on Liberty* (Basil Blackwell, Oxford, 1984), Chapter 2.

7 Anarchism

1. WHAT IS ANARCHISM?

With anarchism the individual human being becomes sovereign. The individual's sphere of freedom is not only inviolable, it is also unlimited. Anarchism is liberalism driven to its extreme. It is, in this crucial respect, instant Marxism: the state will not 'wither away'; it has to be abolished. Anarchism is 'the philosophy of a new social order based on liberty unrestricted by man-made law; the theory that all forms of government rest on violence, and are therefore wrong and harmful, as well as unnecessary.'[1]

Obviously the anarchist view stands in the sharpest possible contrast to the conservative attitude we have just been considering. It would still be quite wrong to think that it is compatible with any of the alternatives to conservatism. Socialism is equally condemned, as is democracy: 'What is called democracy and is alleged to be the government of the people by themselves is in fact the government of the people by elected rulers ...'[2]

The anarchist alternative, however, is not the Hobbesian state of nature of isolated individuals at war with each other. Anarchists start from the assumption that human beings are naturally social and cooperative. They are quite capable of creating a harmonious society which will maintain its own order. It is in fact the imposition of state authority which creates conflicts and antagonisms and so disturbs the harmonious development of society. As Bakunin writes: 'We are convinced that all the richness of the intellectual, moral and material development of man, just like his apparent independence—that all this is the product of life in society.'[3]

There is a considerable diversity of perspectives under the label of 'anarchism'. Indeed, it has been noted that there is no basic statement of principles to which all anarchists pay allegiance. This is held to be an advantage because it makes anarchism a free and open movement, undogmatic and therefore avoiding the exclusion or expulsion of dissidents. The French anarchist Sébastien Faure wrote: 'There is not, and cannot be, a libertarian creed or catechism.'[4] In the same vein Proudhon, often seen as the 'founder' of anarchism as an explicit doctrine, wrote: 'As for a system, I don't have one, and I explicitly reject the idea that I might have one.'[5] In a famous letter written to Marx in 1846 he proposed: 'Once we have abolished all *a priori* dogmatism, let us not think of indoctrinating the people in our turn.'[6]

The most important division within anarchist thought is between *individualist* and *collectivist* anarchists. The classical protagonist of the former is the German Max Stirner with his book *Der Einzige und sein Eigentum (The Ego and his Own)* where he proclaims his absolute and unrestricted right of action. The individual human being is the centre of his world. He has neither responsibility or any duty to God nor to the world. He is responsible for himself and to himself alone. '*Ich hab mein Sach' auf Nichts gestellt*,' declared Stirner ('I've set my cause on nothing'). He has been called 'the most existentialist of all past philosophers'.[7]

Some individualist American anarchists, like Benjamin Tucker (1854–1939), accept free-market ideas, seeing the market and free exchange as means of actualising their autonomy.[8] Starting from a radical Protestant background, Tucker came to deny the existence of God because that existence implied the principle of authority. While Tucker agitated for the improvement of workers' conditions, though rejecting strike action, he maintained that capitalism encouraged anarchist ideas. Every person should be an equal competitor in the marketplace. By contrast every activity of the state represented a crime against individual liberty.[9] In recent times 'anarcho-capitalists' recommend the market as an alternative to the state in so far as the market may provide protection of the individual's 'natural rights' (i.e. security of life and property) by some form of private insurance.[10] The discussion on such lines has been stimulated by Robert Nozick's book *Anarchy, State and Utopia* thought Nozick rather favours a 'minimal state' which, he argues, can be established without violating any person's rights.[11]

Our quotations in the present chapter, however, will be taken from anarchists of the collectivist kind. Such anarchists, like Bakunin, Kropotkin and Proudhon, emphasise human sociability, the capacity and desire of people to act in concert with one another in self-regulating groups, associations or cooperatives. Such decentralised units would form the basis of a future social order. Bakunin called himself an 'anti-authoritarian collectivist'. He wished the means of production to be owned collectively. There should be no individual capitalists, but neither should ownership of the means of production be placed in the hands of the state.

There can still be said to exist a common anarchist perspective shared by individualists and collectivists alike. The same Sébastien Faure who denied the existence of a libertarian creed offered a definition of a 'common characteristic' revealed by all anarchists. Their 'uniting point' was 'the negation of the principle of Authority in social organisations and the hatred of all constraints in institutions founded on that principle'. This led Faure to the conclusion that 'whoever denies Authority and fights against it is an Anarchist'.[12]

2. THE CRITIQUE OF THE STATE

The chief representative of that authority and power which encroach on the freedom of men and women is the state. The state deprives them of part of their property by taxation. It regulates behaviour. It forces people to kill or be killed in war. Its authority is as relentless as it is ubiquitous. It rules 'from above'. Besides, state power inevitably involves what the Russian anarchist Kropotkin called 'the concentration of many functions of the life of societies in the hands of a few'.[13] State power means minority rule:

In creating a highly complex state machine, and requiring practice to become acquainted with the mechanism, such a system leads to the formation of a class especially concerned with state management, which, using its acquired experience, begins to deceive the rest for its personal advantage.[14]

That governing class in turn obstructs what Bakunin demanded, namely 'the free organisation of the working masses from the bottom upwards'.[15]

Like Marx, anarchists see the state as a specialised apparatus of coercion standing over and above society, frustrating society's self-management. State power is domination in its own right; it controls society and smothers its initiative. As Marx said, the state chokes society. Unlike Marxists, however, anarchists reject the notion of a transitional state, the 'dictatorship of the proletariat'. State socialism would merely continue, in fact intensify, the tyranny of the state. In the anarchist view the state continually extends its grip and augments its power. This is a process evidenced by the whole development of modern history.

In his 1896 essay 'The State. Its Historic Role', Kropotkin offers a survey of the growth of state power. The picture presented shows the development of 'natural' self-regulating social units, villages, groups and communes, thwarted and suppressed by the intrusion of the state. In tribal society, 'the state was no more part of those tribes than it is of the society of bees or ants, or of our contemporaries the Patagonians and the Eskimos.' Tribal society gave way to a society based on the village commune; in turn there developed the communes or free cities of the Middle Ages. They represent Kropotkin's idea of a free society. Such a society was based on the principles of decentralisation and federation. 'In these cities, sheltered by their conquered liberties, inspired by the spirit of free agreement and of free initiative, a whole new civilisation grew up and flourished in a way unparalleled to this day.' Each city had its own freedom and inside each city were 'thousands of brotherhoods and guilds' governed by their own members. Communes or cities could federate or associate with each other as they saw fit. Group association and self-determination formed the basic principles of society.

The crucial point came when this free association of communes was menaced and eventually destroyed by the rise of the modern state. The state principles were centralisation and total sovereignty. The decentralised liberties of cities and guilds were no longer tolerated. The concept of 'subject' was introduced. Rule 'from above' took over from spontaneous self-regulation. The agents of this change were 'the new barbarians': the military chief, the Roman judge and the priest.

And in the shadow of this double indoctrination of the Roman jurist and the priest, the federalist spirit which had created the free commune, the spirit of initiative and free association, was dying out and giving place to the spirit of discipline and to pyramidal authoritarian organisation.[16]

The state now took the decisions. *Diktat* from above was substituted for rule from below.

Kropotkin's picture of medieval cities might appear somehow idealised but it illustrates a crucial point, which is that anarchists by no means underrate the importance of social order and of social organisations to sustain that order. Only the organisations must rest on a voluntary basis and all their members must actively participate in them.

'What anarchists do reject is the institutionalisation of organisation, the establishment of a special group of people whose function is to organise other people.'[17] This implies the rejection of the state and of its bureaucracy. The form of the state, whether it is monarchical or democratic, autocratic or constitutional, all this does not matter. Anarchists reject representation. As the French anarchist Elisée Reclus, writing at the time of the Paris Commune, put it: 'Whether he becomes an absolute monarch, a constitutional prince or simply an elected member endowed with a small portion of sovereignty, the candidate whom you elect to the throne or to the parliamentary seat will be your superior.'[18] All states are despotic; they further the interests not of the people but of a small group of power holders. The state, Kropotkin said, was 'an obstacle to the social revolution, the greatest hindrance to the birth of a society based on equality and liberty, as well as the historic means designed to prevent their blossoming'.[19]

In place of a society dominated by the state anarchists have offered a wide variety of pictures illustrating the future society. Here too certain basic themes seem to be common. Freed from the grip of the state, society will be able to organise itself. It will be run on decentralised lines and the constituent groups will be sufficiently small to allow individual participation. Anarchists recommend federalism, meaning that local or occupational groups associate with other groups in a free federation. Such a bond would not impair the autonomy of the basic units.

A recent account of this subject points out that stateless societies have indeed existed for thousands of years in prehistoric, and some also in historic, times. They all were able to preserve social order without resorting to a concentration of force.[20] Amongst the means they employed, which might still be considered available in an ideal anarchy, were 'reciprocity' (i.e. arrangements for mutual aid and the sharing of goods or services) and signs of approval or disapproval, the latter evoking feelings of guilt or shame. In order to be effective, all these and similar social controls require a true 'community' which in turn can only be established within small societies. States, by their centralising activities, undermine community: they absorb or destroy stateless societies. The fact 'inspires little optimism about the viability of anarchy in a crowded world and even less optimism about the prospects for the emergence and durability of an anarchy set in a sea of states.'[21]

Within classical anarchism a more optimistic prognosis was indeed made by Proudhon (1809–65). Proudhon is well known, like Bakunin, because of Marx's quarrels with him, but he is an important thinker in his own right. In the course of the 1848 revolution Proudhon was a member of the Constituent Assembly. The experience seems to have been rather disillusioning, though after June 1848 he was extremely popular with the workers.[22] Proudhon's chief concern was justice of which social justice was an essential aspect.[23] He also believed in the progress of humanity, a progress running through three stages of which the first was a primitive communism, the second the age of private property, the third and final stage an age of 'liberty'. At that final stage society would be organised on 'mutualist' lines. 'Mutualism' was one of Proudhon's basic ideas. He defined 'the regime of mutuality' as involving and constituting 'economic right', or as he put it, 'the application of justice to political economy'.[24] Such justice, broadly speaking, implied that the workers and producing classes should get out of society what they had put in and contributed through their labour. In terms of organisation, society would be composed of workers' associations or cooperatives. Within each mutualist association the workers would be joint owners of the productive apparatus and entitled to a share in its product. Each mutualist cooperative would exchange its products with other cooperatives. In that way a centralised state would become redundant. Within the cooperative the workers were co-owners. They would develop their skills and educate themselves; the mutualist society would be an association of producers. The aim as Proudhon saw it was to 'make the worker joint owner of the industrial machine and share in its profits instead of being chained to it like a slave'.[25]

Proudhon's solution to the problem of social organisation was thus a form of workers' control which would achieve the aim of social justice. It would not be a state collectivist or governmental organisation. Proudhon insisted that the associated workers had no need of a state: 'We want no more government of man by man any more than we want the exploitation of man by man,' he wrote; 'socialism is the opposite of governmentalism.'[26] The mines, canals and railways should be handed over to workers' associations. These should work on their own responsibility to form 'a vast federation of associations united in the common bond of the democratic and social republic'.[27] In a similar vein Bakunin wrote:

The future social organisation must be made solely from the bottom upwards, by the free association or federation of workers, firstly in their unions, then in the communes, regions, nations, and finally in a great federation, international and universal. Then alone will be realised the true and life-giving order of freedom and the common good...[28]

Nevertheless, Proudhon's views and similar anarchist ideas must be assessed in terms of the contemporary critique which we have outlined above. It would then appear that the particular cooperatives could well develop into true 'communities' which as such would need no state interference. The position, however, is different with respect to the interrelations of those cooperatives (or associations) and even more so with respect to wider societies whether they are called a federation or a social republic. These comprehensive units would in turn require social controls and, consequently, an agency to maintain the controls. Such an agency would, to all intents and purposes, be the equivalent of a state. It could not be provided in terms of the anarchist perspective and it seems to follow that with all due respect we shall have to find a place for the anarchist proposal in the realm of utopia.

On the other hand, the anarchist view of a free society may, in a first approximation, remind us of Marx's idea of a post-revolutionary society for which, as we have mentioned, he took the constitution of the Paris Commune as a model. Ultimately, however, the anarchist longing and the vision which inspired Marx coincide on a still higher level when, as the latter hoped and predicted, humanity will have reached a higher degree of intellectual and moral perfection.

The immediate question that arises here is the relationship of anarchism and Marxism, that is to say, the question whether anarchists can regard the Marxist revolution as a suitable route towards their own goal.

3. ANARCHISM AND REVOLUTION

Anarchists stood in line with socialists in the revolutionary struggles of the nineteenth century. Bakunin (1814–76) took part in the 1848 revolution in Germany. He was in France in 1870 when after the catastrophic defeat of the army at Sedan the Republic was proclaimed. His Social-Democratic Alliance was affiliated to the First International, but the cooperation came to an end when Bakunin was expelled from the International at the Hague Congress in 1872. The break was the final result of a long-standing quarrel with Marx, but behind the clash of personalities loomed the irreconcilable conflict of anarchist and Marxist attitudes to the state and to the question of organisation in general.[29]

An important point in the anarchist view has always been the idea that the means used to produce social change will affect the end. A libertarian society cannot be produced by an authoritarian organisation. Hence follows the rejection by anarchists of the Marxist emphasis on political parties as necessary elements in the revolutionary process. Anarchists exalt spontaneous mass action; they are critical of what they regard as an elitist and authoritarian organisation. They are hostile to political parties, whether these are of the Leninist vanguard type or social-democratic mass parties. The latter in any case are condemned as top-heavy and bureaucratic.

Such principles determined the political means which could, and should, be used for the transformation of society. The anarchist emphasis was on spontaneity. Participation in state institutions, including electoral activity where that was possible in democratic states, was refused. Anarchists called for 'abstentionism', which meant rejection of the vote and of party politics. Participation, it was argued , would seem to legitimise the system and help to perpetuate it. Besides, representation necessarily created a gap between the representatives and the masses who had elected them and who would come to be dominated by them. In the already quoted letter of Elisée Reclus to a fellow anarchist, Jean Grave, three points are made urging people not to vote: to vote means to abdicate one's sovereignty, to be duped by legislators who pretend to be omniscient, and finally to be betrayed by them as they are sure to be corrupted in the dishonest atmosphere of parliamentary assemblies.[30]

All these anarchist arguments contradict the Marxist view that organisation and political action are essential stages in the revolutionary struggle of the working class. The most acrimonious dispute, however, arose over the question of the state and state power. It will be remembered that Marx assumed that a transitional state (called 'the dictatorship of the proletariat') would emerge as the result of the socialist revolution. The workers would have to capture political power in order to start the advance towards a communist society. Only gradually would the state 'wither away'. This was enough for the anarchists to stigmatise the Marxists as 'statists'. 'The modern radical,' wrote Kropotkin, 'is a centralist, statist and rabid Jacobin. And the socialists fall in step.' The anarchists' hope was 'the destruction of the state, and new life starting again in thousands of centres on the principle of the lively initiative of the individual and groups and that of free agreement'.[31] The argument was that it would be impossible to use the state and the capture of state power as means for the creation of a libertarian society. Both Proudhon and Bakunin accused the communists of wishing to take over the state, not to destroy it. For Proudhon communism meant 'oppression and slavery'. True, by communists he meant the supporters of Louis Blanc rather than those of Marx. 'They take everything back to the sovereignty of the people, to the right of the collectivity,' Proudhon wrote, 'their notion of power or of the state is absolutely the same as that of their former masters.'[32]

Bakunin's criticism of Marx has already been mentioned in the course of the analysis of the Marxist theory of the state. Bakunin made a distinction between 'revolutionary socialists or collectivists' (by which, in this context, he meant anarchists) and 'the authoritarian communists who are supporters of the absolute power of the state' (i.e. Marxists). Both wanted 'a new social order based solely on the organisation of collective work'.[33] Bakunin, however, envisaged not only a different strategy of revolution. He had in mind a different 'line-up' of revolutionary forces, going well beyond the industrial working class which Marx and his followers considered the main agent of revolutionary change. In general, anarchists have looked at groups sympathetic to social change in a different way from Marx. It has been the oppressed, the dispossessed, all those with nothing to lose, who have been regarded by the anarchists as the agents of libertarian change. The gist of Bakunin's argument was that the communist revolution, as Marx anticipated it, would result in the dictatorship of the working class over the rest of society. This dictatorship would not be exercised by the class as such, but by individual intellectuals or by workers who had ceased to be workers on becoming professional rulers. They 'would then come to regard the whole blue-collared world from governmental heights, and would not represent the people but themselves.... Anyone who does not see this does not know anything about human nature.'[34]

Both Proudhon and Bakunin also accused Marx of trying to create an over-centralised revolutionary movement. Marx, they said, had tried to increase the power of the General Council of the First International, reducing the autonomy of the constituent sections, in order to secure the dominating influence of his supporters. So there could be no peace between the 'authoritarian' Marxists and the true 'anti-authoritarian collectivists', i.e. the anarchists. As far as the main argument goes, Marxists, of course, could reply that such a small-scale decentralised economy as the anarchists had in mind would only be appropriate at a low level of production. Advanced production, which socialism needed as the heir to capitalism, would require planning and centralised coordination. Engels argued to that effect in his short piece *On Authority*: 'Wanting to abolish authority in large-scale industry is tantamount to wanting to abolish industry itself, to destroy the power loom in order to return to the spinning wheel.'[35]

This still does not refute the anarchists' claim that the 'dictatorship of the proletariat' might turn out to be more than a temporary phenomenon. Once a structure of power and authority has been established, those filling its leading positions will be reluctant to abandon them. This may in fact remind us of the elitist argument. Or, as David Miller puts the case of the anarchists: the Marxists 'fail to see that political systems have their own dynamics which allow them to escape from the control of any economic class, however powerful.'[36] The danger which the anarchists identify as 'statism' is that the socialist project may lead, indeed in the anarchist opinion *will* lead, to an inflation and extension of state power, and to the overriding of individual rights for the sake of collective goods. In this sense, that is as a warning, Anthony Arblaster may be right in saying that 'the anarchist contribution is, knowing what we do of the history of socialism in this century, quite simply indispensable.'[37]

Returning to the topic of means and ends, a modern anarchist may be called as witness. Emma Goldman, in her critique of the Russian Revolution, clearly expressed the principle of 'prefiguration', i.e. that the means that are used prefigure or anticipate the final result. She claimed that the Bolsheviks adhered to the principle that 'the end justifies all means'. Against that she wrote:

All human experience teaches that methods and means cannot be separated from the ultimate aim. The means employed become, through individual habit and social practice, part and parcel of the final purpose; they influence it, modify it, and presently the aims and means become identical.

She concluded: 'No revolution can ever succeed as a factor of liberation unless the *Means* used to further it be identical in spirit and tendency with the *Purposes* to be achieved.'[38]

There remains the question: How do anarchists imagine that the transformation of society which they do so ardently desire could ever happen? They repudiate the political road, if by 'political' is meant the activity of political parties, participation in elections and representative assemblies. There are many answers then to the above question, but no unified plan of action emerges. In classical anarchist theory there should in fact be no plan because everything is expected from the spontaneous action of the masses. 'We are convinced that revolution is only sincere, honest and real, in the hands of the masses,' wrote Bakunin.[39] Social action of the people themselves, organised non-hierarchically in groups, associations or syndicalist trade unions, such is the method recommended to arrive at a libertarian society.

Where an autocracy pushed oppression to its extreme and the hoplessness of the political situation drove people to despair, as happened in pre-revolutionary Russia, anarchists resorted to individual acts of terrorism and assassination, sometimes known as 'propaganda by the deed'. Such tactics were also tried by some anarchists in France from 1892 to 1894. These were vain efforts which could lead nowhere. Even more futile is a terrorism of more recent date which in fact misuses the anarchist label in so far as its revolt is not directed so much against the state but rather against society.

Today it could be said that the true protagonists of anarchist ideas are peaceful people. They no longer make bombs nor do they incite the masses. Their weapons are those of rational argument, attempts at persuasion, education and propaganda. Where possible, they want to set an example by 'direct action'. But such action does not involve acts of violence or of destruction. It rather is a sort of private action performed in small groups or voluntary associations without the mediation of official institutions. It is action in the social, not in the political, field. The idea is to show what can be done, even in a small way, outside state control and state power. Anarchists know they will have to wait a long time for the application of their ideas on a larger scale.

4. CONCLUSIONS

We can find no reason to modify the statement that anarchist theory contains utopian elements and is of little relevance to the practice of everyday politics. It does not follow, however, that anarchism is altogether an insignificant phenomenon. It is in fact important both from a practical and theoretical point of view.

We started our investigations with the thesis that the state is a coercive institution which has a monopoly of the legitimate use of force. It is a matter of practical experience to notice how its authority is often stretched beyond its legitimate limits. Beyond its task of maintaining a social order the state imposes controls and restrictions on society either arbitrarily or bureaucratically. For Kropotkin the state was an institution which worked 'to shackle the development of local and individual initiative, to crush existing liberties, to prevent their new blossoming'.[40] By contrast, once freed from the state 'local and individual initiative' would flourish. It could of course be objected that some power would be needed to deal with anti-social elements. The anarchist claim is that social groups would be able to deal with these and similar problems without employing any state power. Yet might not their *social* controls become just as oppressive as any *state* controls? As Miller observes: 'The anarchist idea of moral self-regulation' through 'informally arranged arbitration and discipline' may have certain disadvantages compared with settling disputes through a state system of centralised legal regulation. Decisions may be arbitrary and there might originate a 'tyranny of the majority' more stifling than a system of impersonal legal rules.[41]

Nevertheless, the anarchist perspective functions as a corrective and it contains a warning against the misuse of political power. It criticises state power and exposes the tendency of any state system to perpetuate itself. It emphasises the fact that the power-holders will always try to maintain their power. It urges people to look out for 'libertarian' alternatives of participatory activities independent of the centralised state system. Anarchists also, though they are not alone in this respect, have pointed out the possibly corrupting and debilitating effects of parliamentary as well as of bureaucratic party politics.

The anarchist critique is especially relevant with respect to socialist ideas and projects, and it should be heeded by Marxists. The charge is that Marxists rather want to take over the state while anarchists, in Bakunin's words, 'do not accept, even in the process of revolutionary transition, either constituent assemblies, provisional governments or so-called revolutionary dictatorships'.[42] Marxists may rightly reply that the literal acceptance of such a prescription would condemn them to political sterility, a fate that actually has befallen the anarchists. However, the danger of an omnipotent socialist state exists and has been evidenced by the evolution of the Russian Soviet Republic. This, of course, is not to say that the danger is unavoidable nor that the evolution of the Russian state is completed.

In this sense, if merely as a permanent corrective, we may appreciate Herbert Read's writing of the 'necessity of anarchism'. Anarchism, he observed, is no longer the anarchism of Bakunin and Kropotkin: 'Since Kropotkin's time anarchism has evolved to meet modern conditions and as practical politics is known as syndicalism.'[43] In fact, since the distant days of pre-1914 French syndicalism and the CNT in the Spanish Civil War, libertarian ideas have emerged again, for example, in the student revolt and the 'Events' of May 1968 in France. Hobsbawm too notices their revival and he finds 'two powerful reasons which explain the vogue for anarchism: the crisis of the world communist movement after Stalin's death and the rise of revolutionary discontent among students and intellectuals ...'[44]

'Anarchism has valuable lessons to teach,' Hobsbawm adds, because it has—in practice rather than in theory—been unusually sensitive to the spontaneous elements in mass movements.'[45] Beyond its permanent critique of all state systems and all power-holders, anarchism offers an inspiring vision of a true community of men and women in a free society, but it also brings into focus some important problems concerning democracy and the idea of democratic freedom. It may make us think of the curtailment of our freedom of action even in a democratic society, of the ultimate justification of the majority principle and of the rights that remain to the defeated minority. Robert Paul Wolff writing *In Defence of Anarchism* has summarised these problems well though their discussion goes beyond the scope of the present book.[46]

NOTES

1. Emma Goldman, quoted in *Reinventing Anarchy*, edited by Howard J. Ehrlich *et al.* (Routledge and Kegan Paul, London, 1979), p. 29.
2. Ibid., p. 45.
3. M. Bakunin, 'The Paris Commune and the Idea of the State', in Michael Bakunin, *Selected Writings*, edited and introduced by Arthur Lehning (Jonathan Cape, London, 1973), p. 208.
4. Sébastien Faure, *Encyclopédie anarchiste* (n.d.), in George Woodcock (ed.), *The Anarchist Reader* (Fontana, London, 1977), p. 62.
5. P.J. Proudhon, *Oeuvres choisis* (ed. Jean Bancal) (Gallimard, Collection Idées, Paris, 1967), p. 46.
6. Ibid., p. 89.
7. Herbert Read, *Anarchy and Order* (Souvenir Press, London, 1974), p. 165. On Stirner, see M. Stirner, *The Ego and His Own*, translated by S.T. Byington (Jonathan Cape, London, 1921); and R.W.K. Paterson, *The Nihilistic Egoist: Max Stirner* (Oxford University Press, Oxford, 1971).
8. On individualist anarchism in general, see Chapter 3 of David Miller, *Anarchism* (Dent, London, 1984).
9. On Benjamin Tucker see David DeLeon, *The American as Anarchist* (Johns Hopkins University Press, Baltimore and London, 1978), pp. 68–76.
10. Michael Taylor, *Community, Anarchy and Liberty* (Cambridge University Press, Cambridge, 1982), p. 59.
11. Robert Nozick, *Anarchy, State and Utopia* (Blackwell, Oxford, 1974).
12. Faure, in Woodcock (ed.), *Anarchist Reader*, p. 62.
13. Kropotkin, *The State, its Historic Role*, in P.A. Kropotkin, *Selected Writings on Anarchism and Revolution*, edited by Martin Miller (MIT Press, Massachusetts, 1970), p. 213.
14. Kropotkin, 'Must we occupy ourselves with an examination of the ideal of a future system?' (1873), in *Selected Writings*, ed. Miller, p. 61.
15. Bakunin, 'On Marx and Marxism', in *Selected Writings*, p. 270.

16. Kropotkin, *The State, its Historic Role*, in *Selected Writings*, ed. Miller, pp. 218, 233, 241.
17. *Reinventing Anarchy*, p. 48.
18. Elisée Reclus, letter to Jean Grave, 26 September 1885 (published in *Le Révolté*, 11 October 1885), in Elisée Reclus, *Correspondance*, 3 Vols. (Paris, 1911–25), Vol. II, p. 364.
19. Kropotkin, *The State, its Historic Role*, in *Selected Writings*, ed. Miller, p. 221.
20. Taylor, *Community, Anarchy and Liberty*, Chapter 2.
21. Ibid., p. 139.
22. See R.L. Hoffman, *Revolutionary Justice: the Social and Political Theory of P.-J. Proudhon* (University of Illinois Press, Urbana, 1972), p. 137; John Plamenatz, *The Revolutionary Movement in France, 1815–1871* (Longman, London, 1952), pp. 89–90.
23. One of his main works was *De la Justice dans la Révolution et dans l'Église* (4 vols, 1858). Proudhon is best known as the author of *What is Property?* (1840–41), where the answer provided was that property is theft. It should be noted, however, that Proudhon did not mean this to apply to a person's private possessions, but to the opportunity property gave to that person to exploit other people's labour and gain the fruits thereof.
24. Proudhon, *Oeuvres choisis*, p. 103.
25. Ibid., p. 113.
26. Ibid., p. 120.
27. Ibid., p. 120.
28. Bakunin, 'Paris Commune and the Idea of the State', in *Selected Writings*, p. 206.
29. For an account of the clash and the history of the First International, see G.D.H. Cole, *A History of Socialist Thought*, Vol. II: *Marxism and Anarchism, 1850–1890* (Macmillan, London, 1954). On Bakunin, see Aileen Kelly, *Mikhail Bakunin. A Study in the Psychology and Politics of Utopianism* (Clarendon Press, Oxford, 1982).
30. Elisée Reclus, *Correspondance*, Vol. II, pp. 364–6.
31. Kropotkin, *The State, its Historic Role*, in *Selected Writings*, ed. Miller, p. 264.
32. Proudhon, *De la capacité politique des classes ouvrières*, introduction by M. Leroy (Marcel Rivière, Paris, 1924), p. 113.
33. Bakunin, 'Paris Commune and the Idea of the State', in *Selected Writings*, p. 197.
34. Bakunin, 'On Marx and Marxism', in *Selected Writings*, p. 269.
35. F. Engels, 'On Authority', in K. Marx and F. Engels, *Selected Works*, 3 vols (Progress Publishers, Moscow, 1973), Vol. 2, p. 377.
36. Miller, *Anarchism*, p. 82.
37. Anthony Arblaster, 'The Relevance of Anarchism', in *The Socialist Register 1971*, edited by R. Miliband and J. Saville, p. 182.
38. Emma Goldman, *My Further Disillusionment with Russia* (1924), in Woodcock (ed.), *The Anarchist Reader*, pp. 160–1.
39. Bakunin, 'On Marx and Marxism', in *Selected Writings*, p. 237.

40. Kropotkin, *The State, its Historic Role*, in *Selected Writings*, ed. Miller, p. 259.
41. Miller, *Anarchism*, pp. 173–9.
42. Bakunin, 'On Marx and Marxism', in *Selected Writings*, p. 237.
43. Herbert Read, 'The Necessity of Anarchism', in Herbert Read, p. 99.
44. E.J. Hobsbawm, *Revolutionaries* (Weidenfeld and Nicolson, London, 1973), p. 84.
45. Ibid., p. 89.
46. Robert Paul Wolff, *In Defense of Anarchism* (Harper and Row, New York, 1970).

Bibliography

Albertoni, E.A., *Gaetano Mosca. Storia di una dottrina politica. Formazione e interpretazione* (Giuffrè, Milan, 1978).

Albertoni, E.A. (ed.), *Studies on the Political Thought of Gaetano Mosca* (Giuffrè, Milan, 1982).

Ali, T. (ed.), *The Stalinist Legacy. Its Impact on Twentieth-Century Politics* (Penguin, Harmondsworth, 1984).

Allison, L. *Right Principles. A conservative philosophy of politics* (Blackwell, Oxford, 1984).

Anderson, P. *Considerations on Western Marxism* (New Left Books, London, 1976).

Arblaster, A. 'The Relevance of Anarchism'. *The Socialist Register 1971*, edited by R. Miliband and J. Saville (Merlin, London, 1971).

Arblaster, A. *The Rise and D.·cline of Western Liberalism* (Blackwell, Oxford, 1984).

Aron, R. *Progress and Disillusion* (Penguin, Harmondsworth, 1972).

Avineri, S. *The Social and Political Thought of Karl Marx* (Cambridge University Press, Cambridge, 1986).

Bachrach, P. *The Theory of Democratic Elitism. A Critique* (University of London Press, London, 1969).

Bachrach, P. and Baratz, M.S. *Power and Poverty. Theory and Practice* (Oxford University Press, New York, 1970).

Bagehot, W. *The English Constitution* (Introduction by R.H.S. Crossman) (Collins, The Fontana Library, 1963).

Bahro, R. *The Alternative in Eastern Europe* (New Left Books, London, 1978).

Bakunin, M. *Selected Writings* (ed. A. Lehning) (Jonathan Cape, London, 1973).

Beetham, D. 'Beyond Liberal Democracy'. *The Socialist Register 1981*, edited by R. Miliband and J. Saville (Merlin, London, 1981) pp. 190–206.

Beetham, D. 'From Socialism to Fascism: The Relation Between Theory and Practice in the Work of Robert Michels'. *Political Studies* XXV (1977), pp. 3–24, 161–81.

Beetham, D. *Marxists in Face of Fascism* (Manchester University Press, Manchester, 1983).

Beetham, D. *Max Weber and the Theory of Modern Politics* (2nd edition) (Polity Press, Cambridge, 1985).

Beetham, D. 'Michels and his critics'. *European Journal of Sociology* XXII (1981), pp. 81–99.

Bellis, P. *Marxism and the USSR: the theory of proletarian dictatorship and the Marxist analysis of Soviet society* (Macmillan, London, 1979).

Berger, S. (ed.) *Organizing Interests in Western Europe* (Cambridge University Press, Cambridge, 1981).

Berlin, I. *Four Essays on Liberty* (Oxford University Press, Oxford, 1969).

von Beyme, K. *Political Parties in Western Democracies* (Gower, Aldershot, 1985).

Birnbaum, P. *Les Sommets de l'état* (Seuil, Paris, 1977) (English translation: *The Heights of Power. An essay on the power elite in France*. University of Chicago Press, Chicago, 1982.)

Blackburn, R. (ed.) *Ideology in Social Science* (Fontana/Collins, London, 1972).

Blackburn, R. *Revolution and Class Struggle. A Reader in Marxist Politics* (Fontana, 1977).

Blake, R. *The Conservative Party from Peel to Thatcher* (Fontana Press, London, 1985).

Bottomore, T. and Goode, P. (eds.) *Austro-Marxism* (Clarendon Press, Oxford, 1978).

Bottomore, T.B. *Elites and Society* (Penguin, Harmondsworth, 1966).

Bottomore, T.B. *Political Sociology* (Hutchinson, London, 1979).

Bracher, K.D. *The German Dictatorship. The Origins, Structure and Effects of National Socialism* (Penguin, Harmondsworth, 1973).

Broszat, M. *The Hitler State* (Longman, London and New York, 1981).

Brus, W. *Socialist Ownership and Political Systems* (Routledge and Kegan Paul, London, 1975).

Buck, P.W. (ed.) *How Conservatives Think* (Penguin, Harmondsworth, 1975).

Burke, E. *Reflections on the Revolution in France* (Penguin, Harmondsworth, 1968).

Carr, E.H. *The Bolshevik Revolution 1917–1923*, Vol. I (Macmillan, London, 1950).

Cawson, A. *Corporatism and Political Theory* (Blackwell, Oxford, 1986).

Claudin, F. *Eurocommunism and Socialism* (New Left Books, London, 1978).

Claudin, F. *The Communist Movement from Comintern to Cominform* (Penguin, Harmondsworth, 1975).

Cohen, G.A. *Karl Marx's Theory of History. A Defence* (Clarendon Press, Oxford, 1978).

Cohen, S.F., Rabinowitch, A. and Sharlet, R. (eds.) *The Soviet Union Since Stalin* (Macmillan, London, 1980).

Cole, G.D.H. *A History of Socialist Thought*: Vol. II, *Marxism and Anarchism, 1850–1890* (Macmillan, London, 1954).

Connolly, W.E. (ed.) *Legitimacy and the State* (Blackwell, Oxford, 1984).

Crick, B. *The Reform of Parliament* (Weidenfeld & Nicolson, London, 1970).

Crosland, C.A.R. *The Future of Socialism* (Jonathan Cape, London, 1976).

Cummins, I. *Marx, Engels and National Movements* (Croom Helm, London, 1980).

Dahl, R.A. *A Preface to Economic Democracy* (Polity Press, Oxford, 1985).

Dahl, R.A. *Modern Political Analysis*, 3rd edition (Prentice-Hall, Englewood Cliffs, 1976).

Dahl, R.A. (ed.) *Political Oppositions in Western Democracies* (Yale University Press, New Haven and London, 1966).

Dahl, R.A. *Who Governs? Democracy and Power in an American City* (Yale University Press, New Haven and London, 1961).

Davis, H.B. *Nationalism and Socialism* (Monthly Review Press, New York, 1967).

De Felice, R. *Fascism. An Informal Introduction to its Theory and Practice* (Transaction Books, New Brunswick, N.J., 1977).

De Felice, R. *Interpretations of Fascism* (Harvard University Press, Cambridge, Mass. 1977).

Deleon, D. *The American as Anarchist* (Johns Hopkins University Press, Baltimore and London, 1978).

Deutscher, I. *The Prophet Outcast. Trotsky: 1929–1940* (Oxford University Press, London, 1970).

Dogan, M. and Rose, R. (eds.) *European Politics, A Reader* (Macmillan, London, 1971).

Draper, H. *Karl Marx's Theory of Revolution*. Vol. I: *State and Bureaucracy* (Monthly Review Press, New York and London, 1977).

Duverger, M. *Political Parties* (Methuen, London, 1954).

Duverger, M. *The Study of Politics* (Thomas Crowell, New York, 1972).

Ehrlich, H.J. *et al.* (eds.) *Reinventing Anarchy* (Routledge and Kegan Paul, London, 1979).

Eldridge, J.E.T. *C. Wright Mills* (Ellis Horwood, Chichester, 1983).

Engels, F., Lafargue, P. and L. *Correspondance,* Vol. II (1887-1890) (Editions Sociales, Paris, 1956).

Finer, S.E. *Anonymous Empire. A Study of the Lobby in Great Britain* (Pall Mall Press, London, 1966).

Finley, M.I. *Democracy Ancient and Modern* (Chatto & Windus, London, 1985).

Fiori, G. *Antonio Gramsci, Life of a Revolutionary* (New Left Books, London, 1970).

Fleming, M. *The Anarchist Way to Socialism. Elisée Reclus and Nineteenth-Century European Anarchism* (Croom Helm, London, 1979).

Freeman, M. *Edmund Burke and the Critique of Political Radicalism* (Blackwell, Oxford, 1980).

Freeman, M. 'Edmund Burke and the Sociology of Revolution'. *Political Studies* XXV (1977), pp. 459–473.

Galbraith, J.K. *American Capitalism* (Penguin, Harmondsworth, 1963).

Gamble, A. 'The Free Economy and the Strong State', *The Socialist Register 1979*, eds. R. Miliband and J. Saville (Merlin, London, 1979).

Gerth, H.H. and Wright Mills, C. (eds.) *From Max Weber: Essays in Sociology* (Routledge and Kegan Paul, London, 1948).

Giddens, A. and Held, D. (eds.) *Classes, Power and Conflict* (Macmillan, Basingstoke, 1982).

Godechot, J. (ed.) *La Pensée révolutionnaire en France et en Europe 1780–1799* (Armand Colin, Paris, 1964).

Gray, J. *Hayek on Liberty* (Blackwell, Oxford, 1984).

Green, P. *Retrieving Democracy* (Methuen, London, 1985).

Griffith, J.A.G. *The Politics of the Judiciary* (3rd edition) (Fontana Press, 1985).

Halévy, E. *A History of the English People in the 19th Century*, 6 Vols (Cass, London, 1949–52).

Hall, S. and Jacques, M. (eds.) *The Politics of Thatcherism* (Lawrence and Wishart, London, 1983).

Harding, N. *Lenin's Political Thought* (Macmillan, London, 1983).

Harding, N. (ed.) *The State in Socialist Society* (Macmillan, London, 1984).

Harris, N. *Competition and the Corporate Society. British Conservatives, the State, and Industry, 1945–64* (Methuen, London, 1972).

Havel, V. *The Power of the Powerless. Citizens against the State in Central-Eastern Europe* (Hutchinson, London, 1985).

Hayek, F. *The Constitution of Liberty* (Routledge and Kegan Paul, London, 1960).

Hegel, G.W.F. *The Philosophy of History* (Dover Publications, New York, 1956).

Held, D. *et al.* (eds.) *States and Societies* (Martin Robertson, Oxford, 1983).

Hobsbawm, E.J. *Revolutionaries* (Weidenfeld and Nicolson, London, 1973).

Hoffman, R.L. *Revolutionary Justice: The Social and Political Theory of P.-J. Proudhon* (University of Illinois Press, Urbana, 1972).

Holmes, L. *Politics in the Communist World* (Clarendon Press, Oxford, 1986).

Hosking, G. *A History of the Soviet Union* (Fontana Press, Collins, London, 1985).

Hough, J.F. *The Soviet Union and Social Science Theory* (Harvard University Press, Cambridge, Mass., 1977).

Hough, J. and Fainsod, M. *How the Soviet Union is Governed* (Harvard University Press, Cambridge, Mass., 1980).

Hunt, R.N. *The Political Ideas of Marx and Engels*, 2 Vols (Macmillan, London, 1975 and 1984).

Huntingdon, S.P. *Political Order in Changing Societies* (Yale University Press, New Haven and London, 1968).

Huntingdon, S.P. and Moore, C.H. (eds.) *Authoritarian Politics in Modern Society: The Dynamics of Established One-Party Systems* (Basic Books, New York and London, 1970).

Ionescu, G. and de Madariaga, I. *Opposition* (C.A. Watts, London, 1968).

Jessop, B. 'The Capitalist State and the Rule of Capital: Problems in the Analysis of Business Associations', *West European Politics* 6(2) April 1983, pp. 139–63.

Johnstone, M. 'Marx and Engels and the Concept of the Party', *The Socialist Register 1967*, edited by R. Miliband and J. Saville, (Merlin, London, 1967), pp. 121–58.

Jones, T. *Lloyd George* (Geoffrey Cumberledge, Oxford University Press, 1951).

Jordon, B. *The State. Authority and Autonomy* (Blackwell, Oxford, 1985).

Kariel, H.S. 'Pluralism', *International Encyclopedia of the Social Sciences*, edited by D.L. Shils. (Macmillan and Free Press, New York, 1968).

Kelly, A. *Mikhail Bakunin* (Clarendon Press, Oxford, 1982).

Kershaw, I. *Popular Opinion and Political Dissent in the Third Reich:*

Bavaria 1933–1945 (Clarendon Press, Oxford, 1983).

Kolakowski, L. *Main Currents of Marxism*, 3 Vols (Clarendon Press, Oxford, 1978).

Kornhauser, W.A. *The Politics of Mass Society* (Routledge, London, 1960).

Kropotkin, P.A. *Selected Writings on Anarchism and Revolution*, edited by M. Miller (MIT Press, Massachusetts, 1970).

Lane, B.M. and Rupp, L.J. (eds.) *Nazi Ideology Before 1933, A Documentation* (Manchester University Press, Manchester, 1978).

Laqueur, W. (ed.) *Fascism: A Reader's Guide* (Penguin, Harmondsworth, 1979).

Laski, H. *A Grammar of Politics* (Allen and Unwin, London, 1970).

Le Bon, G. *The Psychology of Revolution* (T. Fisher Unwin, London, 1913).

Leftwich, A. (ed.) *What is Politics? The Activity and its Study* (Blackwell, Oxford, 1984).

Lenin, V.I. *The Proletarian Revolution and the Renegade Kautsky* (Progress Publishers, Moscow, 1976).

Lenin, V.I. *Selected Works in One Volume* (Lawrence and Wishart, London, 1969).

Lenin, V.I. *What is to be Done? Collected Works*, Vol. 5 (Lawrence and Wishart, London, 1961).

Liebman, M. *Leninism under Lenin* (Merlin Press, London, 1975).

Lindblom, C.E. *Politics and Markets. The World's Political-Economic Systems* (Basic Books, New York, 1977).

Linden, C.A. *Khrushchev and the Soviet Leadership, 1957–1964* (Johns Hopkins University Press, Baltimore, 1960).

Linz, J.L. *The Breakdown of Democratic Regimes: Crisis, Breakdown and Re-equilibration* (Johns Hopkins University Press, Baltimore and London, 1978).

Linz, J.L. and Stepan, A. (eds.) *The Breakdown of Democratic Regimes: Europe* (Johns Hopkins University Press, Baltimore and London, 1978).

Lively, J. and Rees, J. (eds.) *Utilitarian Logic and Politics* (Oxford University Press, Oxford, 1978).

Locke, J. *Two Treatises of Government*, edited by P. Laslett (Cambridge University Press, Cambridge, 1967).

Löwy, M. *Georg Lukács – From Romanticism to Bolshevism* (New Left Books, London, 1979).

Lukács, G. *The Destruction of Reason* (Merlin Press, London, 1980).

Lukács, G. *History and Class Consciousness* (Merlin, London, 1971).

Lukes, S. *Essays in Social and Political Theory* (Macmillan, London, 1977).

Lukes, S. *Individualism* (Blackwell, Oxford, 1973).

Lukes, S. *Power. A Radical View* (Macmillan, London, 1974).

Luxemburg, R. *The Russian Revolution*, and *Leninism or Marxism?*, introduced by B.D. Wolfe (University of Michigan Press, Ann Arbor, 1961).

Lyttelton, A. (ed.) *Italian Fascisms, from Pareto to Gentile* (Jonathan Cape, London, 1973).

Lyttelton, A. *The Seizure of Power. Fascism in Italy 1919–1929* (Weidenfeld and Nicolson, London, 1973).

Macpherson, C.B. *Burke* (Oxford University Press, Oxford, 1980).

Macpherson, C.B. *The Life and Times of Liberal Democracy* (Oxford University Press, Oxford, 1977).

Macpherson, C.B. *The Real World of Democracy* (Clarendon Press, Oxford, 1966).

Magraw, R. *France 1814–1915, The Bourgeois Century* (Fontana, 1983).

Maguire, J.M. *Marx's Theory of Politics* (Cambridge University Press, Cambridge, 1978).

Manley, J.F. 'Neo-Pluralism: A Class Analysis of Pluralism I and Pluralism II', *American Political Science Review* 77 (1983), pp. 368–83.

Mannheim, K. *Essays on Sociology and Social Psychology* (Routledge and Kegan Paul, London, 1953).

Marcuse, H. *One-Dimensional Man. Studies in the Ideology of Advanced Industrial Society* (Routledge and Kegan Paul, London, 1968).

Marsh, D. 'Interest Group Activity and Structural Power: Lindblom's *Politics and Markets*', *West European Politics* 6(2) April 1983, pp. 3–14.

Marx, K. *Capital*, 3 Vols (Lawrence and Wishart, London, 1970–74).

Marx, K. *Early Writings* (Penguin, Harmondsworth, 1975).

Marx, K. *Grundrisse* (Penguin, Harmondsworth, 1973).

Marx, K. and Engels, F. *Selected Correspondence* (Progress Publishers, Moscow, 1975).

Marx, K. and Engels, F. *Selected Works*, in 3 Vols (Progress Publishers, Moscow, 1973).

Marx, K. *Surveys from Exile* (Penguin, Harmondsworth, 1973).

Marx, K. *The First International and After* (Penguin, Harmondsworth, 1974).

Marx, K. *The Revolutions of 1848* (Penguin, Harmondsworth, 1973).

Marx, K. and Engels, F. *The Holy Family*, in Karl Marx and Frederick Engels, *Collected Works*, Vol. 4 (Lawrence and Wishart, London, 1975).

Matthias, E. and Morsey, R. (eds.) *Das Ende der Parteien 1933* (Droste Verlag, Düsseldorf, 1960).

Maurras, C. *Kiel et Tanger 1895–1905. La République française devant l'Europe* (Librairie Nationale Française, Paris, 1913).

McLellan, D. *Marxism after Marx, an introduction* (Macmillan, London, 1979).

McLellan, D. *The Thought of Karl Marx, an introduction* (Macmillan, London, 1971).

Medvedev, R, *Let History Judge. The Origins and Consequences of Stalinism* (Spokesman Books, Nottingham, 1976).

Medvedev, R. *On Socialist Democracy* (Macmillan, London, 1975).

Meisel, J.H. *The Myth of the Ruling Class* (University of Michigan Press, Ann Arbor, 1962).

Merquior, J.G. *Western Marxism* (Paladin, London, 1986).

Michels, R. *Political Parties* (Dover Publications, New York, 1959).

Miliband, R. *Capitalist Democracy in Britain* (Oxford University Press, Oxford, 1982).

Miliband, R. *Class Power and State Power* (Verso, London, 1983).

Miliband, R. *Marxism and Politics* (Oxford University Press, London, 1977).

Miliband, R. *The State in Capitalist Society* (Weidenfeld and Nicolson, London, 1969).

Mill, J.S. *Three Essays* ('On Liberty'; 'Representative Government'; 'The Subjection of Women') (Oxford University Press, Oxford, 1975).

Miller, D. *Anarchism* (J.M. Dent, London and Melbourne, 1984).

Mills, C.W. *Power, Politics and People* (Oxford University Press, New York, 1963).

Mills, C.W. *The Power Elite* (Oxford University Press, New York, 1956).

Mills, C.W. *The Sociological Imagination* (Penguin, Harmondsworth, 1970).

Minkin, L. *The Labour Party Conference* (Manchester University Press, Manchester, 1980).

Mommsen, W.J. *The Age of Bureaucracy* (Blackwell, Oxford, 1974).

Morris-Jones, W.H. 'In Defence of Apathy', *Political Studies* 2 (1954), pp. 25–37.

Mosca, G. *The Ruling Class (Elementi di Scienza Politica)* (McGraw Hill, New York, 1939).

Muir, R. *How Britain is Governed. A Critical Analysis of Modern Developments in the British System of Government* (Constable, London, 1930).

Neumann, F. *The Democratic and the Authoritarian State* (Free Press, New York, 1957).

Nicolet, C. *L'Idée républicaine en France* (Gallimard, Paris, 1982).

Nisbet, R. *Conservatism* (Open University Press, Milton Keynes,

1986).

Noakes, J. and Pridham, G. (eds.) *Documents on Nazism 1919–1945* (Jonathan Cape, London, 1974).

Norton, P. and Aughey, A. *Conservatives and Conservatism* (Temple Smith, London, 1981).

Nove, A. *The Economics of Feasible Socialism* (Allen and Unwin, London, 1983).

Nozick, R. *Anarchy, State and Utopia* (Blackwell, Oxford, 1974).

Offe, C. 'Structural Problems of the Capitalist State' in K. von Beyme (ed.), *German Political Studies*, Vol. I (Sage, London, 1974).

Olsen, M.E. (ed.) *Power in Societies* (Macmillan, New York, 1970).

O'Sullivan, N. *Conservatism* (Dent, London, 1976).

Panitch, L. *Working-Class Politics in Crisis. Essays on Labour and the State* (Verso, London, 1986).

Parekh, B. (ed.). *Bentham's Political Thought* (Croom Helm, London, 1973).

Pareto, V. *The Mind and Society. A Treatise on General Sociology* (Dover Publications, New York, 1963).

Pareto, V. *Sociological Writings*, selected and introduced by S.E. Finer (Pall Mall Press, London, 1966).

Parry, G. *Elites and Society* (Allen and Unwin, London, 1969).

Parsons, T. *The Structure of Social Action* (The Free Press, Glencoe, 1949).

Paterson, R.W.K. *The Nihilistic Egoist: Max Stirner* (Oxford University Press, Oxford, 1971).

Pelczynski, Z. and Gray, J. (eds.) *Conceptions of Liberty in Political Philosophy* (Athlone Press, London, 1984).

Pizzorno, A. (ed.) *Political Sociology* (Penguin Books, Harmondsworth, 1971).

Plamenatz, J. *The Revolutionary Movement in France 1815–1871* (Longman, London, 1952).

Polsby, N. *Community Power and Political Theory* (Yale University Press, New Haven and London, 1963).

Popper, K. *The Poverty of Historicism* (Routledge and Kegan Paul, London, 1957).

Poulantzas, N. *Fascism and Dictatorship* (New Left Books, London, 1974).

Poulantzas, N. *The Crisis of the Dictatorships: Portugal, Greece, Spain* (New Left Books, London, 1976).

Proudhon, P.J. *De la capacité politique des classes ouvrières* (Marcel Rivière, Paris, 1924).

Proudhon, P.J. *Oeuvres choisis, textes présentés par Jean Bancal* (Gallimard, Paris, 1967).

Przeworski, A. *Capitalism and Social Democracy* (Cambridge University Press, Cambridge, 1985).

Quinton, A.M. *The Politics of Imperfection* (Faber, London, 1978).

Read, H. *Anarchy and Order* (Souvenir Press, London, 1974).

Reclus, E. *Correspondance*, 3 Vols (Paris, 1911–25).

Rousseau, J-J. *The Social Contract and Discourses* (Everyman edition) (Dent, London, 1968).

Rowbotham, S., Segal, L. and Wainwright, H. *Beyond the Fragments. Feminism and the Making of Socialism* (Merlin Press, London, 1979).

Runciman, W.G. *Social Science and Political Theory* (Cambridge University Press, Cambridge, 1965).

Rutland, P. *The Myth of the Plan. Lessons of the Soviet Planning Experience* (Hutchinson, London, 1985).

Salvadori, M. *Karl Kautsky and the Socialist Revolution 1880–1938* (New Left Books, London, 1979).

Sartori, G. 'Anti-Elitism Revisited'. *Government and Opposition* 13 (1978), pp. 58–80.

Schumpeter, J.A. *Capitalism, Socialism and Democracy* (Allen and Unwin, London, 1943).

Scruton, R. *The Meaning of Conservatism* (Penguin, Harmondsworth, 1980).

Skilling, H.G. and Griffiths, F. (eds.) *Interest Groups in Soviet Politics* (Princeton University Press, Princeton, N.J., 1971).

Smith, G. *Politics in Western Europe* (Heinemann, London, 1972).

Sorel, G. *Reflections on Violence* (Collier-Macmillan, London, 1972).

Stirner, M. *The Ego and His Own* (Jonathan Cape, London, 1921).

Suleiman, E. *Politics, Power and Bureaucracy in France. The Administrative Elite* (Princeton University Press, Princeton, 1974).

Tawney, R.H. *Equality* (Allen and Unwin, London, 1964).

Taylor, M. *Community, Anarchy and Liberty* (Cambridge University Press, Cambridge, 1982).

Therborn, G. 'The Rule of Capital and the Rise of Democracy'. *New Left Review* 103 (1977), pp. 3–41.

Thompson, E.P. *Writing by Candlelight* (Merlin Press, London, 1980).

Tiersky, R. *Ordinary Stalinism: democratic centralism and the question of communist political development* (Allen and Unwin, London, 1985).

de Tocqueville, A. *Democracy in America* (edited by J.P. Mayer and Max Lerner), (Collins, The Fontana Library, 1968).

de Tocqueville, A. *The Ancien Régime and the French Revolution* (Collins, The Fontana Library, 1966).

Trotsky, L. *The Revolution Betrayed* (Pathfinder Press, New York, 1970).

Trotsky, L. *The Struggle against Fascism in Germany* (Penguin, Harmondsworth, 1975).

Tucker, R.C. (ed.) *Stalinism: Essays in Historical Interpretation* (Norton, New York, 1977).

Unger, A.L. *Constitutional Development in the USSR: a guide to the Soviet Constitution* (Methuen, London, 1980).

Unger, A.L. *The Totalitarian Party: Party and People in Nazi Germany and Soviet Russia* (Cambridge University Press, Cambridge, 1974).

Urry, J. and Wakeford, J. (eds.) *Power in Britain. Sociological Readings* (Heinemann, London, 1973).

Useem, M. *The Inner Circle. Large Corporations and the Rise of Business Political Activity in the U.S. and U.K.* (Oxford University Press, New York, 1984).

Vile, M.J.C. *Constitutionalism and the Separation of Powers* (Clarendon Press, Oxford, 1967).

Voslensky, M. *Nomenklatura: Anatomy of the Soviet Ruling Class* (Bodley Head, London, 1985).

Walzer, M. *Obligations. Essays on Disobedience, War and Citizenship* (Harvard University Press, Cambridge, Mass., 1971).

Weber, M. *Gesammelte Politische Schriften* (J.C.B. Mohr (Paul Siebeck), Tübingen, 1971).

Weber, M. *Selections in Translation*, edited by W.G. Runciman (Cambridge University Press, Cambridge, 1978).

White, R.J. (ed.) *The Conservative Tradition* (A. & C. Black, London, 1964).

White, S. and Nelson, D. (eds.) *Communist Politics, A Reader* (Macmillan, London, 1986).

Williams, R. *Towards 2000* (Penguin, Harmondsworth, 1985).

Williamson, P.J. *Varieties of Corporatism* (Cambridge University Press, Cambridge, 1985).

Wolff, R.P. *In Defense of Anarchism* (Harper and Row, New York, 1970).

Woodcock, G. (ed.) *The Anarchist Reader* (Fontana/Collins, 1977).

Woodhouse, A.S.P. (ed.) *Puritanism and Liberty* (Dent, London, 1974).

Wrong, D.H. *Power, Its Forms, Bases and Uses* (Blackwell, Oxford, 1979).

Name Index

Subject Index